Integrated Chinese

CHENG & TSUI PUBLICATIONS OF RELATED INTEREST

Making Connections: Enhance Your Listening Comprehension in Chinese (Paperback & Audio CD Set)
Madeline K. Spring

▲ Includes lessons for *Integrated Chinese* users.

Simplified Characters 978-0-88727-366-7
Traditional Characters 978-0-88727-365-0

Chinese BuilderCards: The Lightning Path to Mastering Vocabulary
Song Jiang and Haidan Wang

▲ Includes vocabulary from *Integrated Chinese*.

Simplified Characters 978-0-88727-434-3
Traditional Characters 978-0-88727-426-8

The Way of Chinese Characters: The Origins of 400 Essential Words
Jianhsin Wu, illustrated by Chen Zheng and Chen Tian

▲ Characters correspond to vocabulary from *Integrated Chinese*.

Paperback 978-0-88727-527-2

Cheng & Tsui Chinese-Pinyin-English Dictionary for Learners
Wang Huan, Editor-in-Chief

Paperback 978-0-88727-316-2

Cheng & Tsui Chinese Character Dictionary
Wang Huidi, Editor-in-Chief

Paperback 978-0-88727-314-8

Crossing Paths: Living and Learning in China,
An Intermediate Chinese Course
Hong Gang Jin and De Bao Xu, with Der-lin Chao, Yea-fen Chen, and Min Chen

Paperback & Audio CD Set 978-0-88727-370-4

Please visit www.cheng-tsui.com for more information on these and many other language-learning resources, or for information on web-based and downloadable products.

LEVEL 1
Part 1

Integrated Chinese
中文听说读写

Simplified Character Edition

TEXTBOOK

Expanded 2nd Edition

Tao-chung Yao and Yuehua Liu
Liangyan Ge, Yea-fen Chen, Nyan-Ping Bi,
Xiaojun Wang and Yaohua Shi

CHENG & TSUI COMPANY ▲ BOSTON

Expanded Second Edition

18 17 16 15 14 13 4 5 6 7 8 9 10

Published by
Cheng & Tsui Company, Inc.
25 West Street
Boston, MA 02111-1213 USA
Fax (617) 426-3669
www.cheng-tsui.com
"Bringing Asia to the World"™

Library of Congress Cataloging-in-Publication Data

Integrated Chinese = [Zhong wen ting du shuo xie].
Simplified character edition. Level 1, part 1 / Tao-chung Yao ... [et al.].— 2nd ed.
p. cm. — (C&T Asian language series)
Chinese and English.
Includes index.
ISBN 0-88727-533-8 — ISBN 0-88727-459-5
1. Chinese language—Textbooks for foreign speakers—English. I. Title: Zhong wen ting du shuo xie. II. Yao, Daozhong. III. Series: C&T Asian languages series.
PL1129.E5I683 2005
495.1'82421—dc22

2004063505

The *Integrated Chinese* series includes books, workbooks, character workbooks, audio products, multimedia products, teacher's resources, and more. Visit www.cheng-tsui.com for more information on the other components of *Integrated Chinese*.

Printed in the United States of America

THE INTEGRATED CHINESE SERIES

The *Integrated Chinese* series is a two-year course that includes textbooks, workbooks, character workbooks, audio CDs, CD-ROMs, DVDs and teacher's resources.

Textbooks introduce Chinese language and culture through a series of dialogues and narratives, with culture notes, language use and grammar explanations, and exercises.

Workbooks follow the format of the textbooks and contain a wide range of integrated activities that teach the four language skills of listening, speaking, reading and writing.

Character Workbooks help students learn Chinese characters in their correct stroke order. Special emphasis is placed on the radicals that are frequently used to compose Chinese characters.

Audio CDs include the narratives, dialogues and vocabulary presented in the textbooks, as well as pronunciation and listening exercises that correspond to the workbooks.

Teacher's Resources contain helpful guidance and additional activities online.

Multimedia CD-ROMs are divided into sections of listening, speaking, reading and writing, and feature a variety of supplemental interactive games and activities for students to test their skills and get instant feedback.

Workbook DVD shows listening comprehension dialogues from the Level 1 Part 1 Workbook, presented in contemporary settings in color video format.

PUBLISHER'S NOTE

When *Integrated Chinese* was first published in 1997, it set a new standard with its focus on the development and integration of the four language skills (listening, speaking, reading and writing). Today, to further enrich the learning experience of the many users of *Integrated Chinese* worldwide, the Cheng & Tsui Company is pleased to offer the revised, updated and expanded second edition of *Integrated Chinese*. We would like to thank the many teachers and students who, by offering their valuable insights and suggestions, have helped *Integrated Chinese* evolve and keep pace with the many positive changes in the field of Chinese language instruction. *Integrated Chinese* continues to offer comprehensive language instruction, with many new features.

The Cheng & Tsui Asian Language Series is designed to publish and widely distribute quality language learning materials created by leading instructors from around the world. We welcome readers' comments and suggestions concerning the publications in this series. Please contact the following members of our Editorial Board, in care of our Editorial Department (e-mail: editor@cheng-tsui.com):

CONTENTS

PREFACE

The *Integrated Chinese* series is an acclaimed, best-selling introductory course in Mandarin Chinese. With its holistic, integrated focus on the four language skills of listening, speaking, reading, and writing, it teaches all the basics beginning and intermediate students need to function in Chinese. *Integrated Chinese* helps students understand how the Chinese language works grammatically, and how to use Chinese in real life.

The Chinese title of *Integrated Chinese*, which is simply 中文听说读写 (*Zhōngwén Tīng Shuō Dú Xiě*), reflects our belief that a healthy language program should be a well-balanced one. To ensure that students will be strong in all skills, and because we believe that each of the four skills needs special training, the exercises in the *Integrated Chinese* Workbooks are divided into four sections of listening, speaking, reading, and writing. Within each section, there are two types of exercises, namely, traditional exercises (such as fill-in-the-blank, sentence completion, translation, etc.) to help students build a solid foundation, and communication-oriented exercises to prepare students to face the real world.

How *Integrated Chinese* Has Evolved

Integrated Chinese (IC) began, in 1993, as a set of course materials for beginning and intermediate Chinese courses taught at the East Asian Summer Language Institute's Chinese School, at Indiana University. Since that time, it has become a widely used series of Chinese language textbooks in the United States and beyond. Teachers and students appreciate the fact that IC, with its focus on practical, everyday topics and its numerous and varied exercises, helps learners build a solid foundation in the Chinese language.

What's New in the Second Edition

Thanks to all those who have used *Integrated Chinese* and given us the benefit of their suggestions and comments, we have been able to produce a second edition that includes the following improvements:

- ▲ Typographical errors present in the first edition have been corrected, and the content has been carefully edited to ensure accuracy and minimize errors.
- ▲ The design has been revised and improved for easier use, and the Textbooks feature two colors.
- ▲ **Revised illustrations** and **new photos** provide the reader with visual images and relevant cultural information.
- ▲ Many **new culture notes** and examples of **functional expressions** have been added.

- **Grammar and phonetics explanations** have been rewritten in more student-friendly language.
- **Workbook listening and reading sections** have been revised.
- **A new flexibility for the teaching of characters** is offered. While we believe that students should learn to read all of the characters introduced in the lessons, we are aware that different Chinese programs have different needs. Some teachers may wish to limit the number of characters for which students have responsibility, especially in regards to writing requirements. To help such teachers, we have identified a number of lower-frequency Chinese characters and marked them with a pound sign (#) in the vocabulary lists. Teachers might choose to accept *pinyin* in place of these characters in homework and tests. The new edition adds flexibility in this regard.
- **The Level 1 Workbooks** have been reorganized. The Workbook exercises have been divided into two parts, with each part corresponding to one of the dialogues in each lesson. This arrangement will allow teachers to more easily teach the dialogues separately. They may wish to use the first two or three days of each lesson to focus on the first dialogue, and have students complete the exercises for the first dialogue. Then, they can proceed with the second dialogue, and have students complete the exercises for the second dialogue. Teachers may also wish to give separate quizzes on the vocabulary associated with each dialogue, thus reducing the number of new words students need to memorize at any one time.
- **Level 2 offers full text in simplified and traditional characters.** The original Level 2 Textbook and Workbook, which were intended to be used by both traditional- and simplified-character learners, contained sections in which only the traditional characters were given. This was of course problematic for students who were principally interested in learning simplified characters. This difficulty has been resolved in the new edition, as we now provide both traditional and simplified characters for every Chinese sentence in both the Textbook and the Workbook.

Basic Organizational Principles

In recent years, a very important fact has been recognized by the field of language teaching: the ultimate goal of learning a language is to communicate in that language.

Integrated Chinese is a set of materials that gives students grammatical tools and also prepares them to function in a Chinese language environment. The materials cover two years of instruction, with smooth transitions from one level to the next. They first cover everyday life topics and gradually move to more abstract subject matter. The materials are not limited to one method or one approach, but instead they blend several teaching approaches that can produce good results. Here are some of the features of *Integrated Chinese* which make it different from other Chinese language textbooks:

Integrating Pedagogical and Authentic Materials
All of the materials are graded in *Integrated Chinese.* We believe that students can grasp the materials better if they learn simple and easy to control language items before the more difficult or complicated ones. We also believe that students should be taught some authentic materials even in the first year of language instruction. Therefore, most of the pedagogical materials are actually simulated authentic materials. Real authentic materials (written by native Chinese speakers for native Chinese speakers) are incorporated in the lessons when appropriate.

Integrating Written Style and Spoken Style
One way to measure a person's Chinese proficiency is to see if s/he can handle the "written style" (书面语, shūmiànyǔ) with ease. The "written style" language is more formal and literal than the "spoken style" (口语, kǒuyǔ); however, it is also widely used in news broadcasts and formal speeches. In addition to "spoken style" Chinese, basic "written style" expressions are gradually introduced in *Integrated Chinese.*

Integrating Traditional and Simplified Characters
We believe that students should learn to handle Chinese language materials in both the traditional and the simplified forms. However, we also realize that it could be rather confusing and overwhelming to teach students both the traditional and the simplified forms from day one. A reasonable solution to this problem is for the student to concentrate on one form, either traditional or simplified, at the first level, and to acquire the other form during the second level. Therefore, for Level 1, *Integrated Chinese* offers two editions of the Textbooks and the Workbooks, one using traditional characters and one using simplified characters, to meet different needs.

We believe that by the second year of studying Chinese, all students should be taught to read both traditional and simplified characters. Therefore, the text of each lesson in Level 2 is shown in both forms, and the vocabulary list in each lesson also contains both forms. Considering that students in a second-year Chinese language class might come from different backgrounds and that some of them may have learned the traditional form and others the simplified form, students should be allowed to write in either traditional or simplified form. It is important that the learner write in one form only, and not a hybrid of both forms.

Integrating Teaching Approaches
Realizing that there is no one single teaching method which is adequate in training a student to be proficient in all four language skills, we employ a variety of teaching methods and approaches in *Integrated Chinese* to maximize

the teaching results. In addition to the communicative approach, we also use traditional methods such as grammar-translation and direct method.

Online Supplements to Integrated Chinese

Integrated Chinese is not a set of course materials that employs printed volumes only. It is, rather, a network of teaching materials that exist in many forms. Teacher keys, software, and more are posted for *Integrated Chinese* users at www.webtech.cheng-tsui.com, Cheng & Tsui Company's online site for downloadable and web-based resources. Please visit this site often for new offerings.

Other materials are available at the IC website, http://eall.hawaii.edu/yao/icusers/, which was set up by Ted Yao, one of the principal *Integrated Chinese* authors, when the original edition of *Integrated Chinese* was published. Thanks to the generosity of teachers and students who are willing to share their materials with other *Integrated Chinese* users, this website is constantly growing, and has many useful links and resources. The following are some of the materials created by the community of *Integrated Chinese* users that are available at the *Integrated Chinese* website.

- ▲ Links to resources that show how to write Chinese characters, provide vocabulary practice, and more.
- ▲ *Pinyin* supplements for all *Integrated Chinese* books. Especially useful for Chinese programs that do not teach Chinese characters.
- ▲ Preliminary activities for an activity book for *Integrated Chinese* Level 1 (in progress), by Yea-fen Chen, Ted Yao and Jeffrey Hayden. (http://eall.hawaii.edu/yao/AB/default.htm)
- ▲ Teacher's resources.

About the Format

Considering that many teachers might want to teach their students how to speak the language before teaching them how to read Chinese characters, we decided to place the *pinyin* text before the Chinese-character text in each of the eleven lessons of the Level 1 Part 1 Textbook.

Since *pinyin* is only a vehicle to help students learn the pronunciation of the Chinese language and is not a replacement for the Chinese writing system, it is important that students can read out loud in Chinese by looking at the Chinese text and not just the *pinyin* text. To train students to deal with the Chinese text directly without relying on *pinyin,* we moved the *pinyin* text to the end of each lesson in the Level 1 Part 2 Textbook. Students can refer to the *pinyin* text to verify a sound when necessary.

We are fully aware of the fact that no two Chinese language programs are identical and that each program has its own requirements. Some schools will cover a lot of material in one year while some others will cover considerably less. Trying to meet the needs of as many schools as possible, we decided to cover a wide range of material, both in terms of vocabulary and grammar, in *Integrated Chinese*. To facilitate oral practice and to allow students to communicate in real-life situations, many supplementary vocabulary items are added to each lesson. However, the characters in the supplementary vocabulary sections are not included in the Character Workbooks. In the Character Workbooks, each of the characters is given a frequency indicator based on the *Hànyǔ Pínlǜ Dà Cídiǎn* (汉语频率大辞典). Teachers can decide for themselves which characters must be learned.

Acknowledgments

Since publication of the first edition of *Integrated Chinese,* in 1997, many teachers and students have given us helpful comments and suggestions. We cannot list all of these individuals here, but we would like to reiterate our genuine appreciation for their help. We do wish to recognize the following individuals who have made recent contributions to the *Integrated Chinese* revision. We are indebted to Tim Richardson, Jeffrey Hayden, Ying Wang and Xianmin Liu for field-testing the new edition and sending us their comments and corrections. We would also like to thank Chengzhi Chu for letting us try out his "Chinese TA," a computer program designed for Chinese teachers to create and edit teaching materials. This software saved us many hours of work during the revision. Last, but not least, we want to thank Jim Dew for his superb professional editorial job, which enhanced both the content and the style of the new edition.

As much as we would like to eradicate all errors in the new edition, some will undoubtedly remain, so please continue to send your comments and corrections to editor@cheng-tsui.com, and accept our sincere thanks for your help.

ABBREVIATIONS FOR GRAMMAR TERMS

abbr	*Abbreviation*
adj	*Adjective*
adv	*Adverb*
av	*Auxiliary verb*
ce	*Common expression*
coll	*Colloquialism*
conj	*Conjunction*
exc	*Exclamation*
interj	*Interjection*
m	*Measure word*
n	*Noun*
np	*Noun phrase*
nu	*Numeral*
p	*Particle*
pn	*Proper noun*
pr	*Pronoun*
prefix	*Prefix*
prep	*Preposition*
ono	*Onomatopoeic*
qp	*Question particle*
qpr	*Question pronoun*
qw	*Question word*
t	*Time word*
v	*Verb*
vc	*Verb plus complement*
vo	*Verb plus object*

ABOUT NOTE REFERENCES

Different types of notes provide explanations for selected expressions in the text. In the dialogues, expressions followed by a superscript numeral are explained in notes directly below the text; expressions followed by a superscript "G" plus a numeral are explained in grammar notes in the grammar section of the lesson. "F" refers to "Functional Expressions" explained in the pages that follow the dialogues.

Introduction

I. Chinese Pronunciation

A Chinese syllable is composed of an initial and a final. Initials consist of consonants or semi-vowels; finals consist of vowels or vowels plus one of the two nasal sounds -[n] or -[ng]. In addition to an initial and a final, each Chinese syllable has a tone.

A. SIMPLE FINALS

There are six simple finals: **a**, **o**, **e**, **i**, **u**, **ü**

▲ When it is pronounced by itself, **a** is a central vowel. The tongue remains in a natural, relaxed position.

▲ **o** is a rounded semi-high back vowel. The lips are round when pronouncing **o**.

▲ **e** is an unrounded semi-high back vowel. To produce this vowel, first pronounce **o**, and then change the shape of the mouth from rounded to unrounded. At the same time spread the lips apart, as if you were smiling. This vowel is different from "e" in English, which is pronounced with the tongue raised slightly forward.

▲ **i** is an unrounded high front vowel. The tongue is raised higher than it would be to pronounce its counterpart in English.

▲ **u** is a rounded high back vowel. The tongue is raised higher than it would be to pronounce its counterpart in English.

▲ **ü** is a rounded high front vowel. To produce this vowel, first pronounce **i**, then modify the shape of the mouth from unrounded to rounded.

In the *pinyin* system **i** also represents two additional special vowels. One is a front apical vowel, the other a back apical vowel. Both of these vowels are homorganic with the very limited sets of initials with which they can co-occur (see below, **z**, **c**, **s** and **zh**, **ch**, **sh**, **r**). In our discussion of phonetics, we sometimes write these special vowels with an italicized ***i*** to distinguish it from the ordinary high front vowel **i**.

Note

In this book, Chinese sounds are represented by *pinyin*. The *pinyin* system uses twenty-five of the twenty-six letters of the Roman alphabet. Although *pinyin* symbols are thus the same as English letters, the actual sounds they represent can be very different from their English counterparts. Be careful to distinguish them.

B. INITIALS

There are twenty-one initial consonants in Chinese:

1.	**b**	**p**	**m**	**f**
2.	**d**	**t**	**n**	**l**
3.	**g**	**k**	**h**	
4.	**j**	**q**	**x**	
5.	**z**	**c**	**s**	
6.	**zh**	**ch**	**sh**	**r**

In addition, the semi-vowels **y** and **w** also function as initials.

B.1: b, p, m, f

b is a bilabial unaspirated plosive. Note that the Chinese **b** is different from its English counterpart; it is not voiced. There are no voiced plosives in Chinese.

p is a bilabial aspirated voiceless plosive. In other words, there is a strong puff of breath when the consonant is pronounced. When pronouncing **b** and **p**, the lips are closed lightly between the upper teeth and lower teeth.

m is a bilabial nasal sound, produced in the same manner as an English **m**.

f is a labio-dental fricative. To produce this sound, press the upper teeth against the lower lip, and let the breath flow out with friction, just as in pronouncing an English **f**.

Notes

Only the simple finals **a**, **o**, **i**, and **u** and the compound finals that start with **a**, **o**, **i**, or **u** can be combined with **b**, **p**, and **m**; only the simple finals **a**, **o**, and **u** and the compound finals that start with **a**, **o**, or **u** can be combined with **f**. When these initials are combined with **o**, there is actually a short **u** sound in between. For instance, the syllable **bo (b^{u}o)** actually includes a very short **u** sound between **b** and **o**.

PRACTICE

B.1.a

ba	**bi**	**bu**	**bo**
pa	**pi**	**pu**	**po**
ma	**mi**	**mu**	**mo**
fa	**fu**	**fo**	

B.1.b b vs. p

ba	**pa**	**bu**	**pu**
po	**bo**	**pi**	**bi**

B.1.c m vs. f

ma	**fa**	**mu**	**fu**

B.1.d b, p, m, f

bo	**po**	**mo**	**fo**
fu	**mu**	**pu**	**bu**

B.2: d, t, n, l

When producing **d**, **t**, **n**, the tip of the tongue touches the upper teeth ridge. The tongue is raised more to the front than it would be to pronounce their English counterparts.

d is a tongue tip alveolar unaspirated plosive. It is voiceless.

t is a tongue tip alveolar aspirated stop. It is voiceless.

n is a tongue tip alveolar nasal. It is produced by placing the tip of the tongue against the ridge behind the upper teeth.

l is a tongue tip alveolar lateral. It is different from the English "**l**." To produce the Chinese **l** the tip of the tongue should touch the alveolar ridge, which is the ridge located at the back of the upper teeth.

Note

Only the simple finals **a**, **i**, **e**, and **u** and the compound finals that start with **a**, **i**, **e**, or **u** can be combined with **d**, **t**, **n**, and **l**; **n** and **l** can also be combined with **ü** and the compound finals that start with **ü**.

PRACTICE

B.2.a

da	**di**	**du**	**de**	
ta	**ti**	**tu**	**te**	
na	**ni**	**nu**	**ne**	**nü**
la	**li**	**lu**	**le**	**lü**

B.2.b d vs. t

da	**ta**	**di**	**ti**
du	**tu**	**de**	**te**

B.2.c l vs. n

lu	**lü**	**nu**	**nü**
lu	**nu**	**lü**	**nü**

B.2.d d, t, n, l

le	**ne**	**te**	**de**
du	**tu**	**lu**	**nu**

B.3: g, k, h

g is an unaspirated voiceless velar stop. **k** is an aspirated voiceless velar stop. When producing **g** and **k**, the back of the tongue is raised against the soft palate.

h is a voiceless velar fricative. When producing **h**, the back of the tongue is raised towards the soft palate. The friction is noticeable. With its English counterpart, however, the friction is not noticeable.

Note

Only the simple finals **a**, **e**, and **u** and the compound finals that start with **a**, **e**, or **u** can be combined with **g**, **k**, and **h**.

PRACTICE

B.3.a

gu	**ge**	**ga**
ku	**ke**	**ka**
hu	**he**	**ha**

B.3.b g vs. k

gu	**ku**	**ge**	**ke**

B.3.c g vs. h

gu	**hu**	**ge**	**he**

B.3.d k vs. h

ke	**he**	**ku**	**hu**

B.3.e g, k, h

gu	**ku**	**hu**
he	**ke**	**ge**

B.4: j, q, x

j is an unaspirated voiceless palatal affricate. To produce this sound, first raise the front of the tongue to the hard palate and press the tip of the tongue against the back of the lower teeth, and then loosen the tongue and let the air squeeze out through the channel thus made. It is unaspirated and the vocal cords do not vibrate. Note that the Chinese **j** is similar to English **j** but unvoiced and articulated, with the tip of the tongue resting behind the lower incisors.

q is an aspirated voiceless palatal affricate. It is produced in the same manner as **j**, but it is aspirated. Note that the Chinese **q** is similar to English **ch** except that it is articulated with the tip of the tongue resting behind the lower incisors.

x is a voiceless palatal fricative. To produce it, first raise the front of the tongue toward (but not touching) the hard palate and then let the air squeeze out. The vocal cords do not vibrate. Note that the Chinese **x** is similar to English **sh** except that it is articulated with the tip of the tongue resting behind the lower incisors.

Note

The finals that can be combined with **j**, **q** and **x** are limited to **i** and **ü** and the compound finals that start with **i** or **ü**. When **j**, **q** and **x** are combined with **ü** or a compound final starting with **ü**, the umlaut is omitted and the **ü** appears as **u**.

PRACTICE

B.4.a

ji	**ju**
qi	**qu**
xi	**xu**

B.4.b j vs. q

ji	**qi**	**ju**	**qu**

B.4.c q vs. x

qi	**xi**	**qu**	**xu**

B.4.d j vs. x

ji	**xi**	**ju**	**xu**

B.4.e j, q, x

ji	**qi**	**xi**
ju	**qu**	**xu**

B.5: z, c, s

z is an unaspirated voiceless apical affricate.

c is an aspirated voiceless apical affricate. The aspiration is strong. Note that c is like the ts sound in "it's hot."

s is a voiceless apical fricative. It is the same as English **s**.

The above group of sounds is pronounced with the tongue touching the back of the upper teeth.

Note

The simple finals that can be combined with **z**, **c**, **s** are **a**, **e**, **u** and the front apical vowel ***i*** (*not* the regular palatal high front vowel **i**).

In pronouncing the syllables ***zi***, ***ci*** and ***si*** the tongue is held in the same position throughout the syllable except that it is slightly relaxed as the articulation moves from the voiceless initial consonant to the voiced vowel.

PRACTICE

B.5.a

za	**zu**	**ze**	**zi**
ca	**cu**	**ce**	**ci**
sa	**su**	**se**	**si**

B.5.b s vs. z

sa	**za**	**su**	**zu**
se	**ze**	**si**	**zi**

B.5.c z vs. c

za	**ca**	**zi**	**ci**
ze	**ce**	**zu**	**cu**

B.5.d s vs. c

sa	**ca**	**si**	**ci**
su	**cu**	**se**	**ce**

B.5.e z, c, s

sa	**za**	**ca**
su	**zu**	**cu**
se	**ze**	**ce**
si	**zi**	**ci**
za	**cu**	**se**
ci	**sa**	**zu**
su	**zi**	**ce**

B.6: zh, ch, sh, r

zh is an unaspirated voiceless blade-palatal affricate. To produce it, first turn up the tip of the tongue against the hard palate, then loosen it and let the air squeeze out the channel thus made. It is unaspirated and the vocal cords do not vibrate. Note that **zh** is similar to English **j** but unvoiced and with the tip of the tongue raised against the back of the gum ridge or front part of the hard palate.

ch is an aspirated voiceless blade-palatal affricate. This sound is produced in the same manner as **zh**, but it is aspirated. Note that **ch** is similar to English **ch** except that it is produced with the tip of the tongue raised against the back of the gum ridge or front part of the hard palate.

sh is a voiceless blade-palatal fricative. To produce this sound, turn up the tip of the tongue toward (but not touching) the hard palate and then let the air squeeze out. The vocal cords do not vibrate. Note that **sh** is similar to English **sh** except that it is produced with the tip of the tongue raised against the back of the gum ridge or front part of the hard palate.

r is a voiced blade-palatal fricative. It is produced in the same manner as **sh**, but it is voiced. The vocal cords vibrate. It is very different from the English "r."

Note

The finals that can be combined with **zh**, **ch**, **sh**, **r** are **a**, **e**, **u** and the back apical vowel ***i***, as well as the compound finals that start with **a**, **e**, or **u**. In pronouncing the syllables **zhi**, **chi**, **shi** and **ri** the tongue is held in the same position throughout the syllable except that it is slightly relaxed as the articulation moves from the initial consonant to the vowel.

PRACTICE

B.6.a

zha	**zhu**	**zhe**	**zhi**
cha	**chu**	**che**	**chi**
sha	**shu**	**she**	**shi**
ru	**re**	**ri**	

B.6.b zh vs. sh

sha	**zha**	**shu**	**zhu**

B.6.c zh vs. ch

zha	**cha**	**zhu**	**chu**

B.6.d ch vs. sh

chu	**shu**	**sha**	**cha**

B.6.e zh, ch, sh

shi	**zhi**	**chi**	**shi**
she	**zhe**	**che**	**she**

B.6.f sh vs. r

shu	**ru**	**shi**	**ri**

B.6.g r vs. l

lu	**ru**	**li**	**ri**

B.6.h sh, r, l

she	**re**	**le**	**re**

B.6.i zh, ch, r

zhe	**re**	**che**	**re**

B.6.j zh, ch, sh, r

sha	**cha**	**zha**	
shu	**zhu**	**chu**	**ru**
zhi	**chi**	**shi**	**ri**
che	**zhe**	**she**	**re**

A REFERENCE CHART FOR INITIALS

	UNASPIRATED STOPS	ASPIRATED STOPS	NASALS	FRICATIVES	VOICED CONTINUANTS
Labials	**b**	**p**	**m**	**f**	**w***
Alveolars	**d**	**t**	**n**		**l**
Dental sibilants	**z**	**c**		**s**	
Retroflexes	**zh**	**ch**		**sh**	**r**
Palatals	**j**	**q**		**x**	**y***
Velars	**g**	**k**		**h**	

*See explanations of **w** and **y** in the "Spelling Rules" section below.

C. COMPOUND FINALS

1.	**ai**	**ei**	**ao**	**ou**					
2.	**an**	**en**	**ang**	**eng**	**ong**				
3.	**ia**	**iao**	**ie**	**iu***	**ian**	**in**	**iang**	**ing**	**iong**
4.	**ua**	**uo**	**uai**	**ui****	**uan**	**un*****	**uang**	**ueng**	
5.	**üe**	**üan**	**ün**						
6.	**er**								

*The main vowel **o** is omitted in the spelling of the final **iu** (**iu** = **iou**). Therefore **iu** represents the sound **iou**. The **o** sound is especially conspicuous in third and fourth tone syllables.
The main vowel **e is omitted in the final **ui** (**ui** = **uei**). Like **iu** above, the **e** sound within **ui** is quite conspicuous in third and fourth tone syllables.
***The main vowel **e** is omitted in **un** (**un** = **uen**).

In Chinese, compound finals are comprised of a main vowel and one or two secondary vowels, or a main vowel and one or two vowels followed by one of the nasal endings **-n** or **-ng**. When the initial vowels are **a**, **e** and **o**, they are stressed. The vowels following are soft and brief. When the initial vowels are **i**, **u** and **ü**, the main vowels come after them. **i**, **u** and **ü** are transitional sounds. If there are vowels or nasal consonants after the main vowels, they should be unstressed as well. In a compound final, the main vowel can be affected by the phonemes before and after it. For instance, the **a** in **ian** is pronounced with a lower degree of aperture and a higher position of the tongue than the **a** in **ma**; and to pronounce the **a** in **ang** the tongue has to be positioned more to the back of the mouth than the **a** elsewhere.

As noted above, in *pinyin* orthography some vowels are omitted for the sake of economy, e.g., **i(o)u**, **u(e)i**. However, when pronouncing those sounds, the vowels must not be omitted.

Spelling Rules

1 If there is no initial consonant before **i**, **i** is written as a semi-vowel, **y**. Thus **ia**, **ie**, **iao**, **iu**, **ian**, **iang** become **ya**, **ye**, **yao**, **you** (note that the **o** cannot be omitted here), **yan**, **yang**. Before **in**, **ing**, and **o**, add **y**, e.g., **yin**, **ying**, **yo**.

2 If there is no initial consonant before **ü**, add a **y** and drop the umlaut: **yu**, **yuan**, **yue**, **yun**.

▲3▲ **u** becomes **w** if not preceded by an initial, e.g., **wa**, **wai**, **wan**, **wang**, **wei**, **wen, weng, wo. u** by itself becomes **wu**.

▲4▲ **ueng** is written as **ong**, if preceded by an initial, e.g., **tong**, **dong**, **nong**, **long**. Without an initial, it is **weng**.

▲5▲ In order to avoid confusion, an apostrophe is used to separate two syllables with connecting vowels, e.g., **shí'èr** (twelve) and the city **Xī'ān** (**shí** and **èr, xī** and **ān** are separate syllables).

PRACTICE

C.1: ai ei ao ou

pai	**lei**	**dao**	**gou**
cai	**mei**	**sao**	**shou**

C.2: an en ang eng ong

C.2.a an vs. ang

tan	**tang**	**chan**	**chang**
zan	**zhang**	**gan**	**gang**

C.2.b en vs. eng

sen	**seng**	**shen**	**sheng**
zhen	**zheng**	**fen**	**feng**

C.2.c eng vs. ong

cheng	**chong**	**deng**	**dong**
zheng	**zhong**	**keng**	**kong**

C.3: ia iao ie iu ian in iang ing iong

C.3.a ia vs. ie

jia	**jie**	**qia**	**qie**
xia	**xie**	**ya**	**ye**

C.3.b ian vs. iang

xian	**xiang**	**qian**	**qiang**
jian	**jiang**	**yan**	**yang**

C.3.c in vs. ing

bin	**bing**	**pin**	**ping**
jin	**jing**	**yin**	**ying**

C.3.d iu vs. iong

xiu	**xiong**	**you**	**yong**

C.3.e ao vs. iao

zhao	**jiao**	**shao**	**xiao**
chao	**qiao**	**ao**	**yao**

C.3.f an vs. ian

chan	**qian**	**shan**	**xian**
zhan	**jian**	**an**	**yan**

C.3.g ang vs. iang

zhang	**jiang**	**shang**	**xiang**
chang	**qiang**	**ang**	**yang**

C.4: ua uo uai ui uan un uang

C.4.a ua vs. uai

shua	**shuai**	**wa**	**wai**

C.4.b uan vs. uang

shuan	**shuang**	**chuan**	**chuang**
zhuan	**zhuang**	**wan**	**wang**

C.4.c un vs. uan

dun	**duan**	**kun**	**kuan**
zhun	**zhuan**	**wen**	**wan**

C.4.d uo vs. ou

duo	**dou**	**zhuo**	**zhou**
suo	**sou**	**wo**	**ou**

C.4.e ui vs. un

tui	**tun**	**zhui**	**zhun**
dui	**dun**	**wei**	**wen**

C.5: üe üan ün

C.5.a ün vs. un

jun	**zhun**	**yun**	**wen**

C.5.b üan vs. uan

xuan	**shuan**	**juan**	**zhuan**
quan	**chuan**	**yuan**	**wan**

C.5.c üe

yue	**que**	**jue**

C.6: er

ger*

*Due to the lack of words with first tone **er** in them, the word "**ger**" (**ge** with **r** ending) is here to give the reader a feel for it. See **D.1 Practice III** below (p. 18) for more examples.

D. TONES

Every Chinese syllable has a tone.

D.1: Four tones

There are four tones in Mandarin Chinese (i.e., 普通话 pǔtōnghuà, "common language" in mainland China; 国语 guóyǔ, "national language" in Taiwan; 华语 Huáyǔ, "the Chinese language" in Singapore and some other places): the first tone (阴平 yīnpíng), the second tone (阳平 yángpíng), the third tone (上声 shǎngshēng), the fourth tone (去声 qùshēng).

The first tone is a high level tone with a pitch value of 55 (see chart below); its tone mark is " ˉ ."

The second tone is a rising tone with a pitch value of 35; its tone mark is " ˊ ."

The citation form of the third tone has a pitch value of 214. However, in normal speech it almost always occurs as a "half third tone" with a pitch value of 21 or (in front of another third tone) transformed into a second tone with the pitch value of 35. Its tone mark is " ˇ ."

The fourth tone is a falling tone with a pitch value of 51; its tone mark is " ˋ ."

In addition to the four tones, there is also a neutral tone (轻声 qīngshēng) in Mandarin Chinese. Neutral tone words include those that do not have fundamental tones (e.g., the question particle **ma**), and those that do have tones when pronounced individually, but are not stressed in certain compounds (e.g., the second **ba** in "**bàba**" or "father"). There are no tone marks for neutral tone syllables. A neutral tone syllable is pronounced briefly and softly, and its pitch value is determined by the stressed syllable immediately before it. A neutral tone following a first tone syllable, as in **māma** 妈妈, carries a pitch tone of 2. When it follows a second tone syllable, a third tone syllable, or a fourth tone syllable, its pitch value will be 3, 4, and 1 respectively.

Tones are very important in Chinese. The same syllable with different tones can have different meanings. For instance, **mā** 妈 is mother, **má** 麻 is hemp, **mǎ** 马 is horse, **mà** 骂 is to scold, and **ma** 吗 is an interrogative particle. The four tones can be diagrammed as follows:

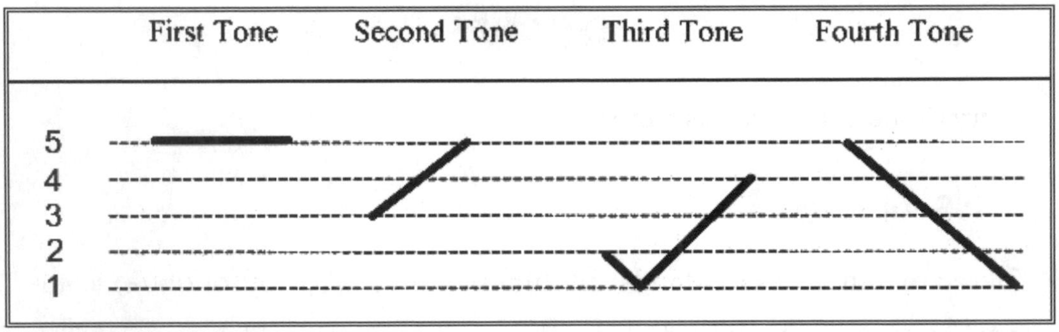

Tone marks are written above the main vowel of a syllable. The main vowel can be identified according to the following sequence: **a-o-e-i-u-ü.** For instance, in **ao** the main vowel is **a**. In **ei** the main vowel is **e**. There is one exception: when **i** and **u** are combined into a syllable, the tone mark is written on the second vowel: **iù**, **uì**.

D.1 PRACTICE I: MONOSYLLABIC WORDS

1.a Four Tones

bī	**bí**	**bǐ**	**bì**
pū	**pú**	**pǔ**	**pù**
dà	**dǎ**	**dá**	**dā**
shè	**shě**	**shé**	**shē**
tí	**tī**	**tǐ**	**tì**
kè	**kě**	**kē**	**ké**
jǐ	**jí**	**jì**	**jī**
gú	**gù**	**gū**	**gǔ**

1.b 1st vs. 2nd

zā	**zá**
chū	**chú**
hē	**hé**
shī	**shí**

1.c 1st vs. 3rd

tū	**tǔ**
mō	**mǒ**
xī	**xǐ**
shā	**shǎ**

1.d 1st vs. 4th

fā	**fà**
dī	**dì**
qū	**qù**
kē	**kè**

1.e 2nd vs. 1st

hú	**hū**
xí	**xī**
zhé	**zhē**
pó	**pō**

1.f 2nd vs. 3rd

gé	**gě**
tí	**tǐ**
jú	**jǔ**
rú	**rǔ**

1.g 2nd vs. 4th

lú	**lù**
mó	**mò**
cí	**cì**
zhé	**zhè**

1.h 3rd vs. 1st

tǎ	**tā**
mǐ	**mī**
gǔ	**gū**
chě	**chē**

1.i 3rd vs. 2nd

chǔ	**chú**
kě	**ké**
xǐ	**xí**
qǔ	**qú**

1.j 3rd vs. 4th

bǒ	**bò**
nǐ	**nì**
chǔ	**chù**
rě	**rè**

1.k 4th vs. 1st

jì	**jī**
là	**lā**
sù	**sū**
hè	**hē**

1.l 4th vs. 2nd

nà	**ná**
zè	**zé**
jù	**jú**
lǜ	**lǘ**

1.m 4th vs. 3rd

sà	**sǎ**
zì	**zǐ**
kù	**kǔ**
zhè	**zhě**

D.1 PRACTICE II: BISYLLABIC WORDS

2.a 1st 1st

chūzū tūchū chūfā

2.b 1st 2nd

chātú xīqí chūxí

2.c 1st 3rd

shēchǐ gēqǔ chūbǎn

2.d 1st 4th

chūsè hūshì jīlǜ

2.e 2nd 1st

shíshī qíjī shíchā

2.f 2nd 2nd

jíhé shépí pígé

2.g 2nd 3rd

jítǐ bóqǔ zhélǐ

2.h 2nd 4th

qítè fúlì chíxù

2.i 3rd 1st

zǔzhī zhǔjī lǐkē

2.j 3rd 2nd

pǔjí zhǔxí chǔfá

2.k 3rd 4th

lǚkè gǔlì tǐzhì

2.l 4th 1st

zìsī qìchē lǜshī

2.m 4th 2nd

fùzá dìtú shìshí

2.n 4th 3rd

zìjǐ bìhǔ dìzhǐ

2.o 4th 4th

mùdì xùmù dàdì

D.1 PRACTICE III: WORDS WITH "ER" SOUND

3.a

érzi érqiě

3.b

ěrduo mù'ěr

3.c

shí'èr èrshí

D.2: Tone sandhi

If two third tone syllables are spoken in succession, the first third tone becomes second tone. This tone change is known as "tone sandhi" in linguistics.

For instance,

xǐlǐ	→	**xílǐ**	(baptism)
chǐrǔ	→	**chírǔ**	(shame)
qǔshě	→	**qúshě**	(accept or reject)

Note

Following standard *pinyin* practice, we do not change the tone marks from third to second tone. Initially you might have to consciously remember that the first syllable actually is pronounced as a second tone syllable, but through pronunciation drills and hearing the language spoken, you will soon be making the sandhi change automatically and unconsciously.

D.2 PRACTICE

chǔlǐ	→	**chúlǐ**	**gǔpǔ**	→	**gúpǔ**
bǐnǐ	→	**bínǐ**	**jǔzhǐ**	→	**júzhǐ**
zǐnǚ	→	**zínǚ**	**zhǐshǐ**	→	**zhíshǐ**

D.3: Neutral tone

The neutral tone occurs in unstressed syllables. It is unmarked. For instance,

chēzi (car)	**māma** (mother, mom)	**chúzi** (cook)
shūshu (uncle)	**lǐzi** (plum)	**shìzi** (persimmon)

The pitch of the neutral tone is determined by the preceding syllable.

D.3 PRACTICE

1.	**māma**	**gēge**	**shīfu**	**chūqu**
2.	**dízi**	**bóbo**	**bízi**	**chúle**
3.	**lǐzi**	**qǐzi**	**dǐzi**	**fǔshang**
4.	**bàba**	**dìdi**	**kèqi**	**kùzi**

E. COMBINATION EXERCISES

I.

shān	**xiān**	**sān**
cháng	**qiáng**	**cáng**
zhǐ	**jǐ**	**zǐ**
lüè	**nüè**	**yuè**
kè	**lè**	**rè**

II.

Zhōngguó	**xīngqī**	**lǜshī**	**zhàopiàn**
zàijiàn	**tóngxué**	**xǐhuan**	**diànshì**
yīnyuè	**kělè**	**yǎnlèi**	**shàngwǔ**
cèsuǒ	**chūntiān**	**xiàwǔ**	**bànyè**
gōngkè	**kāishǐ**	**rìjì**	**cāntīng**
zuìjìn	**xīwàng**	**yīsheng**	**chūzū**
zhōumò	**guānxi**	**dòufu**	**jiéhūn**
liúxué	**nü'ér**	**shénme**	**suīrán**
wǎngqiú	**xǐzǎo**	**niánjí**	**yóuyǒng**

II. Chinese Writing System

A. THE FORMATION OF CHINESE CHARACTERS

Unlike English, which is an alphabetic language, Chinese writing is represented by "characters," each of which represents a meaningful syllable. Characters are traditionally divided into the following six categories:

1. 象形 xiàngxíng   pictographs, pictographic characters

Examples:

人    rén   man

山    shān   mountain

日    rì   sun

月    yuè   moon

木 	mù	tree

2. 指事 zhǐshì self-explanatory characters

Examples:

上 	shàng	above
下 	xià	below

3. 会意 huìyì associative compounds

Examples:

明 	míng	bright
休 	xiū	rest

4. 形声 xíngshēng pictophonetic characters (with one element indicating meaning and the other sound)

Examples: 江，河，饭，姑

5. 转注 zhuǎnzhù mutually explanatory characters

Examples: 老，考

6. 假借 jiǎjiè phonetic loan characters

Examples: 来，我

A popular myth is that Chinese writing is pictographic, and that each Chinese character represents a picture. It is true that some Chinese characters have evolved from pictures, but these comprise only a small proportion of the characters. The vast majority of Chinese characters are pictophonetic characters consisting of a radical and a phonetic element. The radical often suggests the meaning of a character, and the phonetic element indicates its original pronunciation, which may or may not represent its modern pronunciation.

B. BASIC CHINESE RADICALS

Although there are more than fifty thousand Chinese characters in existence, one only needs to know two or three thousand of them to be considered literate. Mastering two or three thousand characters is, of course, a rather formidable task. However, the learning process will be more effective and easier if one knows well the basic components of Chinese characters. Traditionally, Chinese characters are grouped together according to their common components known as "radicals" (部首, bùshǒu). The 214 "Kangxi radicals" have been the standard set of radicals since the publication of the great *Kangxi Dictionary* (康熙字典 *Kāngxī Zìdiǎn*) in 1716, although some contemporary dictionaries, which treat simplified characters as primary forms, have reduced that number to 189. By knowing the radicals and other basic components well, you will find recognizing, remembering and reproducing characters much easier. Knowing the radicals is also a must when using dictionaries, which arrange characters according to their radicals. The following is a selection of forty radicals that everybody should know well when starting to learn characters.

	Chinese radical	*Pinyin*	*English*	*Examples*
1.	人（亻）	rén	man	你，他
2.	刀（刂）	dāo	knife	分，到
3.	力	lì	power	加，助
4.	又	yòu	right hand; again	友，取
5.	口	kǒu	mouth	叫，可
6.	囗**	wéi	enclose	回，因
7.	土	tǔ	earth	在，坐
8.	夕	xī	sunset	外，多
9.	大	dà	big	天，太

**used as radical only, not as a character by itself

10.	女	nǚ	woman	好，妈
11.	子	zǐ	son	字，学
12.	寸	cùn	inch	对，付
13.	小	xiǎo	small	少，尖
14.	工	gōng	labor; work	左，差
15.	幺	yāo	tiny; small	幻，幼
16.	弓	gōng	bow	张，弟
17.	心（忄）	xīn	heart	忙，快
18.	戈	gē	dagger-axe	我，或
19.	手（扌）	shǒu	hand	打，找
20.	日	rì	sun	早，明
21.	月	yuè	moon	有，明
22.	木	mù	wood	李，杯
23.	水（氵）	shuǐ	water	没，洗
24.	火（灬）	huǒ	fire	烧，热
25.	田	tián	field	男，留
26.	目	mù	eye	看，睡
27.	示（礻）	shì	show	社，票
28.	糸（纟）	mì	fine silk	红，素
29.	耳	ěr	ear	取，聊
30.	衣（衤）	yī	clothing	衫，初
31.	言（讠）	yán	speech	说，认
32.	贝	bèi	cowry shell	贵，员

33.	走	zǒu	walk	趣，起
34.	足	zú	foot	跳，跑
35.	金(钅)	jīn	gold	钱，银
36.	门	mén	door	问，间
37.	隹	zhuī	short-tailed bird	售，难
38.	雨	yǔ	rain	雪，零
39.	食(饣)	shí	eat	饭，馆
40.	马	mǎ	horse	骑，驾

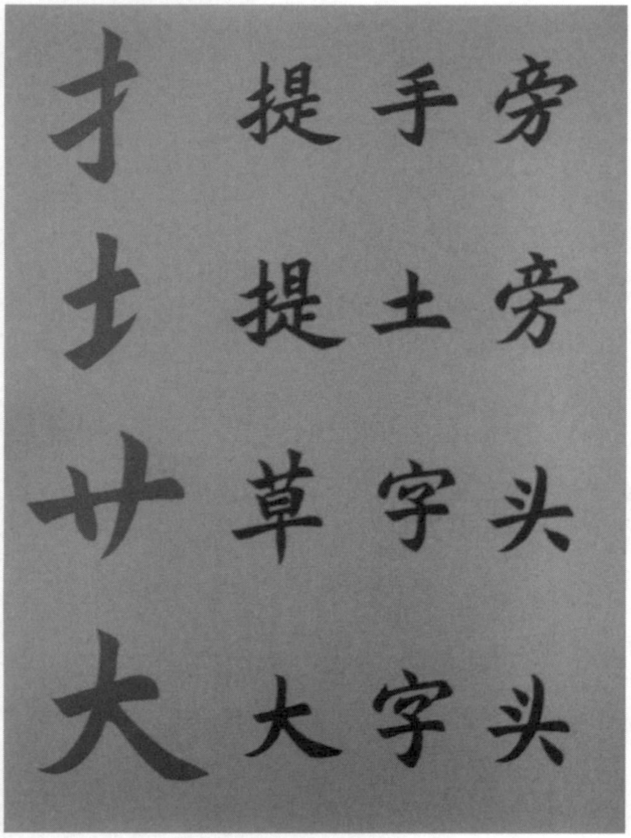

A Chinese radical chart.

C. BASIC STROKES

The following is a list of basic strokes:

	Basic stroke	*Chinese*	*Pinyin*	*English*	*Examples*
1.	"丶"	点	diǎn	dot	小，六
2.	"一"	横	héng	horizontal	一，六
3.	"丨"	竖	shù	vertical	十，中
4.	"丿"	撇	piě	downward left	人，大
5.	"㇏"	捺	nà	downward right	八，人
6.	"㇀"	提	tí	upward	我，江
7.	"乛"	横钩	hénggōu	horizontal hook	你，字
8.	"亅"	竖钩	shùgōu	vertical hook	小，你
9.	"㇂"	斜钩	xiégōu	slanted hook	戈，我
10.	"㇕"	横折	héngzhé	horizontal bend	五，口
11.	"㇗"	竖折	shùzhé	vertical bend	七，亡

Note

With the exception of the "tí" stroke (which moves upward to the right) and the "piě" stroke (which moves downward to the left), all Chinese strokes move from top to bottom, and from left to right.

D. STROKE ORDER

Following is a list of rules of stroke order. When writing a Chinese character, it is important that you follow the rules. Following the rules will make it easier for you to accurately count the number of strokes in a character. Knowing the exact number of strokes in a character will help you find the character in a radical-based dictionary. Also, your Chinese characters will look better if you write them in the correct stroke order!

1. From left to right (川，人)
2. From top to bottom (三)
3. Horizontal before vertical (十)
4. From outside to inside (月)
5. Middle before two sides (小)
6. Inside before closing (日，回)

Note: Learn the correct stroke order of the characters introduced in this book by using the *Integrated Chinese Level 1 Character Workbook.*

III. Useful Expressions

A. CLASSROOM EXPRESSIONS

The following is a list of classroom expressions that you will hear every day in your Chinese class.

1. Nǐ hǎo!	How are you? How do you do?
2. Lǎoshī hǎo!	How are you, teacher?
3. Shàng kè.	Let's begin the class.
4. Xià kè.	The class is over.
5. Dǎkāi shū.	Open the book.
6. Wǒ shuō, nǐmen tīng.	I'll speak, you listen.
7. Kàn hēibǎn.	Look at the blackboard.
8. Duì bu duì?	Is it right?
9. Duì!	Right! Correct!
10. Hěn hǎo!	Very good!
11. Qǐng gēn wǒ shuō.	Please repeat after me.
12. Zài shuō yí cì.	Say it again.
13. Dǒng bu dǒng?	Do you understand?
14. Dǒng le.	Yes, I/we understand.

15. Zàijiàn! Good-bye!

16. Qǐng yòng ______ zàojù! Please make a sentence using ______!

B. SURVIVAL EXPRESSIONS

The following is a list of important expressions that will help you survive in a Chinese language environment. A good language student is constantly learning new words by asking questions. Learn the following expressions well and start to acquire Chinese on your own!

1. Duìbuqǐ!	Sorry!
2. Qǐng wèn...	Excuse me...; May I ask...
3. Xièxie!	Thanks!
4. Zhè shi shénme?	What is this?
5. Wǒ bù dǒng.	I don't understand.
6. Qǐng zài shuō yí biàn.	Please say it one more time.
7. "..." Zhōngguóhuà zěnme shuō?	How do you say "..." in Chinese?
8. "..." shì shénme yìsi?	What does "..." mean?
9. Qǐng nǐ gěi wǒ....	Please give me....
10. Qǐng nǐ gàosu wǒ....	Please tell me....
11. Duìbuqǐ, nín shi shuō...?	Sorry, do you mean...?

C. NUMERALS

Having good control of the Chinese numerals will facilitate your dealing with real life situations such as shopping, asking for time and dates, etc. You can get a head start by memorizing 1 to 10 well now.

1. yī	one	一	6. liù	six	六
2. èr	two	二	7. qī	seven	七
3. sān	three	三	8. bā	eight	八
4. sì	four	四	9. jiǔ	nine	九
5. wǔ	five	五	10. shí	ten	十

Do you know the names of the strokes below? Can you write them properly?

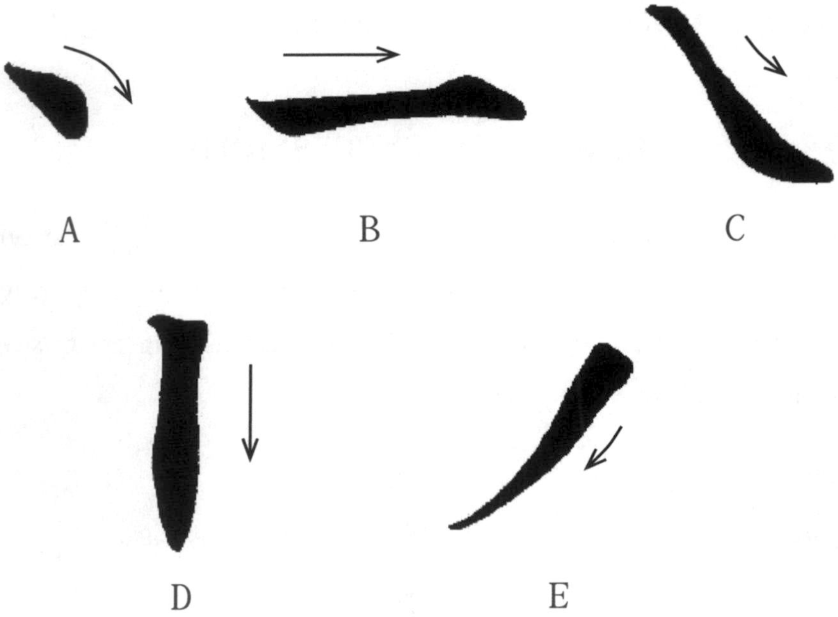

LESSON 1 ▲ Greetings

第一课 ▲ 问好

Dì yí kè ▲ *Wèn hǎo*

你好!

Nǐ hǎo!

Dialogue I: Exchanging Greetings

VOCABULARY

1.	先生	xiānsheng	n	Mr.; husband; teacher
2.	你好	nǐ hǎo	ce	How do you do? Hello!
	你	nǐ	pr	you
	好	hǎo	adj	fine; good; nice; O.K.
3.	小姐	xiǎojie	n	Miss; young lady
4.	请问	qǐng wèn	ce	May I ask...

	请	qǐng	v	please (a polite form of request)
	问	wèn	v	to ask (a question)
5.	您	nín	pr	you (singular; polite)
6.	#贵姓	guì xìng	ce	What is your honorable surname?
	贵	guì	adj	honorable
	姓	xìng	v/n	(one's) surname is...; to be surnamed; surname
7.	我	wǒ	pr	I; me
8.	呢	ne	qp	(an interrogative particle)
9.	叫	jiào	v	to be called; to call
10.	什么	shénme	qpr	what
11.	名字	míngzi	n	name

Proper Nouns

12.	王朋	Wáng Péng	pn	(a personal name)
	王	wáng	n	(a surname); king
13.	李友	Lǐ Yǒu	pn	(a personal name)
	李	lǐ	n	(a surname); plum

DIALOGUE I

Wáng Xiānsheng[(1)] : Nǐ hǎo[(2)]!

Lǐ Xiǎojie: Nǐ hǎo!

Wáng Xiānsheng: Qǐng wèn, nín guì xìng[(3)]?

Lǐ Xiǎojie: Wǒ xìng[(G1)] Lǐ. Nǐ ne[(G2)]?

Wáng Xiānsheng: Wǒ xìng Wáng, jiào[(G3)] Wáng Péng[(4)]. Nǐ jiào shénme míngzi[(5)]?

Lǐ Xiǎojie: Wǒ jiào Lǐ Yǒu.

DIALOGUE I

王先生(1)：　你好(2)！

李小姐：　你好！

王先生：　请问，您贵姓(3)？

李小姐：　我姓(G1)李。你呢(G2)？

王先生：　我姓王，叫(G3)王朋(4)。你叫什么名字(5)？

李小姐：　我叫李友。

A Note on the Notes

▲1▲ The # symbol preceding a character in the vocabulary section suggests that it's a low frequency one. The teacher might want to allow the student to use *pinyin* instead of writing the character when doing homework.

▲2▲ The numbering system for notes in this textbook works as follows:

a. For numbers without any letter in front of them, see the Notes section.

b. For numbers preceded with a "G," see the Grammar section.

c. For the letter "F," see Functional Expressions.

Notes

▲1▲ Most Chinese family names or surnames (姓 xìng) are monosyllabic. There are, however, a few disyllabic family names, written with two characters. The number of Chinese family names is fairly limited. According to the most recent census, the most common family names are Li 李 (Lǐ), Wang 王 (Wáng), Zhang 张 (Zhāng), Liu 刘 (Liú), and Chen 陈 (Chén). Family names also precede official titles or other forms of address: 王先生 (Wáng Xiānsheng, lit. Wang Mister), 李老师 (Lǐ Lǎoshī, lit. Li Teacher), etc. When addressing someone without knowing his or her family name, it is proper to call him 先生 (xiānsheng, Mister) or her 小姐 (xiǎojie, Miss) if she is relatively young.

▴2▴ "你好！" (Nǐ hǎo!) is a common form of greeting. It can be used to address strangers upon first introduction or between old acquaintances. To respond, simply repeat the greeting: "你好！" (Nǐ hǎo!). "你好吗？" (Nǐ hǎo ma? How are you?) is a question usually asked of people you already know. The answer is usually "我很好" (Wǒ hěn hǎo; I am fine).

▴3▴ According to an etymological speculation, the character 姓 (xìng), with a woman radical on the left side and an ideographic component on the right that can mean "to give birth," suggests the matriarchal nature of the society at the time of the character's conception, when family names were inherited matrilineally.

▴4▴ In Chinese, family names (姓 xìng) always precede personal or given names (名 míng). Personal names usually carry auspicious or positive meanings. They can be either monosyllabic, written in one character, or disyllabic, written in two characters. In Chinese a person is seldom referred to by his or her family name alone, especially if the family name is monosyllabic. For example, Wang Peng (王朋 Wáng Péng), should not be referred to simply as Wang.

▴5▴ In China, when you meet someone, it is polite to ask for his or her family name first, rather than his/her full name. Then the question "你叫什么名字？" (Nǐ jiào shénme míngzi? What is your name?) can be asked to find out his or her given name or full name.

Culture Notes

In China the use of given names often suggests a much higher degree of intimacy than in the West. If one's given name is monosyllabic, its use is even more limited, usually confined to writing. For example, Wang Peng's parents can address him as Peng in their letters to him, but at home they would most likely call him Wang Peng, instead of Peng. If he is still a child, they might call him Xiao Peng (lit. Little Peng) or Pengpeng (duplicating the syllable).

Do you know anybody with the following surnames?

毕 (Bì); 蔡 (Cài); 陈 (Chén); 高 (Gāo); 黄 (Huáng); 李 (Lǐ); 林 (Lín); 刘 (Liú); 罗 (Luó); 毛 (Máo); 史 (Shǐ); 王 (Wáng); 吴 (Wú); 谢 (Xiè); 徐 (Xú); 许 (Xǔ); 杨 (Yáng); 姚 (Yáo); 叶 (Yè); 张 (Zhāng); 郑 (Zhèng); 周 (Zhōu)

Dialogue II: Asking One's Status

VOCABULARY

1.	是	shì	v	to be
2.	老师	lǎoshī	n	teacher
3.	吗	ma	qp	(an interrogative particle)
4.	不	bù	adv	not; no
5.	学生	xuésheng	n	student
6.	也	yě	adv	too; also
7.	中国人	Zhōngguórén	n	Chinese people/person
	中国	Zhōngguó	n	China
	人	rén	n	people; person
8.	美国人	Měiguórén	n	American people/person
	美国	Měiguó	n	America

DIALOGUE II

Lǐ Xiǎojie:	Wáng Xiānsheng, nǐ shì[(G4)] lǎoshī ma[(G5)]?
Wáng Xiānsheng:	Bù[(G6)], wǒ bú[(1)] shì lǎoshī, wǒ shì xuésheng. Lǐ Xiǎojie, nǐ ne?
Lǐ Xiǎojie:	Wǒ yě[(G7)] shì xuésheng. Nǐ shì Zhōngguórén ma?
Wáng Xiānsheng:	Shì, wǒ shì Zhōngguórén. Nǐ shì Měiguórén ma?
Lǐ Xiǎojie:	Wǒ shì Měiguórén.

DIALOGUE II

李小姐：王先生，你是(G4)老师吗(G5)？

王先生：不(G6)，我不(1)是老师，我是学生。李小姐，你呢？

李小姐：我也(G7)是学生。你是中国人吗？

王先生：是，我是中国人。你是美国人吗？

李小姐：我是美国人。

Notes

▲1▲ The basic pronunciation of 不 is "bù" with fourth tone. However, when it is placed before another fourth tone syllable, 不 is pronounced in the second tone instead of the fourth. Therefore, 不是 is pronounced "bú shì" rather than "bù shì." In this textbook, the tone for 不 is marked as it is actually pronounced.

Can you identify the "老师" (lǎoshī) and "学生" (xuésheng) in this picture?

SUPPLEMENTARY VOCABULARY

1.	朋友	péngyou	n	friend
2.	太太	tàitai	n	wife; Mrs.
3.	英国	Yīngguó	n	Britain; England
4.	法国	Fǎguó	n	France
5.	日本	Rìběn	n	Japan
6.	德国	Déguó	n	Germany
7.	英国人	Yīngguórén	n	British people/person
8.	法国人	Fǎguórén	n	French people/person
9.	日本人	Rìběnrén	n	Japanese people/person
10.	德国人	Déguórén	n	German people/person
11.	韩国人	Hánguórén	n	Korean people/person
12.	越南人	Yuènánrén	n	Vietnamese people/person

Can you tell their nationalities by their costumes?

What are they saying to each other?

Grammar

[Note: In the grammar explanations in this textbook, the sign * indicates an example sentence that illustrates a grammatical or syntactic mistake.]

1. The Verb 姓 (xìng)

姓 (xìng) is both a noun and a verb. When it is used as a verb, an object must follow it. For example:

(1) A: 您贵姓?

Nín guì xìng?

(What is your surname? lit. Your honorable surname is...?)

B: 我姓王。

Wǒ xìng Wáng.

(My surname is Wang.)

(2) A: 你姓什么?

Nǐ xìng shénme?

(What is your surname? lit. You are surnamed what?)

B: 我姓李。

Wǒ xìng Lǐ.

(My surname is Li.)

姓 (xìng) is usually negated with 不 (bù). [See G.6 below.]

(3) A: 你姓李吗?

Nǐ xìng Lǐ ma?

(Is your family name Li?)

B: 我不姓李。

Wǒ bú xìng Lǐ.

(My surname is not Li.)

Note: When 姓 (xìng; to be surnamed) is used as a verb, an object must follow it. One should therefore never say *我姓 (*Wǒ xìng) or *我不姓 (*Wǒ bú xìng) as a short answer to the question: 你姓李吗? (Nǐ xìng Lǐ ma? Is your family name Li?)

2. Questions Ending with 呢 (ne)

呢 (ne) often follows a noun or pronoun to form a question when the content of the question is already clear from the context.

For example:

(1) 我姓李，你呢?

Wǒ xìng Lǐ, nǐ ne?

(My surname is Li. How about you?)

(2) 我是中国人，你呢?

Wǒ shì Zhōngguórén, nǐ ne?

(I am Chinese. How about you?)

(3) 我是老师，你呢?

Wǒ shì lǎoshī, nǐ ne?

(I am a teacher. How about you?)

Note: When 呢 (ne) is used in this way, there must be some context. In sentence (2) the context is provided by the preceding sentence, "我是中国人" (Wǒ shì Zhōngguórén). Likewise in sentence (3) "我是老师" (Wǒ shì lǎoshī) provides the context.

3. The Verb 叫 (jiào)

The verb 叫 (jiào) has several meanings. It means "to be called" in this lesson. It must be followed by an object.

For example:

(1) A: 你叫什么名字?

Nǐ jiào shénme míngzi?

(What is your name?)

B: 我叫王朋。

Wǒ jiào Wáng Péng.

(My name is Wang Peng.)

叫 (jiào) is usually negated with 不 (bù). [See G.6 below.]

(2) A: 你叫李生吗?

Nǐ jiào Lǐ Shēng ma?

(Is your name Li Sheng?)

B: 我不叫李生。

Wǒ bú jiào Lǐ Shēng.

(My name is not Li Sheng.)

Note: Like 姓 (xìng; to be surnamed), when 叫 (jiào; to be called) is used as a verb, it must take an object. One should therefore never say *我叫 (*Wǒ jiào) or *我不叫 (*Wǒ bú jiào).

From the examples above, we can see that the basic word order in a Chinese sentence runs like this:

Subject + Verb + Object

The word order remains the same in statements and questions. Remember that you don't place the question word at the beginning of a question as you do in English, unless that question word serves as the subject. (See more on word order in Grammar Note 1 in Lesson 4.)

4. The Verb 是 (shì)

In Chinese, 是 (shì) is a verb that can be used to link two nouns, pronouns, or noun phrases that are in some way equivalent.

For example:

(1) A: 你是老师吗？

Nǐ shì lǎoshī ma?

(Are you a teacher?)

B: 我是老师。

Wǒ shì lǎoshī.

(I am a teacher.)

(2) A: 李友是学生。

Lǐ Yǒu shì xuésheng.

(Li You is a student.)

B: 你是美国人吗？

Nǐ shì Měiguórén ma?

(Are you an American?)

是 (shì) is usually negated with 不 (bù). [See G.6 below.]

(3) A: 李友不是中国人。

Lǐ Yǒu bú shì Zhōngguórén.

(Li You is not Chinese.)

B: 王朋不是老师。

Wáng Péng bú shì lǎoshī.

(Wang Peng is not a teacher.)

5. Questions Ending with 吗 (ma)

When 吗 (ma) is added to the end of a declarative statement, that statement is turned into a question. The person who asks a question that ends with 吗 (ma) often has some expectation of the answer. In sentence (1) below, the questioner may expect that the other person is a teacher, and in sentence (2) the questioner may expect that the other person is a student. To answer the question in the affirmative, 是 (shì) is used, while 不 (bù) is used if the answer is negative.

For example:

(1) A: 你是老师吗？

Nǐ shì lǎoshī ma?

(Are you a teacher?)

B: 是，我是老师。

Shì, wǒ shì lǎoshī.

(Yes, I am a teacher.)

C: 不，我不是老师。

Bù, wǒ bú shì lǎoshī.

(No, I am not a teacher.)

D: 不，我是学生。

Bù, wǒ shì xuésheng.

(No, I am a student.)

(2) A: 王友是学生吗？

Wáng Yǒu shì xuésheng ma?

(Is Wang You a student?)

B: 是，王友是学生。

Shì, Wáng Yǒu shì xuésheng.

(Yes, Wang You is a student.)

C: 不，王友不是学生。

Bù, Wáng Yǒu bú shì xuésheng.

(No, Wang You is not a student.)

D: 不，王友是老师。

Bù, Wáng Yǒu shì lǎoshī.

(No, Wang You is a teacher.)

(3) A: 李朋是美国人吗？

Lǐ Péng shì Měiguórén ma?

(Is Li Peng an American?)

B: 是，李朋是美国人。

Shì, Lǐ Péng shì Měiguórén.

(Yes, Li Peng is an American.)

C: 不，李朋不是美国人。

Bù, Lǐ Péng bú shì Měiguórén.

(No, Li Peng is not an American.)

D: 不，李朋是中国人。

Bù, Lí Péng shì Zhōngguórén.

(No, Li Peng is Chinese.)

6. The Negative Adverb 不 (bù)

In Chinese there are two main negative adverbs. One of the two, 不 (bù), occurs in this lesson.

For example:

(1) 不，我不是老师。

Bù, wǒ bú shì lǎoshī.

(No, I am not a teacher.)

(2) 李友不是中国人。

Lǐ Yǒu bú shì Zhōngguórén.

(Li You is not Chinese.)

(3) 老师不姓王。

Lǎoshī bú xìng Wáng.

(The teacher's surname is not Wang.)

(4) 我不叫李中。

Wǒ bú jiào Lǐ Zhōng.

(My name is not Li Zhong.)

7. The Adverb 也 (yě)

The adverb 也 (yě) basically means "too, also" in English. In Chinese, adverbs normally appear after subjects and in front of verbs. They usually cannot precede subjects or follow verbs. The adverb 也 (yě) cannot be put before the subject or at the very end of a sentence.

For example:

(1) 我也是学生。

Wǒ yě shì xuésheng.

(I am a student, too.)

(2) 王朋是学生，李友也是学生。

Wáng Péng shì xuésheng, Lǐ Yǒu yě shì xuésheng.

(Wang Peng is a student. Li You is a student, too.)

(3) 你是中国人，我也是中国人。

Nǐ shì Zhōngguórén, wǒ yě shì Zhōngguórén.

(You are Chinese. I am Chinese, too.)

The following sentences are **incorrect**:

(3) a. *你是中国人，我是中国人也。

Nǐ shì Zhōngguórén, wǒ shì Zhōngguórén yě.

(3) b. *你是中国人，也我是中国人。

Nǐ shì Zhōngguórén, yě wǒ shì Zhōngguórén.

When the adverb 也 (yě) is used together with the negative adverb 不 (bù), 也 (yě) is placed before 不 (bù).

For example:

(4) 王朋不是学生，李友也不是学生。

Wáng Péng bú shì xuésheng, Lǐ Yǒu yě bú shì xuésheng.

(Wang Peng is not a student. Li You is not a student either.)

(5) 你不是中国人，我也不是中国人。

Nǐ bú shì Zhōngguórén, wǒ yě bú shì Zhōngguórén.

(You are not Chinese, and I am not Chinese either.)

PATTERN DRILLS

All the exercises in the Pattern Drills section of each lesson are meant to be **Substitution Drills** unless otherwise noted. The teacher first says a sentence, then gives one or two words. The student uses the word(s) to form a new sentence.

A. 是 (shì)

Example:	Teacher:	Wǒ <u>shì</u> lǎoshī. (xuésheng)
	Student:	Wǒ <u>shì</u> xuésheng.
	Teacher:	我<u>是</u>老师。(学生)
	Student:	我<u>是</u>学生。

1.	Wǒ	shì	Zhōngguó xuésheng.
2.	Nǐ		lǎoshī.
3.	Lǐ Xiǎojie		xuésheng.
4.	Wáng Xiānsheng		lǎoshī.
5.	Wáng Péng		Zhōngguórén.
6.	Lǐ Yǒu		Měiguórén.

1.	我	是	中国学生。
2.	你		老师。
3.	李小姐		学生。
4.	王先生		老师。
5.	王朋		中国人。
6.	李友		美国人。

B. 是…吗 (shì…ma)

1.	Wáng Xiānsheng	shì	xuésheng	ma?
2.	Lǐ Yǒu		Zhōngguórén	
3.	Wáng Péng		Měiguórén	
4.	Lǐ Xiǎojie		Zhōngguó xuésheng	
5.	Wáng Xiānsheng		Měiguó lǎoshī	

1.	王先生	是	学生	吗？
2.	李友		中国人	
3.	王朋		美国人	
4.	李小姐		中国学生	
5.	王先生		美国老师	

C. 吗 (ma)

Provide appropriate questions for speaker A for the answers given by speaker B.

Example: A: Nǐ jiào Wáng Péng ma? B: Bù, wǒ bú jiào Wáng Péng.

A: 你叫王朋吗? B: 不，我不叫王朋。

1. A: ________________ ? B: Bù, Wáng Péng bú shì lǎoshī.
2. A: ________________ ? B: Lǐ Yǒu shì xuésheng.
3. A: ________________ ? B: Wáng Péng shì Zhōngguórén.
4. A: ________________ ? B: Bù, Lǐ Yǒu bú shì Zhōngguórén.
5. A: ________________ ? B: Bù, wǒ bú xìng Lǐ.
6. A: ________________ ? B: Bù, wǒ bú jiào Lǐ Yǒu, wǒ jiào Wáng Yǒu.

1. A: ________________ ? B: 不，王朋不是老师。
2. A: ________________ ? B: 李友是学生。
3. A: ________________ ? B: 王朋是中国人。
4. A: ________________ ? B: 不，李友不是中国人。
5. A: ________________ ? B: 不，我不姓李。
6. A: ________________ ? B: 不，我不叫李友，我叫王友。

D. 也 (yě)

1.	<u>Nǐ shì</u>	xuésheng,	wǒ	<u>yě shì</u>	xuésheng.
2.		lǎoshī,	Wáng Xiānsheng		lǎoshī.
3.		Zhōngguórén,	Lǐ Xiǎojie		Zhōngguórén.
4.		Měiguórén,	Wáng Xiǎojie		Měiguórén.
5.		xuésheng,	Wáng Xiānsheng		xuésheng.
6.		lǎoshī,	Lǐ Xiānsheng		lǎoshī.

1.	<u>你是</u>	学生，	我	<u>也是</u>	学生。
2.		老师，	王先生		老师。
3.		中国人，	李小姐		中国人。
4.		美国人，	王小姐		美国人。
5.		学生，	王先生		学生。
6.		老师，	李先生		老师。

E. 不 (bù)

Answer questions with 不.

Example: Nǐ shì lǎoshī ma? → Wǒ <u>bú</u> shì lǎoshī.

你是老师吗？ → 我<u>不</u>是老师。

1. Lǐ Yǒu shì Zhōngguórén ma?
2. Nǐ shì Wáng Lǎoshī ma?
3. Wáng Péng shì Měiguórén ma?
4. Nǐ jiào Lǐ Yǒu ma?
5. Lǎoshī xìng Wáng ma?

1. 李友是中国人吗?
2. 你是王老师吗?
3. 王朋是美国人吗?
4. 你叫李友吗?
5. 老师姓王吗?

F. 是...不是... (shì ... bú shì...)

1.	Wǒ shì	Lǐ Yǒu,	bú shì	Wáng Péng.
2.		Zhōngguórén,		Měiguórén.
3.		xuésheng,		lǎoshī.
4.		Zhōngguó xuésheng,		Měiguó xuésheng.
5.		Wáng Xiānsheng,		Lǐ Xiānsheng.
6.		Lǐ Xiǎojie,		Wáng Xiǎojie.
7.		Lǐ Lǎoshī,		Wáng Lǎoshī.

1.	我是	李友,	不是	王朋。
2.		中国人,		美国人。
3.		学生,		老师。
4.		中国学生,		美国学生。
5.		王先生,		李先生。
6.		李小姐,		王小姐。
7.		李老师,		王老师。

G. 不是..., 也不是 (bú shì…, yě bú shì...)

1.	Wǒ	bú shì	lǎoshī,	nǐ	yě bú shì	lǎoshī.
2.			Měiguórén,			Měiguórén.
3.			xuésheng,			xuésheng.
4.	Wǒ	bú xìng	Wáng,	nǐ	yě bú xìng	Wáng.
5.	Wǒ	bú jiào	Lǐ Yǒu,	nǐ	yě bú jiào	Lǐ Yǒu.

1.	我	不是	老师，	你	也不是	老师。
2.			美国人，			美国人。
3.			学生，			学生。
4.	我	不姓	王，	你	也不姓	王。
5.	我	不叫	李友，	你	也不叫	李友。

H. 呢 (ne)

1.	Wǒ shì	Zhōngguórén,	nǐ	ne?
2.		Měiguórén,	Wáng Xiǎojie	
3.		xuésheng,	Lǐ Xiānsheng	
4.		Měiguórén,	Wáng Lǎoshī	
5.		lǎoshī,	Lǐ Xiǎojie	

1.	我是	中国人，	你	呢？
2.		美国人，	王小姐	
3.		学生，	李先生	
4.		美国人，	王老师	
5.		老师，	李小姐	

PRONUNCIATION EXERCISES

A. Practice the following initials:

1.	**b**	**p**	**d**	**t**
	bǎo	pǎo	dā	tā
	bān	pān	dí	tí
	bù	pù	duì	tuì
	bō	pō	dīng	tīng
	bēng	pēng	děng	téng
2.	**j**	**q**	**z**	**c**
	jiǎo	qiǎo	zāi	cāi
	jǐng	qǐng	zǎo	cǎo
	jīn	qīn	zì	cì
	jiě	qiě	zé	cè
	jiàn	qiàn	zhè	chè
3.	**sh**	**s**	**x**	
	shēn	sēn	xīn	
	shēng	sēng	xīng	
	shàn	sàn	xiàn	
	shà	sà	xià	

B. Practice the following tones:

tiāntiān	jīnnián	jīnglǐ	shēngqì
xīngqī	fādá	fāzhǎn	shēngdiào

C. Practice the following syllables with neutral tones:

xiānsheng	míngzi	xiǎojie	shénme
wǒ de	nǐ de	tā de	shéi de

D. Practice the following tones:

nǐ hǎo	Lǐ Yǒu	lǎohǔ	zhǎnlǎn
hǎo duō	nǐ lái	hǎo shū	qǐng wèn

English Texts

DIALOGUE I

Mr. Wang:	How do you do? (lit. You well?)
Miss Li:	How do you do?
Mr. Wang:	What's your family name, please? (lit. Please, may I ask... your honorable surname is...?)
Miss Li:	My family name is Li. What's yours? (lit. I am surnamed Li, and you?)
Mr. Wang:	My family name is Wang. My name is Wang Peng. What's your name?
Miss Li:	My name is Li You.

DIALOGUE II

Miss Li:	Mr. Wang, are you a teacher?
Mr. Wang:	No, I'm not a teacher. I'm a student. How about you, Miss Li?
Miss Li:	I'm a student, too. Are you Chinese?
Mr. Wang:	Yes, I'm Chinese. Are you American?
Miss Li:	I'm American.

LESSON 2 ▲ Family

第二课 ▲ 家庭

Dì èr kè ▲ *Jiātíng*

我家有六个人。

Wǒ jiā yǒu liù ge rén.

Dialogue I: Looking at a Family Photo

VOCABULARY

1.	那	nà/nèi	pr	that
2.	张	zhāng	m	(a measure word for flat objects)
3.	照片	zhàopiàn	n	picture; photo
4.	的	de	p	(a possessive, modifying, or descriptive particle)
5.	这	zhè/zhèi	pr	this
6.	爸爸	bàba	n	father; dad

7.	妈妈	māma	n	mother; mom
8.	这个	zhège	pr	this
	个	gè, -ge	m	(a common measure word)
9.	男孩子	nánháizi	n	boy
	男	nán	adj	male
	孩子	háizi	n	child
10.	谁	shéi	qpr	who
11.	他	tā	pr	he; him (May mean either "he/him" or "she/her" when the sex of the person is unknown.)
12.	弟弟	dìdi	n	younger brother
13.	女孩子	nǚháizi	n	girl
	女	nǚ	adj	female
14.	妹妹	mèimei	n	younger sister
15.	她	tā	pr	she
16.	女儿	nǚ'ér	n	daughter
17.	有	yǒu	v	to have; to exist
18.	儿子	érzi	n	son
19.	沒(没)**	méi	adv	not

Note: In the vocabulary section, a hyphen is placed before or after the *pinyin* of a syllable (e.g. "-ge") to indicate a bound form (i.e., something less than an independent word), which is not used alone.

Proper Nouns

20.	小高	Xiǎo Gāo	pn	Little Gao
	小	xiǎo	adj	small; little
	高	gāo	adj	(a surname); tall

**Note that the character méi (not) appears in two forms, 沒 and 没. In writing it, you should use the latter form (没).

DIALOGUE I

(Wang Peng is in Little Gao's room pointing to a picture on the wall.)

Wáng Péng: Xiǎo Gāo(1), nà zhāng(G1) zhàopiàn shì nǐ de ma?

(They both walk toward the picture and then stand in front of it.)

Xiǎo Gāo: Shì. Zhè shì wǒ bàba, zhè shì wǒ māma.

Wáng Péng: Zhège nánháizi shì shéi(G2)?

Xiǎo Gāo: Tā shì wǒ dìdi.

Wáng Péng: Zhège nǚháizi shì nǐ mèimei ma?

Xiǎo Gāo: Bú shì, tā shì Lǐ Xiānsheng de(2) nǚ'ér.

Wáng Péng: Lǐ Xiānsheng yǒu (G3) érzi ma?

Xiǎo Gāo: Tā méiyǒu érzi.

DIALOGUE I

(Wang Peng is in Little Gao's room pointing to a picture on the wall.)

王朋：小高(1)，那张(G1)照片是你的吗？

(They both walk toward the picture and then stand in front of it.)

小高：是。这是我爸爸，这是我妈妈。

王朋：这个男孩子是谁(G2)？

小高：他是我弟弟。

王朋：这个女孩子是你妹妹吗？

小高：不是，她是李先生的(2)女儿。

王朋：李先生有(G3)儿子吗？

小高：他没有儿子。

The picture on the wall in Little Gao's room.

Notes

▲1▲ A familiar and affectionate way of addressing a young person is to add 小 (xiǎo, little; small) to the surname, e.g., 小王 (Xiǎo Wáng, Little Wang), 小李 (Xiǎo Lǐ, Little Li), 小高 (Xiǎo Gāo, Little Gao), etc. Similarly, to address an older peer, 老 (lǎo, old) can be used with the surname, e.g., 老王 (Lǎo Wáng, Old Wang), 老李 (Lǎo Lǐ, Old Li), 老高 (Lǎo Gāo, Old Gao), etc. However, such terms are rarely used to address a relative or a superior.

▲2▲ The particle 的 (de), as an indicator of a possessive relationship, always follows the "possessor" and precedes the "possessed." To that extent, it is equivalent to the "apostrophe + s" structure in English.

Chinese Kinship Terms

Chinese kinship terms are not only gender-specific but also seniority rank-specific, which makes them more precise than their Western counterparts in defining the relationship. If you are interested in learning more about Chinese kinship terms, see the chart in Lesson 22 in Integrated Chinese Level 1, Part 2.

The Chinese School System

In China and Taiwan the school system is similar to that in the United States. A typical education consists of six years of elementary school (小学, xiǎoxué, grades 1–6), six years of middle school (中学 , zhōngxué, grades 7–12), and four years of university (大学, dàxué) or college (学院, xuéyuàn). Middle school is further divided into junior high (初中, chūzhōng, grades 7–9) and senior high (高中, gāozhōng, grades 10–12). Many students also attend kindergarten before they enter the grade school, and some of them continue on to graduate school after college. Now that you have learned that a college student is called 大学生 (dàxuéshēng) in Chinese, can you guess the words for elementary school students, junior high school students, and senior high students?

Dialogue II: Asking about Someone's Family

VOCABULARY

1.	家	jiā	n	family; home
2.	几	jǐ-	qw	how many
3.	哥哥	gēge	n	older brother
4.	两	liǎng	nu	two; a couple of
5.	姐姐	jiějie	n	older sister
6.	和	hé	conj	and
7.	做	zuò	v	to do
8.	英文	Yīngwén	n	the English language
9.	#律师	lǜshī	n	lawyer
10.	都	dōu	adv	both; all
11.	大学生	dàxuéshēng	n	college student
	大学	dàxué	n	university; college
12.	#医生	yīshēng	n	doctor; physician

Proper Nouns

13.	小张	Xiǎo Zhāng	Little Zhang
	张	zhāng	(a surname); (a measure word for flat objects)

DIALOGUE II

Lǐ Yǒu: Xiǎo Zhāng, nǐ jiā(1) yǒu(G4) jǐge(2) rén?

Xiǎo Zhāng: Wǒ jiā yǒu liù ge rén. Wǒ bàba(3), wǒ māma, yí(4) ge(G1) gēge, liǎng(G5) ge jiějie hé(5) wǒ(6). Lǐ Xiǎojie, nǐ jiā yǒu jǐ ge rén?

Lǐ Yǒu: Wǒ jiā yǒu wǔ ge rén: bàba, māma, liǎng ge mèimei hé wǒ. Nǐ bàba māma shì zuò shénme de(7)?

Xiǎo Zhāng: Wǒ māma shì Yīngwén lǎoshī, bàba shì lǜshī, gēge, jiějie dōu(G6) shì dàxuéshēng.

Lǐ Yǒu: Wǒ māma yě shì lǎoshī, wǒ bàba shì yīshēng.

DIALOGUE II

李友：小张，你家(1)有(G4)几个(2)人？

小张：我家有六个人。我爸爸(3)、我妈妈、一(4)个(G1)哥哥、两(G5)个姐姐和(5)我(6)。李小姐，你家有几个人？

李友：我家有五个人。爸爸、妈妈、两个妹妹和我。你爸爸妈妈是做什么的(7)？

小张：我妈妈是英文老师，爸爸是律师，哥哥、姐姐都(G6)是大学生。

李友：我妈妈也是老师，我爸爸是医生。

Notes

▲1▲ In Chinese, 家 (jiā) can refer to one's family as well as one's home. So, one can point to her family picture and say "我家有四个人" (Wǒ jiā yǒu sì ge rén; There are four people in my family), and one can also point to her house and say "这是我的家" (Zhè shì wǒ de jiā; This is my home).

▲2▲ For the number of people in a family, another measure word 口 (kǒu) is also used. The original tone for the measure word 个 (gè) is the falling tone. However, in actual speech it is always pronounced as a neutral tone word.

▲3▲ The possessive particle 的 (de) is usually omitted after a personal pronoun and before a kinship term. Therefore, we say "王朋的妈妈" (Wáng Péng de māma; Wang Peng's mother) with 的 (de) but "我妈妈" (wǒ māma; my mother) without 的 (de).

▲4▲ The numeral "一" (yī, one) is pronounced with the first tone "yī" when it stands alone or comes at the end of a word or sentence. Otherwise, its pronunciation changes according to the following rules: (a) "yī" before a fourth tone syllable becomes second tone. Therefore, "一个" is pronounced "yí gè" rather than "yī gè." (b) "yī" before a syllable in any tone other than the fourth tone becomes fourth tone. The above rules also apply to the numerals "七" (qī, seven) and "八" (bā, eight). However, nowadays few people change tones when pronouncing "七" (qī, seven) and "八" (bā, eight).

▲5▲ Although considered a conjunction and translated as "and," 和 (hé) cannot link two clauses or two sentences as "and" can in English. We say, "我爸爸是老师，我妈妈是医生" (Wǒ bàba shī lǎoshī, wǒ māma shì yīshēng). We don't say, "*我爸爸是老师，和我妈妈是医生" (*Wǒ bàba shì lǎoshī, hé wǒ māma shì yīsheng).

▲6▲ The pause mark, or "series comma," "、" is often used to link two, three or even more parallel words or phrases, e.g., 爸爸、妈妈、两个妹妹和我 (bàba, māma, liǎng ge mèimei hé wǒ; dad, mom, two younger sisters and I). For further discussion of this punctuation mark, see Note 2 for Dialogue I in Lesson 4.

▲7▲ "X 是做什么的" (X shì zuò shénme de) is often used to ask for a person's occupation, where the person is "X."

Culture Notes

In Chinese it is customary to mention the male before the female. Therefore, we say, 爸爸、妈妈，哥哥、姐姐，弟弟、妹妹 (bàba, māma, gēge, jiějie, dìdi, mèimei) instead of 妈妈、爸爸，姐姐、哥哥，妹妹、弟弟 (māma, bàba, jiějie, gēge, mèimei, dìdi), etc.

Whose family is this?

Grammar

1. Measure Words (I)

In Chinese a numeral is not usually followed immediately by a noun. Rather, a measure word is inserted between the number and the noun. There are several hundred measure words in Chinese, but you may hear only two or three dozen in everyday speech. Many nouns are associated with special measure words, which often bear a relationship to the meaning of the given noun. However, the general measure -ge can sometimes be substituted for the special measure. The following are two measure words that we have learned in this lesson.

个 (gè): This is the single most commonly used measure word in Chinese. It is also sometimes used as a substitute for other measure words.

Examples:

(1)	一个人	yí ge rén	a person
(2)	一个学生	yí ge xuésheng	a student
(3)	一个老师	yí ge lǎoshī	a teacher

张 (zhāng): This measure word is associated with objects with flat surfaces.

Examples:

(1)	一张照片	yì zhāng zhàopiàn	a photo
(2)	一张纸 (zhǐ)	yì zhāng zhǐ	a piece of paper
(3)	一张床 (chuáng)	yì zhāng chuáng	a bed

2. Interrogative Pronouns

Interrogative pronouns include 谁 (shéi, who), 什么 (shénme, what), 哪 (nǎ/něi, which) [see L.6], 哪儿 (nǎr, where) [see L.5], 几 (jǐ-, how many), etc. In a question with an interrogative pronoun, the word order is exactly the same as that in a non-interrogative statement. Therefore, when learning to compose a question in Chinese, we can start with a statement and then replace the part of the statement that is in question with the appropriate interrogative pronoun.

For example:

(1) 她是李友。

Tā shì Lǐ Yǒu.

(She is Li You.)

One can replace 她 (tā) with 谁 (shéi):

(2) 谁是李友？

Shéi shì Lǐ Yǒu?

(Who is Li You?)

Here 谁 (shéi) appears in the predicate of the sentence and occupies the same position as 她 (tā) in the corresponding statement. Or one can replace 李友 (Lǐ Yǒu) with 她 (tā):

(3) 她是谁？

Tā shì shéi?

(Who is she?)

谁 (shéi) functions as the object of the sentence and occupies the same position as 李友 (Lǐ Yǒu).

Other examples:

(4) A: 我妈妈是医生。

Wǒ māma shì yīshēng.

(My mother is a doctor.)

B: 你妈妈是做什么的？

Nǐ māma shì zuò shénme de?

(What does your mother do?)

Examples with the verb 有 (yǒu).

(5) A: 王朋有妹妹。

Wáng Péng yǒu mèimei.

(Wang Peng has a younger sister.)

B: 谁有妹妹？

Shéi yǒu mèimei?

(Who has any younger sisters?)

(6) A: 我有三个姐姐。

Wǒ yǒu sān ge jiějie.

(I have three older sisters.)

B: 你有几个姐姐？

Nǐ yǒu jǐ ge jiějie?

(How many older sisters do you have?)

Can you name the family members in Chinese?

3. 有 (yǒu) in the Sense of "to Have" or "to Possess"

有 (yǒu) is always negated with 没 (méi).

Examples:

(1) A: 王先生有一个弟弟。

Wáng Xiānsheng yǒu yí ge dìdi.

(Mr. Wang has a younger brother.)

B: 王先生没有弟弟。

Wáng Xiānsheng méiyǒu dìdi.

(Mr. Wang doesn't have any younger brothers.)

(2) A: 我有两张照片。

Wǒ yǒu liǎng zhāng zhàopiàn.

(I have two photos.)

B: 我没有照片。

Wǒ méiyǒu zhàopiàn.

(I don't have any photos.)

4. 有 (yǒu) in the Sense of "to Exist"

Examples:

(1) 我家有五个人。

Wǒ jiā yǒu wǔ ge rén.

(There are five people in my family.)

(2) 小张家有两个大学生。

Xiǎo Zhāng jiā yǒu liǎng ge dàxuéshēng.

(There are two college students in Little Zhang's family.)

5. The Usage of 二 (èr) and 两 (liǎng)

二 (èr) and 两 (liǎng) both mean "two," but they differ in usage. 两 (liǎng) is used in front of common measure words to express a quantity, e.g., 两个人 (liǎng ge rén, two persons). In counting, one uses "二" (èr): "一， 二， 三， 四......" (yī, èr, sān, sì; one, two, three, four...). "二" (èr) is also used in compound numerals, e.g., 二十二 (èrshí'èr, twenty-two) and 一百二十五 (yìbǎi èrshíwǔ, 125).

Cases involving quadruple digit numbers will be introduced later.

6. 都 (dōu, both; all)

The word 都 (dōu) indicates inclusiveness. As it always occurs in front of a verb, it is classified as an adverb. However, because it refers to something that has been mentioned earlier in the sentence, or in a preceding sentence, it also has a pronoun-like flavor and it must be used at the end of an enumeration.

Examples:

(1) 王朋、高生和李友都是律师。

Wáng Péng, Gāo Shēng hé Lǐ Yǒu dōu shì lǜshī.

(Wang Peng, Gao Sheng and Li You are all lawyers.)

(lit. Wang Peng, Gao Sheng and Li You *all are* lawyers.)

[都 (dōu) refers back to Wang Peng, Gao Sheng and Li You and therefore appears *after* they are mentioned.]

(2) 王朋和李友都不是老师。

Wáng Péng hé Lǐ Yǒu dōu bú shì lǎoshī.

(Neither Wang Peng nor Li You is a teacher.)

(3) 王朋和李友都有弟弟。

Wáng Péng hé Lǐ Yǒu dōu yǒu dìdi.

(Both Wang Peng and Li You have younger brothers.)

(lit. Wang Peng and Li You both have younger brothers.)

(4) 高生和张中都没有妹妹。

Gāo Shēng hé Zhāng Zhōng dōu méiyǒu mèimei.

(Neither Gao Sheng nor Zhang Zhong has younger sisters.)

Note: 没 (méi) is always used to negate 有 (yǒu). However, to say "not all of...have," we say in Chinese "不都有" (bù dōu yǒu) rather than "*没都有" (méi dōu yǒu). Whether the negation word precedes or follows the word 都 (dōu) makes the difference between partial negation and complete negation.

Compare:

A. 他们不都是中国人。

(Tāmen bù dōu shì Zhōngguórén.)

(Not all of them are Chinese.)

B. 他们都不是中国人。

(Tāmen dōu bú shì Zhōngguórén.)

(None of them are Chinese.)

C. 他们不都有弟弟。

(Tāmen bù dōu yǒu dìdi.)

(Not all of them have younger brothers.)

D. 他们都没有弟弟。

(Tāmen dōu méiyǒu dìdi.)

(None of them have younger brothers.)

他们是做什么的？

Tāmen shì zuò shénme de?

PATTERN DRILLS

A. 有 (yǒu, to have) with Measure Words

1.	Wǒ	<u>yǒu</u>	yí	<u>ge</u>	gēge.
2.	Tā		liǎng		jiějie.
3.	Xiǎo Wáng		sān		mèimei.
4.	Xiǎo Lǐ		yí		dìdi.
5.	Xiǎo Zhāng		liǎng		Zhōngguó lǎoshī.
6.	Gāo Lǎoshī		sān		érzi.
7.	Wǒ		liù	<u>zhāng</u>	zhàopiàn.

1.	我	<u>有</u>	一	<u>个</u>	哥哥。
2.	他		两		姐姐。
3.	小王		三		妹妹。
4.	小李		一		弟弟。
5.	小张		两		中国老师。

6.	高老师	三		儿子。
7.	我	六	张	照片。

B. 没有 (méiyǒu, have not)

1.	Lǎo Wáng yǒu	gēge,	méiyǒu	dìdi.
2.		jiějie,		mèimei.
3.		Zhōngguó péngyǒu,		Měiguó péngyǒu.
4.	Xiǎo Lǐ yǒu	gēge,		jiějie.
5.		dìdi,		mèimei.
6.	Wáng Xiánsheng yǒu	mèimei,		jiějie.
7.		jiějie,		dìdi.
8.		nǚ'ér,		érzi.

1.	老王有	哥哥,	没有	弟弟。
2.		姐姐,		妹妹。
3.		中国朋友,		美国朋友。
4.	小李有	哥哥,		姐姐。
5.		弟弟,		妹妹。
6.	王先生有	妹妹,		姐姐。
7.		姐姐,		弟弟。
8.		女儿,		儿子。

C. 有 (yǒu, there is/are)

1.	Wǒ jiā	yǒu	liù	ge rén.
2.	Xiǎo Lǐ jiā		sān	
3.	Zhāng Lǎoshī jiā		liǎng	
4.	Wáng Xiānsheng jiā		sì	

How many children do they have?

5.	Gāo Xiǎojie jiā	bā
6.	Xiǎo Zhāng jiā	wǔ

1.	我家	<u>有</u>	六	<u>个人</u>。
2.	小李家		三	
3.	张老师家		两	
4.	王先生家		四	
5.	高小姐家		八	
6.	小张家		五	

D. Interrogative Pronouns 谁 (shéi, who); 几个 (jǐge, how many); 什么 (shénme, what)

Formulate a question for each of the sentences below using the appropriate interrogative pronoun.

Example: A: <u>Zhè shì shéi?</u> B: Zhè shì wǒ bàba.

A: <u>这是谁?</u> B: 这是我爸爸。

Can you describe this photo in Chinese?

1. A: ____ ? B: Nà shì wǒ jiějie.
2. A: ____ ? B: Xiǎo Zhāng jiā yǒu liù ge rén.
3. A: ____ ? B: Xiǎo Gāo yǒu sān ge jiějie.
4. A: ____ ? B: Wǒ bàba shì lǜshī.
5. A: ____ ? B: Wǒ yǒu liǎng ge Zhōngguó lǎoshī.
6. A: ____ ? B: Tā gēge shì yīshēng.
7. A: ____ ? B: Tā jiào Zhāng Yǒuzhōng.

1. A: ____ ? B: 那是我姐姐。
2. A: ____ ? B: 小张家有六个人。
3. A: ____ ? B: 小高有三个姐姐。
4. A: ____ ? B: 我爸爸是律师。
5. A: ____ ? B: 我有两个中国老师。

6. A: ______________________________ ? B: 他哥哥是医生。

7. A: ______________________________ ? B: 他叫张有中。

E. 都 (dōu, both, all)

Rephrase the sentences with 都.

Example: Wǒ bàba shì yīshēng, tā bàba yě shì yīshēng.

→ Wǒ bàba hé tā bàba dōu shì yīshēng.

我爸爸是医生，他爸爸也是医生。

→ 我爸爸和他爸爸都是医生。

1. Wǒ gēge shì lǜshī, wǒ jiějie yě shì lǜshī. →
2. Wáng Péng shì xuésheng, Lǐ Yǒu yě shì xuésheng. →
3. Wǒ bàba shì lǎoshī, tā bàba yě shì lǎoshī. →
4. Wǒ jiā yǒu sān ge rén, Xiǎo Zhāng jiā yě yǒu sān ge rén. →
5. Wǒ yǒu liǎng ge dìdi, tā yě yǒu liǎng ge dìdi. →
6. Zhège xuésheng shì Zhōngguórén, nàge xuésheng yě shì Zhōngguórén. →
7. Zhè zhāng zhàopiàn shì nǐ de, nà zhāng zhàopiàn yě shì nǐ de. →
8. Wǒ māma xìng Gāo, tā māma yě xìng Gāo. →

1. 我哥哥是律师，我姐姐也是律师。→
2. 王朋是学生，李友也是学生。→
3. 我爸爸是老师，他爸爸也是老师。→
4. 我家有三个人，小张家也有三个人。→

5. 我有两个弟弟，他也有两个弟弟。→
6. 这个学生是中国人，那个学生也是中国人。→
7. 这张照片是你的，那张照片也是你的。→
8. 我妈妈姓高，他妈妈也姓高。 →

F. 都 (dōu, all, both) with 不 (bù, not) or 没有 (méiyǒu, have not)

Rephrase the sentences with 都 plus 不 or 没有.

Examples: Wáng Zhōng shì lǎoshī. Lǐ Shēng shì lǎoshī. Gāo Péng shì yīshēng. (lǜshī)
→ Wáng Zhōng, Lǐ Shēng, Gāo Péng dōu bú shì lǜshī.

Xiǎo Zhāng méiyǒu gēge. Xiǎo Lǐ méiyǒu gēge. Xiǎo Wáng yě méiyǒu gēge.
→ Xiǎo Zhāng, Xiǎo Lǐ, Xiǎo Wáng dōu méiyǒu gēge.

王中是老师。李生是老师。高朋是医生。（律师）
→王中、李生、高朋都不是律师。
小张没有哥哥。小李没有哥哥。小王也没有哥哥。
→小张、小李、小王都没有哥哥。

1. Wǒ bàba shì lǎoshī. Wǒ jiějie shì lǜshī. Wǒ gēge shì yīshēng. (xuésheng)
2. Xiǎo Wáng méiyǒu mèimei. Xiǎo Lǐ méiyǒu mèimei. Xiǎo Zhāng yě méiyǒu mèimei. (mèimei)
3. Wáng Zhōng shì Měiguórén. Lǐ Yǒu shì Měiguórén. Gāo Guì yě shì Měiguórén. (Zhōngguórén)
4. Lǐ Zhōng shì lǎoshī. Wáng Péng bú shì lǎoshī. Gāo Yǒu yě bú shì lǎoshī. (lǎoshī)
5. Wáng Péng méiyǒu zhàopiàn. Lǐ Zhōng méiyǒu zhàopiàn. Gāo Yǒu yě méiyǒu zhàopiàn. (zhàopiàn)
6. Wǒ māma xìng Wáng. Nǐ māma xìng Gāo. Tā bàba xìng Zhāng. (Lǐ)

1. 我爸爸是老师，我姐姐是律师，我哥哥是医生。（学生）
2. 小王没有妹妹，小李没有妹妹，小张也没有妹妹。（妹妹）

3. 王中是美国人，李友是美国人，高贵也是美国人。(中国人)
4. 李中是老师，王朋不是老师，高友也不是老师。(老师)
5. 王朋没有照片，李中没有照片，高友也没有照片。(照片)
6. 我妈妈姓王，你妈妈姓高，她爸爸姓张。(李)

PRONUNCIATION EXERCISES

A. Initials

1.	**zh**	zhè	zhǎo	zhāng	zhuāng
	ch	chè	chǎo	chàng	chuáng
	sh	shè	shǎo	shāng	shuāng
2.	**d**	dà	duō	duì	dōu
	t	tà	tuō	tuì	tōu
3.	**r**	rén	rào	rì	rè

B. The Final "e"

gē	dé	zhè	hē
kē	tè	chē	shé
zé	cè	sè	rè

C. Tones

chénggōng	chángcháng	rénkǒu	xuéxiào
Chángjiāng	Chángchéng	míngxiǎn	chídào

D. The Neutral Tone

māma	shéi de	jiějie	mèimei
tā de	fángzi	nǐ de	dìdi

English Texts

DIALOGUE I

(Wang Peng is in Little Gao's room pointing to a picture on the wall.)

Wang Peng: Little Gao, is that picture yours?

(They both walk toward the picture and then stand in front of it.)

Little Gao: Yes. This is my dad. This is my mom.

Wang Peng: Who is this boy?

Little Gao: This is my younger brother.

Wang Peng: Is this girl your younger sister?

Little Gao: No, she's Mr. Li's daughter.

Wang Peng: Does Mr. Li have any sons?

Little Gao: He has no sons.

DIALOGUE II

Li You: Little Zhang, how many people are there in your family?

Little Zhang: There are six people in my family: my dad, my mom, an older brother, two older sisters and I. How many people are there in your family, Miss Li?

Li You: There are five people in my family: my dad, my mom, my two younger sisters and I. What do your dad and mom do?

Little Zhang: My mom is an English teacher. My dad is a lawyer. My older brother and sisters are all college students.

Li You: My mom is also a teacher. My dad is a doctor.

LESSON 3 ▲ Dates and Time
第三课 ▲ 时间
Dì sān kè ▲ *Shíjiān*

我请你吃晚饭，怎么样？

Wǒ qǐng nǐ chī wǎnfàn, zěnmeyàng?

Dialogue I: Taking Someone Out to Eat on His/Her Birthday

VOCABULARY

1.	九月	jiǔyuè	n	September
	月	yuè	n	month
2.	十二	shí'èr	nu	twelve
3.	#号	hào	m	number in a series; day of the month
4.	星期四	xīngqīsì	n	Thursday

	星期	xīngqī	n	week
5.	天	tiān	n	day
6.	生日	shēngrì	n	birthday
	生	shēng	v	to give birth to; to be born
	日	rì	n	day; the sun
7.	今年	jīnnián	t	this year
	年	nián	n	year
8.	多大	duō dà	ce	how old
	多	duō	adv	how many/much; to what extent
	大	dà	adj	big; old
9.	十八	shíbā	nu	eighteen
10.	#岁	suì	n	year (of age)
11.	请	qǐng	v	to treat (somebody); to invite [see also L.1]
12.	吃	chī	v	to eat
13.	晚饭	wǎnfàn	n	dinner; supper
	晚	wǎn	adj	evening; night; late
	饭	fàn	n	meal; (cooked) rice
14.	吃饭	chī fàn	vo	to eat (a meal)
15.	怎么样	zěnmeyàng	qpr	Is it O.K.? What is it like? How does that sound?
16.	太...(了)	tài...(le)		too; extremely
17.	#谢谢	xièxie	ce	thank you
18.	喜欢	xǐhuan	v	to like, like to; to prefer, prefer to
19.	还是	háishi	conj	or

20.	可是	kěshì	conj	but
21.	好	hǎo	adj	good; O.K.
22.	我们	wǒmen	pr	we
23.	点#钟	-diǎnzhōng	m	o'clock
	点	diǎn	m	o'clock (lit. point, thus "points on the clock")
	钟	zhōng	n	clock
24.	半	bàn	nu	half; half an hour
25.	晚上	wǎnshang	t/n	evening; night
26.	见	jiàn	v	to see
27.	再见	zàijiàn	ce	goodbye; see you again
	再	zài	adv	again

Proper Noun

28.	小白	Xiǎo Bái	pn	Little Bai
	白	bái	adj	white; (a surname)

DIALOGUE I

(Little Gao is talking to Little Bai.)

Xiǎo Gāo: Xiǎo Bái, jiǔyuè shí'èr[(1)] [(G1)] hào[(G2.3)] shì xīngqījǐ[(G2.1)]?

Xiǎo Bái: Shì xīngqīsì.

Xiǎo Gāo: Nà tiān shì wǒ de[(G3)] shēngrì.

Xiǎo Bái: Shì ma? Nǐ jīnnián duō dà[(2)]?

Xiǎo Gāo: Shíbā suì[(3)].

Xiǎo Bái: Xīngqīsì wǒ qǐng nǐ chī wǎnfàn[(G4)], zěnmeyàng?

Xiǎo Gāo: Tài hǎo le. Xièxie, xièxie[(4)].

Xiǎo Bái: Nǐ xǐhuan chī Zhōngguó fàn háishi[(G5)] Měiguó fàn?

Xiǎo Gāo: Wǒ shì Zhōngguórén, kěshì wǒ xǐhuan chī Měiguó fàn.

Xiǎo Bái: Hǎo, wǒmen chī Měiguó fàn.

Xiǎo Gāo: Xīngqīsì jǐ diǎnzhōng?
Xiǎo Bái: Qīdiǎn bàn(G2.6) zěnmeyàng?
Xiǎo Gāo: Hǎo, xīngqīsì wǎnshang jiàn.
Xiǎo Bái: Zàijiàn.

DIALOGUE I

(Little Gao is talking to Little Bai.)

小高：小白，九月十二(1)(G1)号(G2.3)是星期几(G2.1)?

小白：是星期四。

小高：那天是我的(G3)生日。

小白：是吗？你今年多大(2)?

小高：十八岁(3)。

小白：星期四我请你吃晚饭(G4)，怎么样?

小高：太好了。谢谢，谢谢(4)。

小白：你喜欢吃中国饭还是(G5)美国饭?

小高：我是中国人，可是我喜欢吃美国饭。

小白：好，我们吃美国饭。

小高：星期四几点钟?

小白：七点半(G2.6)怎么样?

小高：好，星期四晚上见。

小白：再见!

九　月

日	一	二	三	四	五	六
1	2	3	4	5	6	7
8	9	10	11	12	13	14
15	16	17	18	19	20	21
22	23	24	25	26	27	28
29	30					

Circle Little Gao's birthday.

Notes

▲1▲ Chinese time expressions proceed from the largest to the smallest unit, e.g., 二零零三年九月十二日晚上七点 (èr-líng-líng-sān nián jiǔyuè shí'èr rì wǎnshang qīdiǎn; literally, the year 2003, the ninth month, the twelfth day, the evening, seven o'clock).

▲2▲ To find out someone's age, we ask, 你今年多大？ (Nǐ jīnnián duō dà?). If the person is a child who appears to be under ten, we change the question to 你今年几岁？ (Nǐ jīnnián jǐ suì?). To find out an older person's age, it would be more polite to ask, 您多大年纪/岁数了？ (Nín duō dà niánjì/suìshù le?).

▲3▲ To give one's age, it is correct to say "我十八岁" (Wǒ shíbā suì), but the word 岁 (suì, year of age) can often be dropped. If one is ten years old or younger, however, the word 岁 cannot be dropped. It is **incorrect** to say "*我十" (*Wǒ shí) or "*我八" (*Wǒ bā).

▲4▲ To show gratitude, one can say "谢谢" (xièxie), or "谢谢, 谢谢" (xièxie, xièxie) by repeating the word. The latter one is obviously more polite and exuberant.

Xiao Gao's birthday celebration.

Culture Notes

The traditional Chinese manner of counting age, which is still in use among many (mainly older) people on non-official occasions, is based on the number of the calendar years one has lived *in*, rather than the length of time in actual years that one has lived. For example, a child born in January 2001 can be said to be two years old in January 2002, as he or she has by then lived in two calendar years, 2001 and 2002. But for official purposes, for instance on the census, the child would still be considered as one year old, as that is the actual length of time he or she has lived.

Dialogue II: Inviting Someone to Dinner

VOCABULARY

1.	现在	xiànzài	t	now
2.	刻	-kè	m	quarter (hour); 15 minutes
3.	事	shì	n	matter; affair; business
4.	明天	míngtiān	t	tomorrow
5.	忙	máng	adj	busy
6.	今天	jīntiān	t	today
7.	很	hěn	adv	very
8.	为什么	wèishénme	qpr	why
	为	wèi	prep	for
9.	因为	yīnwei	conj	because
10.	还有	hái yǒu		also there are
	还	hái	adv	also; too; as well
11.	同学	tóngxué	n	classmate
12.	认识	rènshi	v	to know (someone); to recognize

Proper Noun

13.	小李	Xiǎo Lǐ	pn	Little Li

Culture Notes

The traditional Chinese equivalent of the birthday cake is noodles. Because noodles are long, they are considered a symbol of longevity. That is why they are called 长寿面 (chángshòu miàn, longevity noodles). Among the younger generations in urban areas birthday cakes are also becoming quite common.

DIALOGUE II

(Wang Peng and Little Bai are talking to each other.)

Wáng Péng: Xiǎo Bái, xiànzài jǐ diǎnzhōng?

Xiǎo Bái: Wǔ diǎn sān kè.

Wáng Péng: Wǒ liù diǎn yí kè yǒu shì.

Xiǎo Bái: Wáng Péng, nǐ míngtiān máng bu máng(G6)?

Wáng Péng: Wǒ jīntiān hěn máng(1), kěshì míngtiān bù máng. Yǒu shì ma?

Xiǎo Bái: Míngtian wǒ qǐng nǐ chī wǎnfàn, zěnmeyàng?

Wáng Péng: Wèishénme qǐng wǒ chī fàn?

Xiǎo Bái: Yīnwei míngtiān shì Xiǎo Gāo de shēngrì.

Wáng Péng: Shì ma? Hǎo, hái yǒu(G7) shéi?

Xiǎo Bái: Hái yǒu wǒ de tóngxué Xiǎo Lǐ.

Wáng Péng: Nà tài hǎo le! Wǒ yě rènshi Xiǎo Lǐ. Jǐ diǎnzhōng?

Xiǎo Bái: Míngtiān wǎnshang qī diǎn bàn.

Wáng Péng: Hǎo, míngtiān qī diǎn bàn jiàn.

DIALOGUE II

(Wang Peng and Little Bai are talking to each other.)

王朋：小白，现在几点钟？

小白：五点三刻。

王朋：我六点一刻有事。

小白：王朋，你明天忙不忙(G6)？

王朋：我今天很忙(1)，可是明天不忙。有事吗？

小白：明天我请你吃晚饭，怎么样？

王朋：为什么请我吃饭？

小白：因为明天是小高的生日。

王朋：是吗？好。还有(G7)谁？

小白：还有我的同学小李。

王朋：那太好了，我也认识小李。几点钟？

小白：明天晚上七点半。

王朋：好，明天七点半见。

Notes

▲1▲ Although usually translated as "very," the Chinese adverb 很 (hěn) is not quite as strong as its English equivalent. Therefore, the sentence 我很忙 (Wǒ hěn máng)—unless the word 很 (hěn) is stressed—is closer to "I am busy" than "I am *very* busy." There is a tendency in Modern Chinese to compound a monosyllabic adjective with 很, e.g., 很好 (hěn hǎo), 很忙 (hěn máng), etc. Accordingly, we usually say "我很好" (Wǒ hěn hǎo; I am fine) instead of "我好" (Wǒ hǎo) and "她很忙" (Tā hěn máng; She is busy) instead of "她忙" (Tā máng). Also see Grammar Note 2 in Lesson 5.

SUPPLEMENTARY VOCABULARY

1.	分	fēn	m	minute
2.	差	chà	v	to be short of; to be lacking
3.	昨天	zuótiān	t	yesterday
4.	前天	qiántiān	t	the day before yesterday
5.	后天	hòutiān	t	the day after tomorrow
6.	明年	míngnián	t	next year

7.	去年	qùnián	t	last year
8.	前年	qiánnián	t	the year before last
9.	后年	hòunián	t	the year after next
10.	下(个)月	xià(ge)yuè	t	next month
11.	表	biǎo	n	watch
12.	早饭	zǎofàn	n	breakfast
13.	中饭	zhōngfàn	n	lunch

Time Expressions Involving Year and Day

大前天	前天	昨天	今天	明天	后天	大后天
大前年	前年	去年	今年	明年	后年	大后年

Note that the above expressions with 天 (tiān, day) and 年 (nián, year) form two parallel series except for 昨天 (zuótiān, yesterday) and 去年 (qùnián, last year).

Time Expressions Involving Month and Week

上上个月	上个月	这个月	下个月	下下个月
上上个星期	上个星期	这个星期	下个星期	下下个星期

Note that the above expressions with 月 (yuè, month) and 星期 (xīngqī, week) form two parallel series.

Grammar

1. Numbers (0, 11–100)

0: 零 (líng, zero)

11–99: 十一 (shíyī, eleven), 十二 (shí'èr, twelve), 十三 (shísān, thirteen)...二十 (èrshí, twenty), 二十一 (èrshíyī, twenty-one), 二十二 (èrshí'èr, twenty-two), 二十三 (èrshísān, twenty-three)...三十 (sānshí, thirty), 九十一 (jiǔshíyī, ninety-one)...九十九 (jiǔshíjiǔ, ninety-nine)

100, 200, etc.: 一百 (yìbǎi, one hundred), 二百 (èrbǎi, two hundred)

2. Dates and Time

(1) Days of the week

星期一	xīngqīyī	Monday
星期二	xīngqī'èr	Tuesday
星期三	xīngqīsān	Wednesday
星期四	xīngqīsì	Thursday
星期五	xīngqīwǔ	Friday
星期六	xīngqīliù	Saturday
星期日（天）	xīngqīrì (tiān)	Sunday

While 星期 (xīngqī, week) is commonly used in spoken Chinese, 周 (zhōu, week) is usually used in written Chinese. Monday can also be called 周一 (zhōuyī), Tuesday 周二 (zhōu'èr), etc. Weekend is 周末 (zhōumò) in both spoken and written Chinese, and in written Chinese 周日 (zhōurì) is sometimes used to refer to Sunday. In China the week starts on Monday. The question 星期几？ (xīngqījǐ?) is used to ask the day of the week. To answer this question, simply replace the word 几 (jǐ, what, how many) with the number indicating the day of the week, such as 星期四 (xīngqīsì, Thursday), meaning the fourth day of the week. In spoken Chinese the expression 礼拜 (lǐbài, week) is also used. Therefore, 礼拜四 (lǐbàisì) also means Thursday. Both 星期日 (xīngqīrì) and 星期天 (xīngqītiān) mean Sunday. 星期日 (xīngqīrì) is used more in written Chinese whereas 星期天 (xīngqītiān) is used more in spoken Chinese.

(2) Months

一月	yīyuè	January
二月	èryuè	February
三月	sānyuè	March
四月	sìyuè	April
五月	wǔyuè	May
六月	liùyuè	June
七月	qīyuè	July
八月	bāyuè	August
九月	jiǔyuè	September
十月	shíyuè	October
十一月	shíyīyuè	November
十二月	shí'èryuè	December

(3) Days of the month

In spoken Chinese 号 (hào, number) is used to refer to the days of the month. However, in written Chinese 日 (rì, day) is always used.

Examples:

二月五号	èryuè	wǔ hào	February 5	(spoken)
二月五日	èryuè	wǔ rì	February 5	(written)

(4) Year

年 (nián, year) is always included with numbers referring to a year.

Examples:

一七七六年	yī-qī-qī-liù nián	1776
一九九五年	yī-jiǔ-jiǔ-wǔ nián	1995

Note: Unlike in English, where the two years given above are read "seventeen seventy-six" and "nineteen ninety-five" respectively, years in Chinese are pronounced one digit at a time.

(5) Word Order for Dates

To give a date in Chinese, observe the following order (progression from larger to smaller unit):

year	month	day	day of the week
年	月	日	星期
nián	yuè	rì	xīngqī

Example:

一九九五年七月二十六日星期三

(Wednesday, July 26, 1995)

yī jiǔ jiǔ wǔ nián qīyuè èrshíliù rì xīngqīsān

(6) Telling Time

These terms are used to tell time in Chinese: 点钟 (diǎnzhōng, o'clock), 半 (bàn, half hour), 刻 (kè, quarter hour), and 分 (fēn, minute).

Examples:

a. o'clock:

三点钟	sān diǎnzhōng	three o'clock
十一点	shíyī diǎn	eleven o'clock
七、八点钟	qī, bā diǎnzhōng	seven or eight o'clock

Note that 钟 (zhōng) can be omitted from 点钟 (diǎnzhōng).

b. minute:

一点十八(分)	yī diǎn shíbā (fēn)	1:18
两点零七分	liǎng diǎn líng qī fēn	2:07

三点零五(分)	sān diǎn líng wǔ (fēn)	3:05
五点二十(分)	wǔ diǎn èrshí (fēn)	5:20
差十分九点	chà shí fēn jiǔ diǎn	8:50 (ten till nine)

Note: The term 零 (líng, zero) is usually added before a single-digit number of 分 (fēn, minute), e.g., 三点零五分 (sān diǎn líng wǔ fēn). 分 (fēn) can be omitted from the end of the expression if the number for the minutes appears in two syllables. Thus one can say "一点十八" (yī diǎn shíbā) and "三点零五" (sān diǎn líng wǔ), but not "*两点七" (*liǎng diǎn qī) or "*一点十" (*yī diǎn shí).

c. quarter hour:

两点一刻	liǎng diǎn yí kè	2:15	(a quarter past two)
差一刻四点	chà yí kè sì diǎn	3:45	(a quarter till four)
十一点三刻	shíyī diǎn sān kè	11:45	(a quarter till twelve)

d. half hour:

两点半	liǎng diǎn bàn	2:30	(half past two)
八点半	bā diǎn bàn	8:30	(half past eight)
十二点半	shí'èr diǎn bàn	12:30	(half past twelve)

Note that *两刻 (*liǎng kè, two quarters) is *not* used.

e. evening time:

晚上七点（钟）	wǎnshang qī diǎn (zhōng)	7:00 p.m.
晚上八点零五（分）	wǎnshang bā diǎn líng wǔ (fēn)	8:05 p.m.
晚上九点一刻	wǎnshang jiǔ diǎn yí kè	9:15 p.m.
晚上十点半	wǎnshang shí diǎn bàn	10:30 p.m.
晚上差四分十一点	wǎnshang chà sì fēn shíyī diǎn	10:56 p.m.

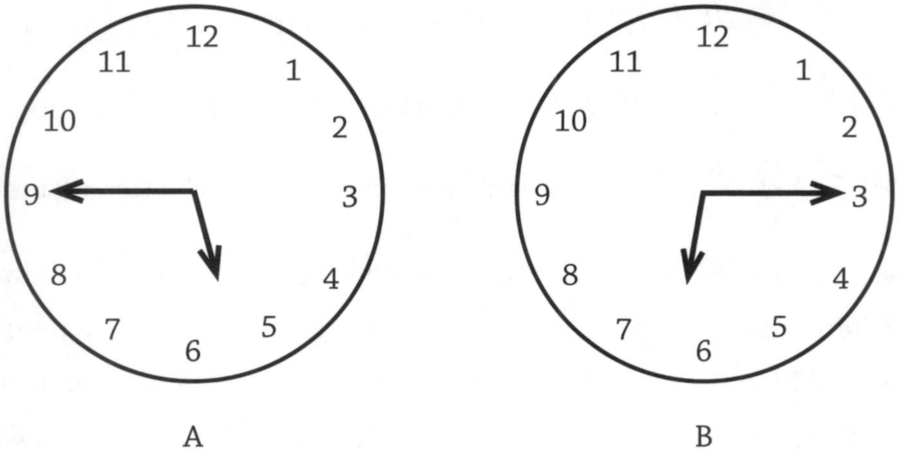

Can you say the times in the pictures above in Chinese?

3. Pronouns as Modifiers and the Usage of 的 (de)

When the personal pronouns 我 (wǒ, I), 你 (nǐ, you), and 他 (tā, he) are followed by a term indicating a close personal relationship such as 妈妈 (māma, mother), 弟弟 (dìdi, younger brother), and 老师 (lǎoshī, teacher), the word 的 (de) can be omitted; e.g., 我妈妈 (wǒ māma, my mother), 你弟弟 (nǐ dìdi, your younger brother), 我们老师 (wǒmen lǎoshī, our teacher). Otherwise 的 (de) is generally required; e.g., 我的生日 (wǒ de shēngrì, my birthday).

4. Pivotal Sentences

In the sentence "我请你吃晚饭" (Wǒ qǐng nǐ chī wǎnfàn; I will treat you to dinner), 你 (nǐ, you) is the object of the verb 请 (qǐng, to treat) as well as the subject of the second verb 吃 (chī, to eat). Therefore, 你 (nǐ, you) can be considered the pivot of the sentence. That is why some people consider this sentence as a type of "pivotal sentence."

Examples:

(1) 明天李生请你吃中国饭。

Míngtiān Lǐ Shēng qǐng nǐ chī Zhōngguófàn.

(Li Sheng is inviting you to eat Chinese food tomorrow.)

(2) 今天晚上我请你和你妹妹吃美国饭，好吗？

Jīntiān wǎnshang wǒ qǐng nǐ hé nǐ mèimei chī Měiguó fàn, hǎo ma?

(How about if I invite you and your younger sister to eat American food tonight?)

5. Alternative Questions

The structure (是)…还是…(shì...háishi..., ...or...) is used to form an alternative question. If there is another verb used in the predicate, the first 是 (shì) can be omitted.

(1) 你是中国人，还是美国人？

Nǐ shì Zhōngguórén, háishi Měiguórén?

(Are you Chinese or American?)

(2) 你哥哥是老师，还是学生？

Nǐ gēge shì lǎoshī, háishi xuésheng?

(Is your older brother a teacher or a student?)

(3) (是)你请我吃饭，还是他请我吃饭？

(Shì) nǐ qǐng wǒ chīfàn, háishi tā qǐng wǒ chīfàn?

(Are you taking me to dinner, or is he?)

(4) A: 他(是)喜欢吃中国饭，还是喜欢吃美国饭？

Tā (shì) xǐhuan chī Zhōngguó fàn, háishi xǐhuan chī Měiguó fàn?

(Does he like to eat Chinese or American food?)

B: 中国饭美国饭他都喜欢。

Zhōngguó fàn Měiguó fàn tā dōu xǐhuan.

(He likes both Chinese food and American food.)

6. Affirmative + Negative (A-not-A) Questions (I)

Besides adding the interrogative particle 吗 (ma) to a declarative sentence, another common way of forming a question in Chinese is to repeat the verb or adjective in its affirmative and negative form.

Example:

(1) 你忙不忙？

Nǐ máng bu máng?

(Are you busy or not?)

(2) 妈妈喜欢不喜欢吃中国饭？

Māma xǐhuan bu xǐhuan chī Zhōngguó fàn?

(Does mother like to eat Chinese food or not?)

(3) 王太太今天有没有事？

Wáng Tàitai jīntiān yǒu méiyǒu shì?

(Does Mrs. Wang have anything to do today or not?)

7. 还有 (hái yǒu, also, too, in addition) + Noun

The word 还有 (hái yǒu) can signify addition. For instance,

(1) 我家有爸爸、妈妈，还有一个妹妹。

Wǒ jiā yǒu bàba, māma, hái yǒu yí ge mèimei.

(In my family there's Dad, Mom, and a younger sister.)

(2) A: 谁喜欢吃美国饭？

Shéi xǐhuan chī Měiguó fàn?

(Who likes to eat American food?)

B: 我、我弟弟，还有我姐姐。

Wǒ, wǒ dìdi, hái yǒu wǒ jiějie.

(I, my younger brother, and also my older sister.)

PATTERN DRILLS

A. Days of the week

(Provide the correct answers based on the calendar below.)

March

Su	M	Tu	W	Th	F	Sa
12	13	14	15	16	17	18

Example: (Sānyuè shíwǔ hào)

A: Sānyuè shíwǔ hào shì xīngqī jǐ?

B: Sānyuè shíwǔ hào shì xīngqīsān.

(三月十五号)

A: 三月十五号是星期几?

B: 三月十五号是星期三。

1. Sānyuè shísān hào
2. Sānyuè shíliù hào
3. Sānyuè shí'èr hào
4. Sānyuè shíqī hào
5. Sānyuè shíbā hào
6. Sānyuè shísì hào

1. 三月十三号
2. 三月十六号
3. 三月十二号

几点钟？

Jǐ diǎnzhōng?

4. 三月十七号
5. 三月十八号
6. 三月十四号

B. Time

1.	<u>Wǒmen</u>	wǔ diǎnzhōng	<u>jiàn</u>.
2.		liù diǎn èrshí fēn	
3.		jiǔ diǎn	
4.		qī diǎn bàn	
5.		bā diǎn shí fēn	
6.		shíyī diǎn sìshí fēn	

1.	<u>我们</u>	五点钟	<u>见</u>。
2.		六点二十分	
3.		九点	
4.		七点半	
5.		八点十分	
6.		十一点四十分	

A Chinese teahouse.

C. 还是 (háishi, or)

Form 还是 *questions with the information given.*

1.	Tā shì xuésheng,	háishi	lǎoshī?
2.	Xiǎo Gāo xǐhuan chī Zhōngguó fàn,		xǐhuan chī Měiguó fàn?
3.	Nǐ de lǎoshī xìng Gāo,		xìng Zhāng?
4.	Nǐ jīnnián shì shíjiǔ,		èrshí?
5.	Tā gēge shì yīshēng,		lǜshī?
6.	Nǐ qǐng wǒ chīfàn,		wǒ qǐng nǐ chīfàn?

1.	他是学生	还是	老师?
2.	小高喜欢吃中国饭,		喜欢吃美国饭?
3.	你的老师姓高,		姓张?
4.	你今年是十九,		二十?
5.	他哥哥是医生,		律师?
6.	你请我吃饭,		我请你吃饭?

What time was this photo taken?

D. 可是 (kěshì, but)

Rephrase the sentences with 可是.

Example: Xiǎo Gāo shì Zhōngguórén. Xiǎo Gāo xǐhuan chī Měiguó fàn.

→ Xiǎo Gāo shì Zhōngguórén, kěshì xǐhuan chī Měiguó fàn.

小高是中国人。小高喜欢吃美国饭。

→小高是中国人，可是喜欢吃美国饭。

1. Wǒ xǐhuan Zhāng Xiǎojie. Wǒ bù xǐhuan Bái Xiǎojie.
2. Wǒ rènshi Wáng Lǎoshī. Wǒ bú rènshi Lǐ Lǎoshī.
3. Wǒ yǒu liǎng ge gēge. Wǒ méiyǒu dìdi.
4. Gāo Lǜshī jīntiān hěn máng. Gāo Lǜshī míngtiān bù máng.
5. Wǒ dìdi shì lǎoshī. Wǒ shì xuésheng.
6. Wǒ qǐng tā chīfàn. Tā bù qǐng wǒ chīfàn.

1. 我喜欢张小姐。我不喜欢白小姐。
2. 我认识王老师。我不认识李老师。
3. 我有两个哥哥。我没有弟弟。

4. 高律师今天很忙。高律师明天不忙。

5. 我弟弟是老师。我是学生。

6. 我请他吃饭。他不请我吃饭。

E. Affirmative + Negative (A-not-A) Questions

Change the questions below into A-not-A questions.

Example: Nǐ shì xuésheng ma?

→Nǐ shì bu shì xuésheng?

你是学生吗?

→你是不是学生?

1. Tā gēge shì yīshēng ma? →
2. Shíyuè wǔ hào shì xīngqīsì ma? →
3. Nǐ qǐng wǒ chī wǎnfàn ma? →
4. Gāo Yīshēng xǐhuan chī Měiguó fàn ma? →
5. Wǒmen jīntiān wǎnshang chī Zhōngguó fàn ma? →
6. Zhāng Lǎoshī jīntiān máng ma? →
7. Wáng Lǜshī rènshi Lǐ Xiǎojie ma? →
8. Xiǎo Bái shì nǐ de tóngxué ma? →

1. 他哥哥是医生吗? →
2. 十月五号是星期四吗? →
3. 你请我吃晚饭吗? →
4. 高医生喜欢吃美国饭吗? →

5. 我们今天晚上吃中国饭吗? →
6. 张老师今天忙吗? →
7. 王律师认识李小姐吗? →
8. 小白是你的同学吗? →

F. 还有 (hái yǒu, also; in addition)

Answer the questions using 还有 and the information in parentheses.

Example: Nǐ rènshi shéi? (Wáng Péng, Xiǎo Gāo)

→ Wǒ rènshi Wáng Péng, hái yǒu Xiǎo Gāo.

你认识谁? (王朋, 小高)

→我认识王朋, 还有小高。

1.	Nǐ qǐng shéi chīfàn?	(Zhāng Yīshēng, Lǐ Lǎoshī, Bái Lǜshī)
2.	Nǐ xǐhuan chī shénme fàn?	(Měiguó fàn, Zhōngguó fàn)
3.	Shéi qǐng nǐ chīfàn?	(Xiǎo Gāo, Xiǎo Lǐ, Xiǎo Wáng)
4.	Shéi xǐhuan chī Zhōngguó fàn?	(Wǒ bàba, wǒ māma, wǒ dìdi)

1.	你请谁吃饭?	(张医生、李老师、白律师)
2.	你喜欢吃什么饭?	(美国饭, 中国饭)
3.	谁请你吃饭?	(小高, 小李, 小王)
4.	谁喜欢吃中国饭?	(我爸爸, 我妈妈, 我弟弟)

PRONUNCIATION EXERCISES

A. The Initial r

shēngrì	rìjì	rèqíng	rénmín
réngrán	ránhòu	ruìlì	ràngbù

B. Finals

1.	**ie**	jiè	xiě	dié	tiě
	ue	jué	xué	quē	qiē
2.	**uo**	duō	tuō	zuò	cuò
	ou	dōu	tóu	zǒu	còu
3.	**u**	dū	tū	zū	cū

C. Two-syllable Words

bàngōng	gànhuó	rìjì	xiànzài
dìqū	dìtú	dàxiě	jiǎozhà

D. The Neutral Tone

yí ge	sān ge	zhè ge	nà ge
tā de	shéi de	wǒ de	nǐ de

E. Tone Sandhi [See Sec. D.2 in the Introduction]

zhǎnlǎn	lǚguǎn	yǔsǎn	děngděng
shǒufǎ	yǔnxǔ	xuǎnjǔ	guǎngchǎng

English Texts

DIALOGUE I

(Little Gao is talking to Little Bai.)

Little Gao: Little Bai, what day is September 12?
Little Bai: It's a Thursday.
Little Gao: That (day) is my birthday.
Little Bai: Really? How old are you this year?
Little Gao: Eighteen.
Little Bai: I'll treat you to dinner on Thursday. How's that?
Little Gao: That would be great. Thank you very much!
Little Bai: Do you like Chinese food or American food?
Little Gao: I'm Chinese, but I like American food.
Little Bai: All right. Let's have American food.

Little Gao:	Thursday at what time?
Little Bai:	How about seven thirty?
Little Gao:	All right. See you Thursday evening.
Little Bai:	See you.

DIALOGUE II

(Wang Peng and Little Bai are talking to each other.)

Wang Peng:	Xiao Bai, what time is it now?
Little Bai:	A quarter to six.
Wang Peng:	I have something to do at a quarter after six.
Little Bai:	Wang Peng, are you busy tomorrow?
Wang Peng:	I'm very busy today, but I won't be tomorrow. What is it?
Little Bai:	I'd like to take you to dinner tomorrow. What do you think?
Wang Peng:	Why are you taking me to dinner?
Little Bai:	Because tomorrow is Little Gao's birthday.
Wang Peng:	Really? Great. (Are you taking) anyone else?
Little Bai:	My classmate Little Li.
Wang Peng:	That's fantastic! I know Little Li, too. At what time?
Little Bai:	Seven thirty tomorrow night.
Wang Peng:	O.K., I'll see you at seven thirty tomorrow.

Can you describe this picture in Chinese?

LESSON 4 ▲ Hobbies

第四课 ▲ 爱好

Dì sì kè ▲ *Àihào*

你喜欢做什么？

Nǐ xǐhuan zuò shénme?

Dialogue I: Talking about Hobbies

VOCABULARY

1.	周末	zhōumò	n	weekend
2.	打球	dǎ qiú	vo	to play ball
	打	dǎ	v	to hit; to strike
	球	qiú	n	ball
3.	看	kàn	v	to watch; to look
4.	电视	diànshì	n	TV

	电	diàn	n	electricity
	视	-shì	n	vision
5.	唱歌(儿)	chàng gē(r)	vo	to sing (a song)
	唱	chàng	v	to sing
	歌	gē	n	song
6.	跳#舞	tiào wǔ	vo	to dance
	跳	tiào	v	to jump
	舞	wǔ	n	dance
7.	#听	tīng	v	to listen
8.	音乐	yīnyuè	n	music
9.	对	duì	adj	right; correct
10.	有时候	yǒu shíhou	ce	sometimes
	时候	shíhou	n	(a point in) time; moment; (a duration of) time
11.	看书	kàn shū	vo	to read books; to read
	书	shū	n	book
12.	电影	diànyǐng	n	movie
	影	yǐng	n	shadow
13.	常常	chángcháng	adv	often
14.	那	nà	conj	in that case; then
15.	去	qù	v	to go
16.	外国	wàiguó	n	foreign country
17.	请客	qǐng kè	vo	to invite someone to dinner; to be the host
18.	昨天	zuótiān	t	yesterday
19.	所以	suǒyǐ	conj	so

DIALOGUE I

(Little Bai is talking to Little Gao.)

Xiǎo Bái:	Xiǎo Gāo, nǐ zhōumò(1) xǐhuan zuò shénme(G1)?
Xiǎo Gāo:	Wǒ xǐhuan dǎ qiú, kàn diànshì(2). Nǐ ne?
Xiǎo Bái:	Wǒ xǐhuan chàng gē, tiào wǔ, hái xǐhuan tīng yīnyuè.
Xiǎo Gāo:	Nǐ yě xǐhuan kàn shū, duì bu duì?
Xiǎo Bái:	Duì, yǒu shíhou yě xǐhuan kàn shū.
Xiǎo Gāo:	Nǐ xǐhuan bu xǐhuan(G2) kàn diànyǐng?
Xiǎo Bái:	Xǐhuan. Wǒ zhōumò chángcháng kàn diànyǐng.
Xiǎo Gāo:	Nà(G3) wǒmen jīntiān wǎnshang qù kàn(G4) yí ge wàiguó diànyǐng, zěnmeyàng?
Xiǎo Bái:	Hǎo. Jīntiān wǒ qǐng kè.
Xiǎo Gāo:	Wèishénme nǐ qǐng kè?
Xiǎo Bái:	Yīnwei zuótiān nǐ qǐng wǒ chīfàn, suǒyǐ jīntiān wǒ qǐng nǐ kàn diànyǐng.

DIALOGUE I

(Little Bai is talking to Little Gao.)

小白：小高，你周末(1)喜欢做什么(G1)？

小高：我喜欢打球、看电视(2)。你呢？

小白：我喜欢唱歌、跳舞，还喜欢听音乐。

小高：你也喜欢看书，对不对？

小白：对，有时候也喜欢看书。

小高：你喜欢不喜欢(G2)看电影？

小白：喜欢。我周末常常看电影。

小高：那(G3)我们今天晚上去看(G4)一个外国电影，怎么样？

小白：好。今天我请客。

小高：为什么你请客？

小白：因为昨天你请我吃饭，所以今天我请你看电影。

Name the hobby depicted in each of the pictures above.

Notes

▲**1**▲ The concept of 周末 (zhōumò) has not always been exactly the same in China and Taiwan as it is in the United States. Until the mid-90s, office workers in China and Taiwan had to work on Saturdays and students had to go to class on Saturday mornings.

▲**2**▲ The series comma (、) is very useful in Chinese. When three or more nouns or pronouns occur in a series, this punctuation mark is used to sepa-

Karaoke.

rate them, while the conjunction 和 (hé) connects the last two items in the series, e.g., 我、你和她 (wǒ, nǐ hé tā; you, she and I); 中国、美国、英国和法国 (Zhōngguó, Měiguó, Yīngguó hé Fǎguó; China, the United States, England and France). The series comma can also be used between two or more verbs, as for example in 我喜欢唱歌、跳舞 (Wǒ xǐhuan chàng gē, tiào wǔ; I like singing and dancing).

Dialogue II: Inviting Someone to Play Ball

VOCABULARY

1.	好久	hǎo jiǔ	ce	a long time
	久	jiǔ	adj	a long time; for a long time
2.	不错	búcuò	adj	not bad; pretty good
	错	cuò	adj	wrong
3.	想	xiǎng	av	to want to; to think

Can you name this sport in Chinese?

4.	觉得*	juéde	v	to feel/think that...
5.	有意思	yǒuyìsi	adj	interesting
	意思	yìsi	n	meaning
6.	只	zhǐ	adv	only
7.	睡#觉*	shuì jiào	vo	to sleep
	睡	shuì	v	to sleep
8.	算了	suàn le	ce	Forget it. Never mind.
9.	找	zhǎo	v	to look for
10.	别人	biérén	n	others; other people; another person
	别（的）	bié (de)	adv	other

*Note that the character 觉 is pronounced in two different ways and has two different meanings: jué "to feel," and jiào "to sleep."

Culture Notes

The Chinese are known for their hospitality, which often finds its strongest expression in connection with meals. After a meal at a restaurant Chinese people often compete with

今天谁请客?

Jīntiān shéi qǐng kè?

their friends or relatives to pay the bill, with everyone insisting that it's their treat today: "今天我请客" (Jīntiān wǒ qǐng kè). For further discussion of Chinese food culture, see Culture Notes in Dialogue I of Lesson 12, in Level 1 Part 2.

DIALOGUE II

(Wang Peng is talking to Little Zhang.)

Wáng Péng: Xiǎo Zhāng, hǎo jiǔ bú jiàn[1], nǐ hǎo ma?

Xiǎo Zhāng: Wǒ hěn hǎo. Nǐ zěnmeyàng?

Wáng Péng: Wǒ yě búcuò. Zhège zhōumò nǐ xiǎng[G5] zuò shénme? Xiǎng bu xiǎng qù dǎ qiú?

Xiǎo Zhāng: Dǎ qiú? Wǒ bù xǐhuan dǎ qiú.

Wáng Péng: Nà wǒmen qù kàn diànyǐng, hǎo ma[G6]?

Xiǎo Zhāng: Kàn diànyǐng? Wǒ juéde kàn diànyǐng yě méiyǒu yìsi[2].

Wáng Péng: Nà nǐ xǐhuan zuò shénme?

Xiǎo Zhāng: Wǒ zhǐ xǐhuan chī fàn, shuì jiào.

Wáng Péng: Nà suàn le[F]. Wǒ qù zhǎo biérén.

DIALOGUE II

(Wang Peng is talking to Little Zhang.)

王朋：小张，好久不见(1)，你好吗？

小张：我很好。你怎么样？

王朋：我也不错。这个周末你<u>想</u>(G5)做什么？想不想去打球？

小张：打球？我不喜欢打球。

王朋：那我们去看电影，<u>好吗</u>(G6)？

小张：看电影？我觉得看电影也没有意思(2)。

王朋：那你喜欢做什么？

小张：我只喜欢吃饭、睡觉。

王朋：那算了(F)。我去找别人。

Note: The (F) sign indicates an idiomatic expression of which more examples are given below, in "Functional Expressions."

FUNCTIONAL EXPRESSIONS

算了 (suàn le; forget it, never mind)

1. A: 明天我们去打球，怎么样？

   (We'll go to play ball tomorrow, how does that sound?)

   Míngtiān wǒmen qù dǎ qiú, zěnmeyàng?

   B: 明天我很忙。 (I'll be busy tomorrow.)

   Míngtiān wǒ hěn máng.

A traditional dance of the Uighur people from Xinjiang Province.

A: 那算了。 (Oh, then never mind.)
Nà suàn le.

2. A: 你今年多大了？ (How old are you this year?)
Nǐ jīnnián duō dà le?

B: 你为什么问我多大了？
(Why do you ask how old I am?)
Nǐ wèishénme wèn wǒ duō dà le?

A: 算了，我不问了。 (Forget it. I'll ask no more.)
Suàn le, wǒ bú wèn le.

Notes

▲1▲ To English speakers, 好久不见 (hǎo jiǔ bú jiàn) may be vaguely reminiscent of the pidgin English expression, "Long time no see," which is said to have had its origin in a word-for-word translation of the Chinese greeting.

▲2▲ The position of negatives in Chinese is not always the same as their counterparts in English. An English speaker would say: "I *don't* think going to the movies is interesting," but Chinese uses the more logical order of negation, as in "我觉得看电影没有意思" (Wǒ juéde kàn diànyǐng méiyou yìsi), which literally means, "I think going to the movies is *not* interesting."

SUPPLEMENTARY VOCABULARY

1.	对了	duì le	ce	That's right!
2.	篮球	lánqiú	n	basketball
3.	网球	wǎngqiú	n	tennis
4.	橄榄球	gǎnlǎnqiú	n	American style football (used in Taiwan)
	橄榄	gǎnlǎn	n	olive
5.	美式足球	Měishì zúqiú	n	American style football (used in mainland China)
6.	棒球	bàngqiú	n	baseball
7.	足球	zúqiú	n	soccer
8.	排球	páiqiú	n	volleyball

Grammar

1. Word Order in Chinese

The basic word order in a Chinese sentence is:

Subject + Adverbial + Verb + Object

Subject (agent of the action) + Adverbial (time, place, manner, etc.) + Verb + Object (receiver of the action)

Examples:

	Subject	Adv. of time		Verb	Object
(1)	他	今天		吃	中国饭。
	Tā	jīntiān		chī	Zhōngguó fàn.
	(He is eating Chinese food today.)				
(2)	我	周末	常常	看	电影。
	Wǒ	zhōumò	chángcháng	kàn	diànyǐng.
	(I often watch movies on weekends.)				

This is the most common word order in a Chinese sentence. (Also see Grammar Note 3 in Lesson 1.) Of course, varying discourse contexts may affect this norm.

2. Affirmative + Negative Questions (II)

In this type of question there can be no adverbials before the verb other than time words. If there is an adverbial—such as 很 (hěn, very), 都 (dōu, all), or 常常 (chángcháng, often)—before the verb, the 吗 type question must be used instead.

(1) 你明天去不去?

Nǐ míngtiān qù bu qù?

(Are you going tomorrow?)

(2) 她今天晚上看不看电视?

Tā jīntiān wǎnshang kàn bu kàn diànshì?

(Is she going to watch TV tonight?)

(3) 他们都是学生吗?

Tāmen dōu shì xuésheng ma?

(Are they all students?)

(3a) *他们都是不是学生?

*Tāmen dōu shì bu shì xuésheng?

(4) 你常常看电影吗?

Nǐ chángcháng kàn diànyǐng ma?

(Do you often go to the movies?)

(4a) *你常常看不看电影?

*Nǐ chángcháng kàn bu kàn diànyǐng?

(5) 张医生很忙吗?

Zhāng Yīshēng hěn máng ma?

(Is Dr. Zhang very busy?)

Having dinner at home.

(5a) *张医生很忙不忙?

*Zhāng Yīshēng hěn máng bu máng?

3. 那(么) (nà{me}) as a Cohesive Device

那(么) (nà{me}) can function as a cohesive device in a dialogue. In other words, 那(么) shows the relationship between a previously-discussed sentence and the current sentence.

For example:

(1) 你今天晚上不想打球，那么我们去看一个外国电影，怎么样?

Nǐ jīntiān wǎnshang bù xiǎng dǎ qiú, nàme wǒmen qù kàn yí ge wàiguó diànyǐng, zěnmeyàng?

(You don't feel like playing ball this evening. Then let's go and see a foreign movie. How does that sound?)

(2) A: 我今天很忙，不想去吃晚饭。

Wǒ jīntiān hěn máng, bù xiǎng qù chī wǎnfàn.

(I'm very busy today. I don't want to go to dinner.)

B: 那明天呢？

Nà míngtiān ne?

(How about tomorrow?)

(3) A: 你喜欢不喜欢吃美国饭？

Nǐ xǐhuan bu xǐhuan chī Měiguó fàn?

(Do you like to eat American food or not?)

B: 不喜欢。

Bù xǐhuan.

(No, I don't.)

C: 那我们吃中国饭，怎么样？

Nà wǒmen chī Zhōngguó fàn, zěnmeyàng?

(Then let's eat Chinese food. How's that sound?)

D: 我也不喜欢。

Wǒ yě bù xǐhuan.

(I don't like it either.)

4. 去 (qù, to go) + Verb

To indicate that the performance of an action involves moving away from the speaker, the 去 (qù) + V construction must be used.

For example:

(1) 我们去看电影。

Wǒmen qù kàn diànyǐng.

(We are going to see a movie.)

(2) 晚上我不去跳舞。

Wǎnshang wǒ bú qù tiào wǔ.

(I will not go dancing tonight.)

(3) 今天我想去打球，你去不去？

Jīntiān wǒ xiǎng qù dǎ qiú, nǐ qù bu qù?

(I would like to play ball today. Do you want to go?)

5. The Auxiliary Verb 想 (xiǎng, to want to)

想 (xiǎng) has several meanings. In this lesson it is a modal verb indicating a desire to do something. It must be followed by a verb, a clause or a whole sentence.

For example:

(1) 你想听音乐吗?

Nǐ xiǎng tīng yīnyuè ma?

(Would you like to listen to some music?)

(2) 今天白老师想打球，可是王老师不想打。

Jīntiān Bái Lǎoshī xiǎng dǎ qiú, kěshì Wáng Lǎoshī bù xiǎng dǎ.

(Today Teacher Bai felt like playing ball, but Teacher Wang didn't.)

(3) 你想不想看中国电影?

Nǐ xiǎng bu xiǎng kàn Zhōngguó diànyǐng?

(Do you feel like going to see a Chinese movie?)

(4) 你想不想听外国音乐?

Nǐ xiǎng bu xiǎng tīng wàiguó yīnyuè?

(Do you feel like listening to some foreign music?)

6. Questions with 好吗 (hǎo ma)

To solicit someone's opinion, we can ask 好吗 (hǎo ma) after stating an idea or suggestion.

For example:

(1) 我们去看电影，好吗?

Wǒmen qù kàn diànyǐng, hǎo ma?

(Let's go see a movie, all right?)

(2) 我们今天晚上吃中国饭，好吗？

Wǒmen jīntiān wǎnshang chī Zhōngguó fàn, hǎo ma?

(We'll eat Chinese food tonight, all right?)

Note: In Taiwan 好不好 (hǎo bu hǎo), instead of 好吗 (hǎo ma), is often used to solicit opinions.

PATTERN DRILLS

A. Subject + Time + Verb + (Object)

1.	Tā dìdi	zhōumò chángcháng	dǎ qiú.
2.	Wáng Péng, Lǐ Yǒu		kàn Zhōngguó diànyǐng.
3.	Gāo Lǎoshī		qǐng xuésheng chī fàn.
4.	Wǒ jiějie		tiào wǔ.
5.	Xiǎo Wáng		kàn diànshì.
6.	Bái Xiǎojie		tīng yīnyuè.

1.	她弟弟	周末常常	打球。
2.	王朋、李友		看中国电影。
3.	高老师		请学生吃饭。
4.	我姐姐		跳舞。
5.	小王		看电视。
6.	白小姐		听音乐。

B. 去 (qù, to go) + Verb

1.	Wǒmen jīntiān wǎnshang	qù	tiào wǔ.
2.			chàng gē.
3.			dǎ qiú.
4.			kàn wàiguó diànyǐng.

5. chī Měiguó fàn.
6. tīng Zhōngguó yīnyuè.

1. 我们今天晚上 去 跳舞。
2. 唱歌。
3. 打球。
4. 看外国电影。
5. 吃美国饭。
6. 听中国音乐。

C. 因为...所以...(yīnwèi...suǒyǐ..., because...therefore...)

Make sentences using 因为...所以....

1.	Yīnwèi	tā shì Zhōngguórén,	suǒyǐ	tā hěn xǐhuan chī Zhōngguó fàn.
2.		tā hěn máng,		tā bú qù kàn diànyǐng.
3.		tā juéde dǎ qiú méiyǒu yìsi,		tā bù xiǎng qù dǎ qiú.
4.		jīntiān de diànshì méiyǒu yìsi,		tā xiǎng qù kàn diànyǐng.
5.		tā xiǎng qù tiào wǔ,		tā bú qù kàn diànyǐng.
6.		tā juéde tīng yīnyuè méiyǒu yìsi,		tā bù tīng yīnyuè.

1.	因为	他是中国人,	所以	他很喜欢吃中国饭。
2.		他很忙,		他不去看电影。
3.		他觉得打球没有意思,		他不想去打球。
4.		今天的电视没有意思,		他想去看电影。
5.		他想去跳舞,		他不去看电影。
6.		他觉得听音乐没有意思,		他不听音乐。

看电影

Kàn diànyǐng

D. 想 (xiǎng, to want to)

1.	Nǐ	<u>xiǎng bu xiǎng</u>	qù dǎ qiú?
2.	Tā		chī Zhōngguó fàn?
3.	Gāo Yīshēng		qù tiào wǔ?
4.	Xiǎo Zhāng de mèimei		tīng yīnyuè?
5.	Lǐ Xiǎojie		qù kàn Měiguó diànyǐng?
6.	Nǐmen		tīng yīnyuè?
7.	Xiǎo Wáng de dìdi		kàn diànshì?

1.	你	<u>想不想</u>	去打球?
2.	他		吃中国饭?
3.	高医生		去跳舞?
4.	小张的妹妹		听音乐?
5.	李小姐		去看美国电影?
6.	你们		听音乐?
7.	小王的弟弟		看电视?

看书

Kàn shū

E. 有意思 (yǒu yìsi, interesting)

1.	Xiǎo Zhāng	juéde	dǎ qiú	hěn yǒu yìsi.
2.	Bái Yīshēng		tiào wǔ	
3.	Zhāng Lǜshī		tīng Zhōngguó yīnyuè	
4.	Lǐ Lǎoshī		kàn wàiguó diànyǐng	
5.	Wáng Xiǎojie		kàn shū	
6.	Xiǎo Gāo de dìdi		kàn diànshì	

1.	小张	觉得	打球	很有意思。
2.	白医生		跳舞	
3.	张律师		听中国音乐	
4.	李老师		看外国电影	
5.	王小姐		看书	
6.	小高的弟弟		看电视	

F. 好吗？ (hǎo ma? O.K.?)

1.	Wǒmen	zhège zhōumò	qù	kàn diànyǐng,	hǎo ma?
2.		míngtiān		tiào wǔ,	
3.		xīngqīsì		chàng gē,	
4.		zhège zhōumò		Gāo Lǎoshī jiā,	
5.		xīngqīliù		dǎ qiú,	
6.		xīngqīwǔ		kàn wàiguó diànyǐng,	
7.		jīntiān wǎnshang		tīng yīnyuè,	

1.	我们	这个周末	去	看电影，	好吗？
2.		明天		跳舞，	
3.		星期四		唱歌，	
4.		这个周末		高老师家，	
5.		星期六		打球，	
6.		星期五		看外国电影，	
7.		今天晚上		听音乐，	

English Texts

DIALOGUE I

(Little Bai is talking to Little Gao.)

Little Bai: What do you like to do on weekends?

Little Gao: I like to play ball and watch TV. How about you?

Little Bai: I like to sing, dance, and listen to music.

Little Gao: You like to read as well, right?

Little Bai: Yes, sometimes I like to read as well.

Little Gao: Do you like to watch movies?

Little Bai: Yes, I do. I often watch movies on weekends.

Little Gao: Then let's go see a foreign movie this evening. How's that sound?

Little Bai:	Fine. I'll treat today.
Little Gao:	Why is it your treat?
Little Bai:	Because you treated me to dinner yesterday, so today I'm treating you to a movie.

DIALOGUE II

(Wang Peng is talking to Little Zhang.)

Wang Peng:	Little Zhang, long time no see. How are you?
Little Zhang:	Great. How about you?
Wang Peng:	I'm fine, too. What would you like to do this weekend? Would you like to play ball?
Little Zhang:	Play ball? I don't like playing ball.
Wang Peng:	Then let's go see a movie. How's that sound?
Little Zhang:	See a movie? I don't think seeing a movie would be much fun either.
Wang Peng:	Then what do you like to do?
Little Zhang:	I only like to eat and sleep.
Wang Peng:	Then forget it. I'll ask somebody else.

我只喜欢睡觉。

Wǒ zhǐ xǐhuan shuì jiào.

LESSON 5 ▲ Visiting Friends

第五课 ▲ 看朋友

Dì wǔ kè ▲ *Kàn péngyou*

Xiao Gao introduces Li You and Wang Peng to his sister, Xiaoyin.

Dialogue: Visiting a Friend's Home

VOCABULARY

1.	呀	ya	p	(an interjectory particle used to soften a question)
2.	进	jìn	v	to enter
3.	快	kuài	adj/adv	fast; quick; quickly
4.	进来	jìnlai	vc	to come in
5.	来	lái	v	to come
6.	#介#绍	jièshào	v	to introduce

7.	一下	yí xià	m	(a measure word used after a verb indicating short duration) [see G1]
8.	高#兴	gāoxìng	adj	happy; pleased
9.	#漂亮	piàoliang	adj	pretty
10.	坐	zuò	v	to sit
11.	在	zài	prep	at; in; on
12.	哪儿	nǎr	qpr	where
13.	工作	gōngzuò	v/n	to work; work; job
14.	学校	xuéxiào	n	school
15.	喝	hē	v	to drink
16.	点(儿)	diǎn(r)	m	a little; a bit; some [see G1]
17.	茶	chá	n	tea
18.	#咖#啡	kāfēi	n	coffee
19.	啤酒	píjiǔ	n	beer
	酒	jiǔ	n	wine; any alcoholic beverage [see Culture Note 3]
20.	吧	ba	p	(a "suggestion" particle; softens the tone of the sentence to which it is appended)
21.	要	yào	v	to want; to have a desire for
22.	杯	bēi	m	cup; glass
23.	可乐	kělè	n	cola
24.	可以	kěyǐ	av	can; may
25.	对不起	duìbuqǐ	ce	I'm sorry.
26.	给	gěi	v	to give
27.	水	shuǐ	n	water

Bringing gifts to a friend's house.

DIALOGUE

Xiǎo Gāo:	Shéi ya?(F)
Wáng Péng:	Shì wǒ, Wáng Péng, hái yǒu Lǐ Yǒu.
Xiǎo Gāo:	Qǐng jìn, qǐng jìn! Lǐ Yǒu, kuài jìnlai! Lái, wǒ jièshào yí xià(G1), zhè shì wǒ jiějie, Gāo Xiǎoyīn.
Lǐ Yǒu:	Xiǎoyīn, nǐ hǎo. Rènshi nǐ hěn gāoxìng(1).
Gāo Xiǎoyīn:	Rènshi nǐmen wǒ yě hěn gāoxìng.
Lǐ Yǒu:	Nǐmen jiā hěn dà(G2), yě hěn piàoliang.
Xiǎo Gāo:	Shì ma(2)(F)? Qǐng zuò, qǐng zuò.
Wáng Péng:	Xiǎoyīn, nǐ zài (G3) nǎr gōngzuò?
Gāo Xiǎoyīn:	Wǒ zài xuéxiào gōngzuò. Nǐmen xiǎng hē diǎnr(G1) shénme? Yǒu chá, kāfēi, hái yǒu píjiǔ.
Wáng Péng:	Wǒ hē píjiǔ ba(G4).
Lǐ Yǒu:	Wǒ bù hē jiǔ. Wǒ yào yì bēi kělè, kěyǐ ma?
Gāo Xiǎoyīn:	Duìbuqǐ, wǒmen méiyǒu kělè.
Lǐ Yǒu:	Nà gěi wǒ yì bēi shuǐ ba.

DIALOGUE

小高： 谁呀？(F)

王朋： 是我，王朋，还有李友。

小高： 请进，请进！李友，快进来！来，我介绍一下(G1)，这是我姐姐，高小音。

李友： 小音，你好。认识你很高兴(1)。

高小音： 认识你们我也很高兴。

李友： 你们家很大(G2)，也很漂亮。

小高： 是吗(2)(F)？请坐，请坐。

王朋： 小音，你在(G3)哪儿工作？

高小音： 我在学校工作。你们想喝点儿(G1)什么？有茶、咖啡，还有啤酒。

王朋： 我喝啤酒吧(G4)。

李友： 我不喝酒。我要一杯可乐，可以吗？

高小音： 对不起，我们没有可乐。

李友： 那给我一杯水吧。

Notes

▲1▲ 认识你很高兴 (Rènshi nǐ hěn gāoxìng) is a translation of the English "I'm happy to meet you," and may therefore sound rather western to some Chinese speakers. However, the traditional Chinese equivalent polite formulae have now generally become obsolete and this expression is often heard.

▲2▲ Although it takes a question mark, 是吗 (shì ma) is not a question here but a mild expression of one's surprise on hearing something unexpected in a conversation. Here it indicates modest acceptance of a compliment, with the intended implication: "Your compliment has taken me by surprise." It could be translated as "Is that so?" "You don't say!" or "Really?" Another phrase which can be used for the same purpose is 哪里 (nǎli). The original meaning of 哪里 (nǎli) is "where?" When paid a compliment, some Chinese people would say, "哪里" (nǎli) or "哪里， 哪里" (nǎli, nǎli). In recent times, however, 哪里 (nǎli) has become somewhat old fashioned.

你们家很大，也很漂亮。

Nǐmen jiā hěn dà, yě hěn piàoliang.

Enjoying refreshments.

FUNCTIONAL EXPRESSIONS

谁呀 (shéi ya? Who is it?)

1. A: (敲门) (Knocking at the door.)

   (Qiāo mén.)

   B: 谁呀? (Who is it?)

   Shéi ya?

   A: 是我，李友。 (It's me, Li You.)

   Shì wǒ, Lǐ Yǒu.

   B: 请进。 (Come in, please.)

   Qǐng jìn.

2. A: (敲门) (Knocking at the door.)

   (Qiāo mén.)

   B: 谁呀? (Who is it?)

   Shéi ya?

   A: 我，小王。 (It's me, Little Wang.)

   Wǒ, Xiǎo Wáng.

矿泉水

Kuàngquánshuǐ

B: 进来。 (Come in.)

Jìnlai.

是吗 (shì ma? Really?)

1. A: 王朋的女朋友很漂亮。

   (Wang Peng's girlfriend is pretty.)

   Wáng Péng de nǚpéngyǒu hěn piàoliang.

   B: 是吗？ 她是学生吗？

   (Really? Is she a student?)

   Shì ma? Tā shì xuésheng ma?

2. A: 你的中文老师不是中国人。

   (Your Chinese teacher is not Chinese.)

   Nǐ de Zhōngwén lǎoshī búshì Zhōngguó rén.

   B: 是吗？ 他是哪国人？

   (Really? What country is he from?)

   Shì ma? Tā shì nǎ guó rén?

   A: 他是美国人。

   (He is American.)

   Tā shì Měiguó rén.

Culture Notes

▲1▲ Generally speaking, in Chinese culture privacy is a less sacrosanct notion than it is in the West. One would not necessarily be considered an intruder if one drops by a friend's place without any warning. Neither are age, marital status, and salary considered off limits in polite conversation. However, all that is changing—particularly among urbanites.

▲2▲ Although tea is the most popular beverage in China, the number of coffee drinkers has been on the rise in recent years, as evidenced by the varieties of coffee on supermarket shelves and the surge of coffee shops, such as Starbucks (星巴克, Xīngbākè), in many Chinese cities.

▲3▲ Although usually translated as "wine," 酒 (jiǔ) applies to all kinds of alcoholic beverages. Among the traditional Chinese rice wines and liquors, the most celebrated is 茅台 (Máotái), a strong liquor with a heady aroma.

Narrative: At a Friend's House

VOCABULARY

1.	玩(儿)	wán(r)	v	to have fun; to play
2.	图书馆	túshūguǎn	n	library
3.	#瓶	píng	m	bottle
4.	一起	yìqǐ	adv	together
5.	#聊天（儿）	liáo tiān(r)	vo	to chat
	#聊	liáo	v	to chat
6.	才	cái	adv	not until, only then
7.	回家	huí jiā	vo	to go home
	回	huí	v	to return

Narrative

Zuótiān wǎnshang, Wáng Péng hé Lǐ Yǒu qù Xiǎo Gāo jiā wánr. Zài Xiǎo Gāo jiā, tāmen rènshile(G5) Xiǎo Gāo de jiějie. Tā jiào Gāo Xiǎoyīn, zài xuéxiào de túshūguǎn gōngzuò. Xiǎo Gāo qǐng Wáng Péng hē(1) píjiǔ, Wáng Péng hēle liǎng píng. Lǐ Yǒu bù hē jiǔ, zhǐ hēle yì bēi shuǐ. Tāmen yìqǐ liáo tiānr, kàn diànshì. Wáng Péng hé Lǐ Yǒu wǎnshang shí'èr diǎn cái(G6) huíjiā.

Narrative

昨天晚上，王朋和李友去小高家玩儿。在小高家，他们认识了(G5)小高的姐姐。她叫高小音，在学校的图书馆工作。小高请王朋喝(1)啤酒，王朋喝了两瓶。李友不喝酒，只喝了一杯水。他们一起聊天儿、看电视。王朋和李友晚上十二点才(G6)回家。

Notes

▲1▲ 喝 (hē) is not always used in the same way as its English equivalent, "to drink." When used intransitively, the English verb often carries the connotation of "drinking alcohol." 喝 (hē), on the other hand, is a transitive verb. Unless it's clear from the context, it always takes an object; in other words, the beverage has to be specified. Therefore, "他常常喝" (Tā chángcháng hē) is a complete sentence only when the beverage has been indicated in the context, e.g.:

A: 他常常喝咖啡吗？

Tā chángcháng hē kāfēi ma?

(Does he often drink coffee?)

B: 他常常喝。

Tā chángcháng hē.

(He often does.)

她在哪儿工作?

Tā zài nǎr gōngzuò?

SUPPLEMENTARY VOCABULARY

1.	打工	dǎ gōng	vo	to work part-time; to do manual work
2.	好吃	hǎochī	adj	good to eat; delicious
3.	好喝	hǎohē	adj	good to drink; tasty
4.	好看	hǎokàn	adj	good-looking
5.	好玩(儿)	hǎowán(r)	adj	fun
6.	可口可乐	Kěkǒukělè	n	Coke
7.	百事可乐	Bǎishìkělè	n	Pepsi
8.	雪碧	Xuěbì	n	Sprite
9.	汽水(儿)	qìshuǐ(r)	n	soft drink; soda pop
10.	矿泉水	kuàngquánshuǐ	n	mineral water

Grammar

1. 一下 (yí xià) and (一) 点儿 ({yì}diǎnr) Moderating the Tone of Voice

Following a verb, both 一下 (yí xià, lit. "once") and (一) 点儿 ({yì }diǎnr, "a bit") can soften a statement. This is similar to a moderated tone of voice in English and is therefore more polite. When used in this way, 一下 (yí xià) modifies the verb, while (一) 点儿 ({yì}diǎnr) modifies the object.

(1) 你看一下，这是谁的照片？

Nǐ kàn yí xià, zhè shì shéi de zhàopiàn?

(Take a look. Whose photo is this?)

(2) 你进来一下。

Nǐ jìnlai yí xià.

(Come in for a minute.)

(3) 你想吃点儿什么？

Nǐ xiǎng chī diǎnr shénme?

(What would you like to eat?)

(4) 你喝一点儿茶吧。

Nǐ hē yīdiǎnr chá ba.

(Have some tea.)

2. Adjectives Used as Predicates

In Chinese an adjective can be used as a predicate without being preceded by the verb 是 (shì, to be).

(1) 我今天很高兴。

Wǒ jīntiān hěn gāoxìng.

(I'm very happy today.)

(2) 他妹妹很漂亮。

Tā mèimei hěn piàoliang.

(His younger sister is very pretty.)

(3) 那个电影很好。

Nàge diànyǐng hěn hǎo.

(That movie is very good.)

(4) 你们学校很大。

Nǐmen xuéxiào hěn dà.

(Your school is very large.)

Note: When an adjective is used as a predicate, it is usually modified by 很 (hěn, very) or some other adverbial modifier. 很 (hěn) is not as strong as its English counterpart "very." In certain contexts Chinese adjectives without some sort of a modifier before them can be inherently comparative.

(5) A: 姐姐漂亮还是妹妹漂亮？

Jiějie piàoliang háishi mèimei piàoliang?

(Who's prettier, the older sister or the younger sister?)

B: 妹妹漂亮。

Mèimei piàoliang.

(The younger sister is prettier).

(6) 妹妹的中文好，我的中文不好。

Mèimei de Zhōngwén hǎo, wǒ de Zhōngwén bù hǎo.

(My younger sister's Chinese is good. Mine is not.)

3. 在 (zài, at; in; on)

Combined with a noun, the preposition 在 (zài) indicates location. When the phrase is placed before a verb, it indicates the location of the action.

(1) 你在哪儿工作？

Nǐ zài nǎr gōngzuò?

(Where do you work?)

(2) 我在这个学校学中文。

Wǒ zài zhège xuéxiào xué Zhōngwén.

(I study Chinese at this school.)

Chinese green tea.

(3) 我不喜欢在家看电影。

Wǒ bù xǐhuan zài jiā kàn diànyǐng.

(I don't like to watch movies at home.)

4. The Particle of Mood 吧 (ba)

吧 (ba) is often used at the end of an imperative sentence to soften the tone.

(1) 你喝茶吧。

Nǐ hē chá ba.

(Have some tea.)

(2) 请进来吧。

Qǐng jìnlai ba.

(Come in, please.)

5. The Particle 了 (le) (I)

The dynamic particle 了 (le) signifies the occurrence of an action or the emergence of a situation. The action or situation usually pertains to the past, but sometimes it can refer to the future. Therefore the use of 了 (le) should not be taken as an equivalent to the past tense in English. In the current lesson, 了 (le) indicates the occurrence of an action. It can be used after a verb or at the end of a sentence.

(1) 妈妈喝了一杯水。

Māma hēle yì bēi shuǐ.

(Mom had a glass of water.)

(2) 昨天晚上我去小高家玩儿了。

Zuótiān wǎnshang wǒ qù Xiǎo Gāo jiā wánr le.

(Yesterday evening I went to Little Gao's home for a visit.)

(3) 星期一小高请我喝了一杯茶。

Xīngqīyī Xiǎo Gāo qǐng wǒ hēle yì bēi chá.

(On Monday Little Gao invited me out for tea.)

(4) 明天我吃了晚饭去看电影。

Míngtiān wǒ chīle wǎnfàn qù kàn diànyǐng.

(Tomorrow I'll go see a movie after I have eaten dinner.)

Note: There is often a specific time phrase in a sentence with the dynamic particle 了 (le)—such as 昨天晚上 (zuótiān wǎnshang, last night) in example (2), 星期一 (xīngqīyī, Monday) in example (3), and 明天 (míngtiān, tomorrow) in example (4). When 了 (le) is embedded between the verb and the object, the object must be preceded by a modifier. The following numeral + measure word is the most common type of modifier for the object:

一杯 (yì bēi, one cup; one glass) example (1)

一瓶 (yì píng, one bottle) example (3)

If there are other phrases or sentences following the object, then the object does not need a modifier. See example (4) above. Also, if the object following 了 (le) is a proper noun, it does not need a modifier, either:

我昨天看了 "Titanic," 那个电影很好。

Wǒ zuótiān kànle "Titanic." Nàge diànyǐng hěn hǎo.

(I saw *Titanic* yesterday. It was very good.)

Name these drinks in Chinese.

To say that an action did not take place in the past, use 没 (有) (méi{yǒu}) instead of 不…了 (bù...le) or 没有…了 (méiyǒu…le) .

For example:

(5) 昨天我没有听音乐。

Zuótiān wǒ méiyǒu tīng yīnyuè.

(I didn't listen to the music yesterday.)

(5a) *昨天我不听音乐了。

Zuótiān wǒ bù tīng yīnyuè le.

(5b) *昨天我没有听音乐了

Zuótiān wǒ méiyǒu tīng yīnyuè le.

Interrogative forms:

(6) A: 你吃了吗?

Nǐ chīle ma?

(Did you eat?)

B: 我没吃。

Wǒ méi chī.

(No, I didn't.)

(7) 你吃饭了没有?

Nǐ chī fànle méiyǒu?

(Have you eaten?)

(8) A: 你喝了几杯水？

Nǐ hēle jǐ bēi shuǐ?

(How many glasses of water did you drink?)

B: 我喝了一杯水。

Wǒ hēle yì bēi shuǐ.

(I drank one glass of water.)

A note on the phrase 认识了 (rènshile): 认识 (rènshi, to know; to be or become acquainted with) is a verb that usually indicates not an action but a state. Thus 认识了 (rènshile) indicates the beginning of a new state, "to become acquainted with." 了 (le) indicates the occurrence of the transition from "not knowing" to "knowing." Compare:

(9) 我认识高小音。

Wǒ rènshi Gāo Xiǎoyīn.

(I know Gao Xiaoyin.)

(10) 我昨天认识了高小音。

Wǒ zuótiān rènshile Gāo Xiǎoyīn.

(I got acquainted with Gao Xiaoyin yesterday.)

6. The Adverb 才 (cái)

才 (cái) indicates that an action or state occurs later than might have been expected.

(1) 我六点请他吃晚饭，他六点半才来。

Wǒ liù diǎn qǐng tā chī wǎnfàn, tā liù diǎn bàn cái lái.

(I invited him to dinner at six. He didn't come till six thirty.)

(2) 我昨天十二点才回家。

Wǒ zuótiān shí'èr diǎn cái huíjiā.

(I didn't go home yesterday till twelve o'clock.)

(3) 她晚上很晚才睡觉。

Tā wǎnshang hěn wǎn cái shuì jiào.

(She goes to bed very late in the evening.)

PATTERN DRILLS

A. 一下 (yí xià)

1.	Wǒ kàn	yí xià.
2.	Nǐ jièshào	
3.	Nǐ zuò	
4.	Wǒ tīng	
5.	Nǐ qù	
6.	Nǐ lái	

1.	我看	一下。
2.	你介绍	
3.	你坐	
4.	我听	
5.	你去	
6.	你来	

B. Adjectives as Predicates

1.	Xiǎo Gāo de	jiā	hěn	piàoliang.
2.	xuéxiào			dà.
3.	yīshēng			máng.
4.	shū			yǒu yìsi.
5.	jiějie			gāoxìng.
6.	dìdi			gāo.
7.	lǎoshī			hǎo.
8.	tóngxué			hǎo.

1.	小高的	家	很	漂亮。
2.	学校			大。

3.	医生	忙。
4.	书	有意思。
5.	姐姐	高兴。
6.	弟弟	高。
7.	老师	好。
8.	同学	好。

C. 在 (zài)

C1:

1.	<u>Wáng Péng hé Lǐ Yǒu zài</u>	túshūguǎn	kàn shū.
2.		jiā	tīng yīnyuè.
3.		túshūguǎn	gōngzuò.
4.		jiā	kàn diànshì.
5.		Xiǎo Gāo jiā	hē kāfēi.
6.		Wáng Lǎoshī jiā	liáo tiān.
7.		Xiǎo Bái jiā	chī fàn.
8.		xuéxiào	dǎ qiú.

1.	<u>王朋和李友在</u>	图书馆	看书。
2.		家	听音乐。
3.		图书馆	工作。
4.		家	看电视。
5.		小高家	喝咖啡。
6.		王老师家	聊天。
7.		小白家	吃饭。
8.		学校	打球。

C2: Answer questions with 在.

Example: Xiǎo Gāo zài nǎr gōngzuò? (xuéxiào)

→ Xiǎo Gāo zài xuéxiào gōngzuò.

小高在哪儿工作?(学校)

→小高在学校工作。

1.	Zhāng Yīshēng zài nǎr tīng yīnyuè?	(jiā)
2.	Xiǎo Wáng zài nǎr dǎ qiú?	(xuéxiào)
3.	Xiǎo Gāo de mèimei zài nǎr kàn shū?	(túshūguǎn)
4.	Xiǎo Lǐ hé Xiǎo Bái zài nǎr kàn diànyǐng?	(xuéxiào)
5.	Wáng Péng hé Lǐ Yǒu zài nǎr liáo tiānr?	(Xiǎo Gāo jiā)
6.	Xiǎo Gāo de jiějie zài nǎr gōngzuò?	(túshūguǎn)
7.	Xiǎo Zhāng zài nǎr shuì jiào?	(jiā)

1.	张医生在哪儿听音乐?	(家)
2.	小王在哪儿打球?	(学校)
3.	小高的妹妹在哪儿看书?	(图书馆)
4.	小李和小白在哪儿看电影?	(学校)
5.	王朋和李友在哪儿聊天儿?	(小高家)
6.	小高的姐姐在哪儿工作?	(图书馆)
7.	小张在哪儿睡觉?	(家)

D. 点儿 (diǎnr)

1.	Nǐ	xiǎng	chī	diǎnr	shénme?
2.	Xiǎo Bái		tīng		
3.	Nǐ		zuò		
4.	Zhāng Lǜshī		chī		
5.	Lǐ Yīshēng, nín		hē		

1.	你	<u>想</u>	吃	<u>点儿</u>	<u>什么</u>？
2.	小白		听		
3.	你		做		
4.	张律师		吃		
5.	李医生，您		喝		

E. 了 (le)

1.	<u>Tā zuótiān wǎnshang</u>	hē	<u>le</u>	sì bēi	shuǐ.
2.		kàn		liǎng ge	diànyǐng.
3.		hē		wǔ bēi	kělè.
4.		hē		liǎng píng	píjiǔ.
5.		hē		liù bēi	chá.
6.		chàng		sān ge	gē.
7.		tiào		yí ge	wǔ.

1	<u>他昨天晚上</u>	喝	<u>了</u>	四杯	水。
2.		看		两个	电影。
3.		喝		五杯	可乐。
4.		喝		两瓶	啤酒。
5.		喝		六杯	茶。
6.		唱		三个	歌。
7.		跳		一个	舞。

F. 才 (cái)

1.	<u>Wǒmen</u>	liù diǎn	chī fàn,	<u>tā</u>	liù diǎn bàn	<u>cái lái</u>.
2.		jiǔ diǎn	tiào wǔ,		shí diǎn	
3.		qī diǎn	kàn diànyǐng,		bā diǎn	
4.		bā diǎn bàn	hē kāfēi,		jiǔ diǎn	
5.		qī diǎn	chī wǎnfàn,		qī diǎn bàn	
6.		jiǔ diǎn shí fēn	dǎ qiú,		jiǔ diǎn bàn	
7.		bā diǎn	tīng yīnyuè,		bā diǎn bàn	
8.		liù diǎn shíwǔ fēn	gōngzuò,		liù diǎn bàn	
9.		wǔ diǎn	qù zhǎo Gāo Lǎoshī,		liù diǎn èrshí fēn	

1	<u>我们</u>	六点	吃饭，	<u>他</u>	六点半	<u>才来</u>。
2.		九点	跳舞，		十点	
3.		七点	看电影，		八点	
4.		八点半	喝咖啡，		九点	
5.		七点	吃晚饭，		七点半	
6.		九点十分	打球，		九点半	
7.		八点	听音乐，		八点半	
8.		六点十五分	工作，		六点半	
9.		五点	去找高老师，		六点二十分	

Make a story out of the four pictures above.
Don't forget to mention the time in each picture!

English Texts

DIALOGUE

Little Gao:	Who is it?
Wang Peng:	It's me, Wang Peng. Li You is here, too.
Little Gao:	Please come in. Please come in, Li You. Let me introduce you to one another. This is my sister, Gao Xiaoyin.
Li You:	How do you do, Xiaoyin! Pleased to meet you.
Gao Xiaoyin:	Pleased to meet you, too.
Li You:	Your home is very big, and very beautiful, too.
Little Gao:	Really? Sit down, please.
Wang Peng:	Xiaoyin, where do you work?
Gao Xiaoyin:	I work at a school. What would you like to drink? We have tea, coffee, and beer.
Wang Peng:	I'll have a beer.
Li You:	I don't drink. Could I have a glass of cola?
Miss Gao:	I'm sorry. We don't have cola.
Li You:	Then please give me a glass of water.

Describe this scene in detail.

Narrative

Last night Wang Peng and Li You went to Little Gao's home for a visit. At Little Gao's home they met Little Gao's older sister. Her name is Gao Xiaoyin. She works at a school library. Little Gao offered beer to Wang Peng. Wang Peng had two bottles of beer. Li You does not drink. She just had a glass of water. They talked and watched TV together. Wang Peng and Li You did not get home until twelve o'clock.

Use what you have learned so far to describe the picture above.
You may also write a dialogue for the conversation that is underway.

LESSON 6 ▲ Making Appointments

第六课 ▲ 约时间

Dì liù kè ▲ *Yuē shíjiān*

您什么时候有空？

Nín shénme shíhòu yǒu kòng?

Dialogue I: Calling One's Teacher

VOCABULARY

1.	给	gěi	prep	to; for [see also L.5]
2.	打电话	dǎ diànhuà	vo	to make a phone call
	电话	diànhuà	n	telephone
	话	huà	n	speech; talk; words
3.	# 喂	wèi/wéi	interj	(on telephone) Hello! Hey!
4.	在	zài	v	to be present; to be at (a place)

5.	就	jiù	adv	the very one (indicating verification of someone mentioned before)
6.	哪	nǎ/něi	qpr	which
7.	位	wèi	m	(a polite measure for people)
8.	下午	xiàwǔ	t	afternoon
9.	时间	shíjiān	t	time
10.	几	jǐ-	nu	some; a few (an indefinite number, usually less than ten)
11.	问题	wèntí	n	question; problem
12.	要	yào	av	will; to be going to
13.	开会	kāi huì	vo	to have a meeting
	开	kāi	v	to hold (a meeting, party, etc.)
14.	上午	shàngwǔ	t	morning
15.	节	jié	m	(a measure word for class period)
16.	课	kè	n	class; lesson
17.	年级	niánjí	n	grade in school
18.	考试	kǎoshì	v/n	to give or take a test; test
	考	kǎo	v	to give or take a test
19.	以后	yǐhòu	t	after
20.	有空(儿)	yǒu kòng(r)	vo	to have free time
21.	要是	yàoshi	conj	if
22.	方便	fāngbiàn	adj	convenient
23.	到…去	dào…qù		to go to (a place)
24.	办公室	bàngōngshì	n	office
25.	行	xíng	adj	all right; O.K.

26.	没问题	méi wèntí	ce	no problem
27.	等	děng	v	to wait; to wait for
28.	不客气	bú kèqi	ce	You are welcome. Don't be (so) polite.
	客气	kèqi	adj	polite

开会

Kāi huì

DIALOGUE I

(Lǐ Yǒu gěi(G1) lǎoshī dǎ diànhuà.)

Lǐ Yǒu: Wèi(F), qǐng wèn, Wáng Lǎoshī zài ma?

Wáng Lǎoshī: Wǒ jiù shì. Nín shì nǎ wèi?

Lǐ Yǒu: Lǎoshī, nín hǎo. Wǒ shì Lǐ Yǒu.

Wáng Lǎoshī: Lǐ Yǒu, nǐ hǎo, yǒu shì ma?

Lǐ Yǒu: Lǎoshī, jīntiān xiàwǔ nín yǒu shíjiān ma? Wǒ xiǎng wèn(1) nín jǐ ge wèntí.

Wáng Lǎoshī: Duìbuqǐ, jīntiān xiàwǔ wǒ yào(G2) kāi huì.

Lǐ Yǒu: Míngtiān ne?

Wáng Lǎoshī: Míngtiān shàngwǔ wǒ yǒu liǎng jié(2) kè, xiàwǔ sān diǎnzhōng yào gěi èr niánjí kǎoshì.

Lǐ Yǒu: Nín shénme shíhou yǒu kòng?

Wáng Lǎoshī: Míngtiān sì diǎn yǐhòu(3) cái yǒu kòng.

Lǐ Yǒu: Yàoshì nín fāngbiàn, sì diǎn bàn wǒ dào nín de bàngōngshì qù, xíng ma?

Wáng Lǎoshī: Sì diǎn bàn, méi wèntí(F). Wǒ zài bàngōngshì děng nǐ.
Lǐ Yǒu: Xièxie(F) nín.
Wáng Lǎoshī: Bú kèqi.

DIALOGUE I

(李友给(G1)老师打电话。)

李友： 喂(F)，请问，王老师在吗？

王老师： 我就是。您是哪位？

李友： 老师，您好。我是李友。

王老师： 李友，你好，有事吗？

李友： 老师，今天下午您有时间吗？我想问(1)您几个问题。

王老师： 对不起，今天下午我要(G2)开会。

李友： 明天呢？

王老师： 明天上午我有两节(2)课，下午三点钟要给二年级考试。

李友： 您什么时候有空？

王老师： 明天四点以后(3)才有空。

李友： 要是您方便，四点半我到您的办公室去，行吗？

王老师： 四点半，没问题(F)。我在办公室等你。

李友： 谢谢(F)您。

王老师： 不客气。

Notes

▲1▲ The verb 问 (wèn, to ask) is not as versatile as its English equivalent "ask," which can be used in two semantic categories only loosely related to each other: making a request and directing a question. Thus we can say "I asked her to dance" as well as "I asked her a question." In Chinese, however, 问 (wèn) is only used in the sense of questioning. To make a request or invitation, 请 (qǐng) is used instead. For the two English sentences above, we have to say in Chinese: "我请她跳舞" (Wǒ qǐng tā tiào wǔ; I ask her to dance) and "我问她一个问题" (Wǒ wèn tā yí ge wèntí; I ask her a question).

▲2▲ The term 节 (jié), which literally means "segment," is here a measure word for class periods. It is not used as a measure for courses, for which the measure word is 门 (mén). Compare 三节课 (sān jié kè, three class periods) with 三门课 (sān mén kè, three courses).

▲3▲ While 以后 (yǐhòu) is translated as "after," it is positioned differently than in English. In English, we say "after four o'clock." The word "after" appears before the time marker "four o'clock." In the Chinese equivalent, 四点以后 (sìdiǎn yǐhòu), the word 以后 (yǐhòu) appears after the time marker. Likewise, we say "before Monday" in English, but "星期一以前" (xīngqīyī yǐqián) in Chinese.

Use the information in Dialogue I to tell what's happening in this picture.

Use the information in Dialogue I to tell what's happening in this picture.

Use the information in Dialogue I to tell what's happening in this picture.

FUNCTIONAL EXPRESSIONS

喂 (wèi, hello) [used on the telephone]

1. A: 喂，哪位？ (Hello! May I ask who's calling?)

   Wèi. Nǎ wèi?

   B: 我是王朋。请问，李友在吗？

   (This is Wang Peng. Is Li You in?)

   Wǒ shì Wáng Péng. Qǐng wèn Lǐ Yǒu zài ma?

   A: 在，你等等，我去叫她。

   (Yes. Just a minute, I'll go get her.)

   Zài, nǐ děngdeng, wǒ qù jiào tā.

2. A: 喂，你找谁？

   (Hello! With whom would you like to speak?)

   Wèi, nǐ zhǎo shéi?

   B: 我找小张。 (I'd like to speak to Little Zhang.)

   Wǒ zhǎo Xiǎo Zhāng.

   A: 我就是。你是谁？ (This is he. Who is this?)

   Wǒ jiù shì. Nǐ shì shéi?

   B: 我是你哥哥。 (This is your older brother.)

   Wǒ shì nǐ gēge.

没问题 (méi wèntí, no problem)

1. 李友：王朋，你今天晚上帮助我练习中文，好吗？

   (Li You: Wang Peng, would you please help me practice Chinese this evening?)

   Lǐ Yǒu: Wáng Péng, nǐ jīntiān wǎngshang bāngzhù wǒ liànxí Zhōngwén, hǎo ma?

王朋：没问题。晚上见。

(Wang Peng: No problem. See you this evening.)

Wáng Péng: Méi wèntí. Wǎnshang jiàn.

2. A: 你给我介绍一个女朋友，好吗？

(Can you help find me a girlfriend?)

Nǐ gěi wǒ jièshào yíge nǚpéngyou, hǎo ma?

B: 没问题。 (No problem.)

Méi wèntí.

谢谢！ (Xièxie! Thanks!)

1. A: 小李，你的电话。 (Little Li, your phone call.)

Xiǎo Lǐ, nǐ de diànhuà.

B: 谢谢！ (Thanks!)

Xièxie!

A: 不客气。 (You're welcome.)

Bú kèqi.

2. A: 小李，请喝茶。 (Please have some tea, Little Li.)

Xiǎo Lǐ, qǐng hē chá.

B: 多谢！ (Thanks a lot.)

Duō xiè.

A: 不谢。 (No need to thank [me].)

Bú xiè.

3. A: 小李，这是你的可乐。

(Little Li, this is your cola.)

Xiǎo Lǐ, zhèshì nǐde kělè.

B: 谢谢！ (Thanks!)

Xièxie.

A: 没事儿。 (No problem.)

Méi shìr.

4. A: 小李，你的中文书。

(Little Li, your Chinese book.)

Xiǎo Lǐ, nǐde Zhōngwén shū.

B: 谢了。 (Thanks.)

Xiè le.

A: 不用谢。 (No need to thank [me].)

Búyòng xiè.

Use the information in Dialogue I to tell what's happening in this picture.

Culture Notes

About Chinese phone etiquette: The receiver of the call usually does not identify herself immediately on picking up the phone as some people like to do in the United States. Instead, she would only say "喂" (wèi) and let the caller initiate the conversation.

Dialogue II: Calling a Friend for Help

VOCABULARY

1.	帮忙	bāng máng	vo	to help; to do someone a favor
2.	别客气	bié kèqi	ce	Don't be so polite!
	别	bié		don't [see G3]
3.	下个星期	xiàge xīngqī	t	next week
	下	xià		below; next
4.	中文	Zhōngwén	n	the Chinese language
	文	wén	n	language; script; written language
5.	帮	bāng	v	to help
6.	#练习	liànxí	v	to practice
7.	说	shuō	v	to say; to speak
8.	啊	a	p	(a sentence-final particle of exclamation, interrogation, etc.)
9.	但是	dànshì	conj	but
10.	得	děi	av	must; to have to
11.	知道	zhīdao	v	to know [see also Note 4 for Dialogue II below]
12.	回来	huílai	vc	to come back

DIALOGUE II

Lǐ Yǒu: Wèi, qǐng wèn, Wáng Péng zài ma?

Wáng Péng: Wǒ jiù shì. Nǐ shì Lǐ Yǒu ba(1)? Yǒu shì ma?

Lǐ Yǒu: Wǒ xiǎng qǐng nǐ bāng máng.

Wáng Péng: Bié(G3) kèqi, yǒu shénme shì?

Lǐ Yǒu:	Wǒ xiàge xīngqī(2) yào kǎo Zhōngwén(3), nǐ bāng wǒ liànxí shuō Zhōngwén, hǎo ma?
Wáng Péng:	Hǎo a, dànshì nǐ děi(G4) qǐng wǒ hē kāfēi.
Lǐ Yǒu:	Hē kāfēi, méi wèntí. Jīntiān wǎnshang nǐ yǒu kòngr ma?
Wáng Péng:	Jīntiān wǎnshang yǒu rén qǐng wǒ chīfàn, bù zhīdao(4) shénme shíhou huílai(G5). Wǒ huílai yǐhòu gěi nǐ dǎ diànhuà ba.
Lǐ Yǒu:	Hǎo ba, wǒ děng nǐ de diànhuà.

DIALOGUE II

李友：	喂，请问，王朋在吗？
王朋：	我就是。你是李友吧(1)？有事吗？
李友：	我想请你帮忙。
王朋：	别(G3)客气，有什么事？
李友：	我下个星期(2)要考中文(3)，你帮我练习说中文，好吗？
王朋：	好啊，但是你得(G4)请我喝咖啡。
李友：	喝咖啡，没问题。今天晚上你有空儿吗？
王朋：	今天晚上有人请我吃饭，不知道(4)什么时候回来(G5)。我回来以后给你打电话吧。
李友：	好吧，我等你的电话。

Notes

▲1▲ Compare the questions "你是李友吧？" (Nǐ shì Lǐ Yǒu ba?) and "你是李友吗？" (Nǐ shì Lǐ Yǒu ma?). While in the latter question the speaker does not lean toward either the positive or the negative answer, the use of 吧 (ba) in the former question suggests that the speaker expects a confirmation of his assumption: "I guess you are Li You. Am I right?"

▲2▲ The expression 下个星期 (xiàge xīngqī, next week) literally means "the week below." By the same token, 上个星期 (shàngge xīngqī, last week) literally means "the week above." The 个 (gè) in the above expressions can be omitted, e.g., 下个星期 (xiàge xīngqī) and 下星期 (xià xīngqī) both mean "next week." The same formula is used in the expressions for "next month" (下个月, xiàge yuè) and "last month" (上个月, shàngge yuè) as well, but the 个 (gè) is usually kept. To the Chinese people, the elapse of time is perceived as a downward movement. Hence the month that has passed is the one "up" and the month ahead is the one "down." However, for "last year" the term 去年 (qùnián, lit. the gone year) is used, rather than *上年 (*shàngnián). For "next year" the term 明年 (míngnián, lit. bright year) is used, rather than *下年 (*xiànián). Also, for "yesterday" and "tomorrow," 昨天 (zuótiān) and 明天 (míngtiān) are used, instead of *上天 (*shàngtiān) and *下天 (*xiàtiān). For a review of such time expressions, see the tables on page 81 in Lesson 3.

▲3▲ The Chinese language is referred to both as 中文 (Zhōngwén) and as 汉语 (Hànyǔ). The latter term refers to the predominant ethnic group in China, the Han. There is also a difference in nuance between 语 (yǔ, speech) and 文 (wén, writing), but 汉语 (Hànyǔ) and 中文 (Zhōngwén) are generally considered synonymous.

▲4▲ Although both 知道 (zhīdao) and 认识 (rènshi) translate as "to know," the two terms are not synonymous. 知道 (zhīdao) means "to know (a fact), while 认识 (rènshi) means "to know, be acquainted with (usually a person) or a written character." The object of 知道 (zhīdao) can sometimes be a person as well, but the meaning is different. The sentence "我知道他" (Wǒ zhīdao tā) suggests knowledge about that person: "I know who he is." It does not indicate personal acquaintance as does the word 认识 (rènshi).

Tell a story based on this picture.

Tell a story based on this picture.

SUPPLEMENTARY VOCABULARY

1.	中午	zhōngwǔ	t	noon
2.	法文	Fǎwén	n	the French language
3.	日文	Rìwén	n	the Japanese language
4.	德文	Déwén	n	the German language
5.	韩国	Hánguó	n	Korea
6.	韩文	Hánwén	n	the Korean language
7.	俄国	Éguó	n	Russia
8.	俄文	Éwén	n	the Russian language
9.	西班牙	Xībānyá	n	Spain
10.	西班牙文	Xībānyáwén	n	the Spanish language
11.	意大利	Yìdàlì	n	Italy
12.	意大利文	Yìdàlìwén	n	the Italian language
13.	葡萄牙	Pútáoyá	n	Portugal
14.	葡萄牙文	Pútáoyáwén	n	the Portuguese language
15.	希腊	Xīlà	n	Greece
16.	希腊文	Xīlàwén	n	the Greek language
17.	拉丁文	Lādīngwén	n	Latin
18.	越南	Yuènán	n	Vietnam
19.	菲律宾	Fēilǜbīn	n	the Philippines
20.	泰国	Tàiguó	n	Thailand
21.	马来西亚	Mǎláixīyà	n	Malaysia
22.	夏威夷	Xiàwēiyí	n	Hawaii

Grammar

1. The Preposition 给 (gěi)

给 (gěi) can be a verb or a preposition. In Chinese, prepositions are generally combined with nouns or pronouns to form prepositional phrases, which appear before verbs as adverbials.

(1) 他给我打了一个电话。

Tā gěi wǒ dǎle yí gè diànhuà.

(He gave me a call.)

(2) 他是谁？请你给我们介绍一下。

Tā shì shéi? Qǐng nǐ gěi wǒmen jièshào yí xià.

(Who is he? Please introduce us.)

(3) 你有你姐姐的照片吗？给我看一下，行吗？

Nǐ yǒu nǐ jiějie de zhàopiàn ma? Gěi wǒ kàn yí xià, xíng ma?

(Do you have a picture of your older sister? Can you let me have a look?)

2. The Auxiliary Verb 要 (yào, will; be going to) (I)

[See also L.9 G1]

The auxiliary verb 要 (yào) has several meanings. In this lesson, 要 (yào) indicates a future action.

(1) 明天我要去小白家玩。

Míngtiān wǒ yào qù Xiǎo Bái jiā wán.

(Tomorrow I'm going to visit Little Bai.)

(2) 今天晚上妹妹要去看电影。

Jīntiān wǎnshang mèimei yào qù kàn diànyǐng.

(This evening my younger sister is going to see a movie.)

(3) 下午我们要开会。

Xiàwǔ wǒmen yào kāi huì.

(This afternoon we are going to have a meeting.)

A public phone in Taiwan.

3. 别 (bié, don't)

别 (bié, don't) is used to advise someone to refrain from doing something.

(1) 你别说！

Nǐ bié shuō!

(Don't tell.)

(2) 别进来！

Bié jìnlai!

(Don't come in.)

(3) 那个电影没有意思，你别看。

Nàge diànyǐng méiyǒu yìsi, nǐ bié kàn.

(That movie is boring. Don't go see it.)

An office building at a college.

4. The Auxiliary Verb 得 (děi, must)

The modal verb 得 (děi) means "need" or "must."

(1) 老师三点钟给你打了一个电话，你得给老师回个电话。

Lǎoshī sān diǎnzhōng gěi nǐ dǎle yí ge diànhuà, nǐ děi gěi lǎoshī huí ge diànhuà.

(The teacher called you at three o'clock. You'd better call him back.)

(2) 我有事，得去学校。

Wǒ yǒu shì, děi qù xuéxiào.

(I've some business [to attend to]. I must go to the school.)

Note: The negative form of 得 (děi, must) is 不用 (bú yòng, need not) or 不必 (bú bì, need not), not 不得 (bù děi). Therefore, the correct way to say "You don't have to go to the school" in Chinese is A, and not B, below.

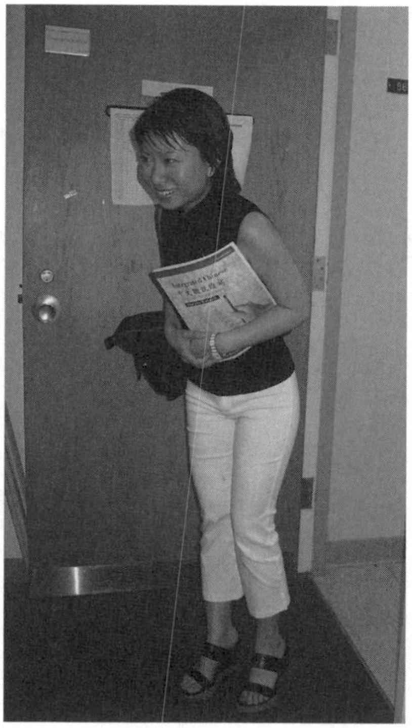

Did she hear 进来 (jìnlai) or 进去 (jìnqu) when she knocked at the door?

A. 你不用去学校。 (Nǐ bú yòng qù xuéxiào.)

or 你不必去学校。 (Nǐ bú bì qù xuéxiào.)

B. *你不得去学校。 (*Nǐ bù děi qù xuéxiào.)

5. Directional Complements (I)

来/去 (lái/qù, to come/go) can serve as a directional complement after such verbs as 进 (jìn, to enter) and 回 (huí, to return). 来 (lái, to come) signifies movement toward the speaker. 去 (qù, to go) signifies movement away from the speaker.

(1) [**A** is at home on the phone.]

A: 你什么时候回来?

Nǐ shénme shíhou huílai?

(When are you coming home?)

B: 我六点回去。

Wǒ liù diǎn huíqu.

(I'm going back home at six.)

(2) [**A** is outside, and **B** is inside. **A** knocks on the door.]

进来。

Jìnlai. (Come in.)

(3) [Both **A** and **B** are outside. **A** tells **B** to go inside.]

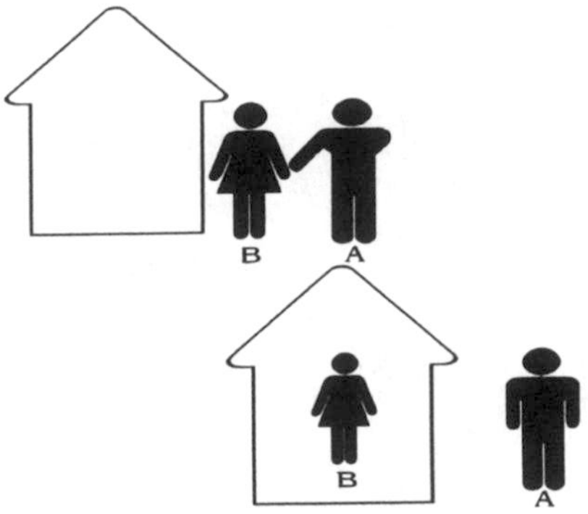

进去。

Jìnqu. (Go in.)

PATTERN DRILLS

A. 给 (gěi) as a Preposition

1.	Wǒ	gěi nǐmen	jièshào yí xià.
2.	Lǐ Lǎoshī		kàn tā de shū.
3.	Xiǎo Gāo		kàn tā bàba māma de zhàopiàn.
4.	Xiǎo Wáng		tīng Zhōngguó yīnyuè.
5.	Tā		jièshào yí ge péngyou.
6.	Gāo Xiǎoyīn		hē Zhōngguó chá.

1.	我	<u>给你们</u>	介绍一下。
2.	李老师		看她的书。
3.	小高		看他爸爸妈妈的照片。
4.	小王		听中国音乐。
5.	她		介绍一个朋友。
6.	高小音		喝中国茶。

B. 要 (yào) Indicating a Future Action

1.	Míngtiān	<u>wǒ yào</u>	qù tiào wǔ.
2.	Zhège zhōumò		qù zhǎo Gāo Xiǎoyīn.
3.	Jīntiān wǎnshang		qǐng Wáng Péng hē kāfēi.
4.	Míngtiān xiàwǔ		qù Lǐ Lǎoshī de bàngōngshì.
5.	Jīntiān xiàwǔ		wèn Xiǎo Bái yí ge wèntí.
6.	Míngtiān wǎnshang		qù Xiǎo Zhāng de xuéxiào kàn diànyǐng.
7.	Míngtiān shàngwǔ		qù Xiǎo Gāo jiā liànxí Zhōngwén.
8.	Zhège zhōumò		gěi Wáng Lǎoshī dǎ diànhuà.
9.	Zhège zhōumò		gěi Xiǎo Gāo jièshào yí ge péngyou.

1.	明天	<u>我要</u>	去跳舞。
2.	这个周末		去找高小音。
3.	今天晚上		请王朋喝咖啡。
4.	明天下午		去李老师的办公室。
5.	今天下午		问小白一个问题。
6.	明天晚上		去小张的学校看电影。
7.	明天上午		去小高家练习中文。
8.	这个周末		给王老师打电话。
9.	这个周末		给小高介绍一个朋友。

A public phone in China.

C. 要是 (yàoshi, if)

1.	Yàoshi	nǐ jīntiān méiyǒu kòngr, míngtiān	zěnmeyàng?
2.		nǐ bù xiǎng kàn diànshì, wǒmen tīng yīnyuè,	
3.		nǐ juéde dǎ qiú méiyǒu yìsi, wǒmen qù kàn diànyǐng,	
4.		nǐ bù xǐhuan tiào wǔ, wǒmen liáo tiānr,	
5.		jīntiān bù fāngbiàn, míngtiān,	
6.		bù xǐhuan hē chá, wǒmen hē píjiǔ,	
7.		nǐ jīntiān qǐng wǒ hē kāfēi, wǒ míngtiān qǐng nǐ kàn diànyǐng,	
8.		nǐ xiǎng wèn wǒ wèntí, xiàwǔ lái wǒ de bàngōngshì,	

1.	要是	你今天没有空儿，明天	怎么样？
2.		你不想看电视，我们听音乐，	
3.		你觉得打球没有意思，我们去看电影，	
4.		你不喜欢跳舞，我们聊天儿，	

5. 今天不方便，明天

6. 不喜欢喝茶，我们喝啤酒，

7. 你今天请我喝咖啡，我明天请你看电影，

8. 你想问我问题，下午来我的办公室，

D. 别 (bié, don't) and 得 (děi, must)

1.	Nǐ bié	dǎ qiú,	nǐ děi	kàn shū.
2.		hē chá,		shuì jiào.
3.		kàn diànshì,		gěi Wáng Lǎoshī dǎ diànhuà.
4.		shuì jiào,		kàn shū.
5.		liáo tiān,		qù kāi huì.
6.		hē píjiǔ,		kǎo shì.
7.		chī fàn,		dǎ qiú.
8.		qù Xiǎo Gāo jiā,		zài jiā děng nǐ bàba māma de diànhuà.
9.		liáo tiānr,		liànxí Zhōngwén.

1.	你别	打球，	你得	看书。
2.		喝茶，		睡觉。
3.		看电视，		给王老师打电话。
4.		睡觉，		看书。
5.		聊天，		去开会。
6.		喝啤酒，		考试。
7.		吃饭，		打球。
8.		去小高家，		在家等你爸爸妈妈的电话。
9.		聊天儿，		练习中文。

Using a 手机 (shoǔjī), cellular phone.

E. 得 (děi, have to, must)

1.	Jīntiān	wǒ děi	qù zhǎo Wáng Lǎoshī.
2.	Jīntiān wǎnshang		qù Xiǎo Gāo jiā liànxí Zhōngwén.
3.	Zhège zhōumò		qù túshūguǎn kàn shū.
4.	Jīntiān xiàwǔ		qù xuéxiào kāi huì.
5.	Míngtiān wǎnshang		qù Xiǎo Bái jiā chī wǎnfàn.
6.	Míngtiān shàngwǔ		qù Wáng Lǎoshī de bàngōngshì.
7.	Míngtiān xiàwǔ		hé Wáng Péng liànxí Zhōngwén.
8.	Míngtiān wǎnshang		qù xuéxiào liànxí chàng gē.
9.	Jīntiān wǎnshang		zài jiā liànxí tiào wǔ.

1.	今天	我得	去找王老师。
2.	今天晚上		去小高家练习中文。
3.	这个周末		去图书馆看书。
4.	今天下午		去学校开会。
5.	明天晚上		去小白家吃晚饭。

6.	明天上午	去王老师的办公室。
7.	明天下午	和王朋练习中文。
8.	明天晚上	去学校练习唱歌。
9.	今天晚上	在家练习跳舞。

English Texts

DIALOGUE I

(Li You is on the phone with her teacher.)

Li You:	Hello, is Teacher Wang in?
Teacher Wang:	This is he. Who's this, please?
Li You:	Teacher, how are you? This is Li You.
Teacher Wang:	Li You, how are you? What can I do for you?
Li You:	Teacher, are you free this afternoon? I'd like to ask you a few questions.
Teacher Wang:	I'm sorry. This afternoon I have to go to a meeting.
Li You:	What about tomorrow?
Teacher Wang:	Tomorrow morning I have two classes. Tomorrow afternoon at three o'clock I have to give an exam to the second-year class.
Li You:	When will you be free?
Teacher Wang:	I won't be free until after four o'clock tomorrow.
Li You:	If it's convenient for you, I'll go to your office at four thirty. Is that all right?
Teacher Wang:	Four thirty? No problem. I'll wait for you in my office.
Li You:	Thank you.
Teacher Wang:	You're welcome.

DIALOGUE II

(Li You and Wang Peng are talking on the phone.)

Li You:	Hello, is Wang Peng there?
Wang Peng:	This is he. Is this Li You? What's up?
Li You:	I'd like to ask you a favor.

Wang Peng:	Don't be so polite. What is it?
Li You:	Next week I have a Chinese exam. Could you help me practice speaking Chinese?
Wang Peng:	Sure, but you must invite me to drink some coffee.
Li You:	Invite you to drink some coffee? No problem. Are you free this evening?
Wang Peng:	This evening someone is taking me to dinner. I don't know when I'll be back. Why don't I call you after I get back?
Li You:	O.K. I'll wait for your call.

LESSON 7 ▲ Studying Chinese
第七课 ▲ 学中文
Dì qī kè ▲ *Xué Zhōngwén*

我中国字写得太慢！

Wǒ Zhōngguó zì xiě de tài màn!

Dialogue I: Asking about an Examination

VOCABULARY

1.	跟	gēn	conj	and
2.	说话	shuō huà	vo	to talk
3.	上个星期	shàngge xīngqī	t	last week [see Note 2 for Dialogue 2 in L.6]
4.	得	de	p	(a structural particle) [see G1]
5.	帮助	bāngzhù	v	to help
6.	#复习	fùxí	v	to review

7.	字	zì	n	character
8.	写	xiě	v	to write
9.	慢	màn	adj	slow
10.	教	jiāo	v	to teach
11.	怎么	zěnme	qpr	how
12.	就	jiù	adv	(indicates that something takes place sooner than expected)
13.	学	xué	v	to study
14.	笔	bǐ	n	pen
15.	难	nán	adj	difficult
16.	快	kuài	adj	quick; fast
17.	哪里	nǎli	ce	You flatter me. Not at all. (a polite reply to a compliment) [also see Note 2 for the Dialogue in L.5]
18.	第	dì	prefix	(a prefix for ordinal numbers)
19.	#预习	yùxí	v	to preview
20.	语法	yǔfǎ	n	grammar
21.	容易	róngyì	adj	easy
22.	多	duō	adj	many; much
23.	懂	dǒng	v	to understand
24.	生词	shēngcí	n	new words
25.	汉字	Hànzì	n	Chinese character
26.	有一点儿	yǒu yìdiǎnr	ce	a little; somewhat [also see G5]
27.	不谢	bú xiè	ce	Don't mention it. Not at all. You're welcome.

DIALOGUE I

(Wáng Péng gēn Lǐ Yǒu shuōhuà.)

Wáng Péng:	Lǐ Yǒu, nǐ shàngge xīngqī kǎoshì kǎo de(G1) zěnmeyàng?
Lǐ Yǒu:	Kǎo de búcuò, yīnwèi nǐ bāngzhù(1) wǒ fùxí, suǒyǐ kǎo de búcuò. Dànshì lǎoshī shuō wǒ Zhōngguó zì xiě de tài(G2) màn!
Wáng Péng:	Shì ma? Yǐhòu wǒ gēn nǐ yìqǐ liànxí xiě zì, jiāo nǐ zěnme xiě, hǎo bu hǎo(2)?
Lǐ Yǒu:	Nà tài hǎo le! Wǒmen xiànzài jiù(G3) xiě. Gěi nǐ bǐ.
Wáng Péng:	Hǎo, wǒ jiāo nǐ xiě "nán" zì.
Lǐ Yǒu:	Nǐ xiě zì xiě de hěn hǎo, yě hěn kuài.
Wáng Péng:	Nǎli, nǎli(F). Nǐ míngtiān yǒu Zhōngwén kè ma?
Lǐ Yǒu:	Yǒu, míngtiān wǒmen xué dì qī(G4) kè.
Wáng Péng:	Nǐ yùxí le ma?
Lǐ Yǒu:	Yùxí le. Dì qī kè de yǔfǎ hěn róngyì, wǒ dōu dǒng, kěshì shēngcí tài duō, hànzì yě yǒu yìdiǎnr(G5) nán.
Wáng Péng:	Jīntiān wǎnshang wǒ gēn nǐ yìqǐ liànxí ba.
Lǐ Yǒu:	Hǎo, xièxie nǐ.
Wáng Péng:	Bú xiè, wǎnshang jiàn.

DIALOGUE I

(王朋跟李友说话。)

王朋：	李友，你上个星期考试考得(G1)怎么样？
李友：	考得不错，因为你帮助(1)我复习，所以考得不错。但是老师说我中国字写得太(G2)慢！
王朋：	是吗？以后我跟你一起练习写字，教你怎么写，好不好(2)？

李友：那太好了！我们现在<u>就</u>(G3)写。给你笔。

王朋：好，我教你写“难”字。

李友：你写字写得很好，也很快。

王朋：哪里，哪里(F)。你明天有中文课吗？

李友：有，明天我们学<u>第七</u>(G4)课。

王朋：你预习了吗？

李友：预习了。第七课的语法很容易，我都懂，可是生词太多，汉字也<u>有一点儿</u>(G5)难。

王朋：今天晚上我跟你一起练习吧。

李友：好，谢谢你。

王朋：不谢，晚上见。

Notes

▲**1**▲ 帮助 (bāngzhù), like 帮 (bāng), takes an object. 帮忙 (bāng máng) does not. Therefore, we say “他帮我练习中文 (Tā bāng wǒ liànxí Zhōngwén)” or “他帮助我练习中文 (Tā bāngzhù wǒ liànxí Zhōngwén).” We don't say “*他帮忙我练习中文 (*Tā bāng máng wǒ liànxí Zhōngwén).” Remember that 帮忙 (bāng máng) is a verb + object compound. It already has an object built into it.

▲**2**▲ The expression 好不好 (hǎo bu hǎo), like 行吗 (xíng ma), means “Is it O.K.?” They are both used to seek approval.

Based on Dialogue I, tell what's happening in this picture.

FUNCTIONAL EXPRESSIONS

哪里，哪里 (năli, năli; You flatter me.)

1. A: 你今天很漂亮。 (You are very pretty today.)

   Nǐ jīntiān hěn piàoliang.

   B: 哪里，哪里。 (You flatter me.)

   Năli, năli.

2. A: 你写汉字写得很漂亮。

   (You write Chinese characters beautifully.)

   Nǐ xiě Hànzì xiě de hěn piàoliang.

   B: 哪里，哪里。 (You flatter me.)

   Năli, năli.

Simplified and Traditional Characters

In the 1950s, as part of the campaign to raise the nation's literacy rate, the government of the People's Republic of China set out to simplify some of the more complex characters, or 汉字 (Hànzì). That accounts for the bifurcation of 简体字 (jiǎntǐzì, simplified

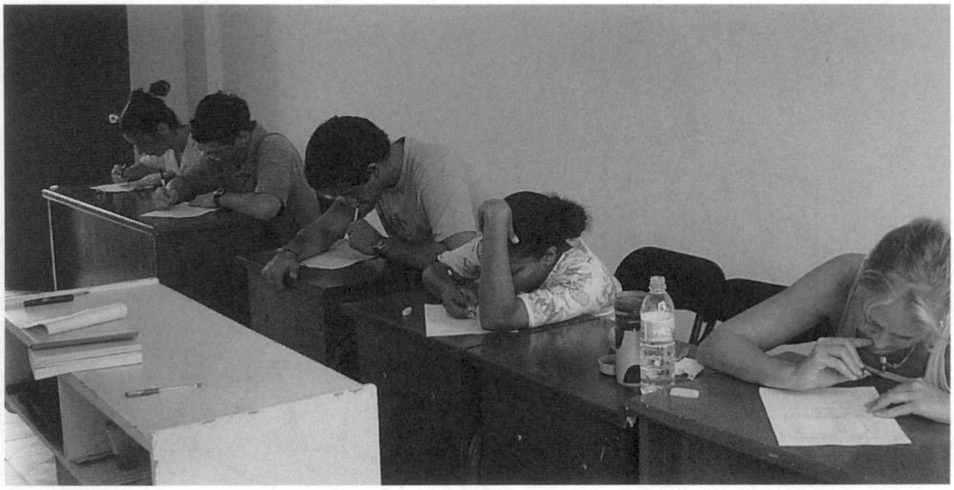

考试
Kǎo shì

characters) and 繁体字 (fántǐzì, traditional characters, or, literally, complex characters). Currently, simplified characters are used in Mainland China and Singapore. However, people in Taiwan, Hong Kong, and most Chinese diasporas still write traditional characters. Most of the simplified characters were actually not new inventions. They had been used at different times in China's long history, and a few of them even have a longer history than their *fantizi* counterparts. The additional burden on Chinese learners caused by this bifurcation is actually not as onerous as it may appear. After all, most of the characters were not affected.

Direction of Chinese Script

Traditionally, the Chinese wrote vertically from top to bottom, and from right to left. Now almost everyone in China writes horizontally from left to right. But the traditional way of writing is still kept alive in calligraphy.

Chinese Writing Brushes

For many centuries the Chinese wrote with a 毛笔 (máobǐ), or "writing brush," as it is called in English. But nowadays people have switched to more convenient Western-style writing instruments such as the 铅笔 (qiānbǐ, pencil), the 钢笔 (gāngbǐ, fountain pen), and the 圆珠笔 (yuánzhūbǐ, ballpoint pen), which is also known in Taiwan

Name these writing instruments.

as 原子笔 (yuánzǐbǐ). The traditional 毛笔 (máobǐ) is now used almost exclusively in calligraphy.

Complex vs. Simplified: ***Examples***

問 學 幾 號 話 寫 難 筆 電 聽
问 学 几 号 话 写 难 笔 电 听

Dialogue II: Preparing for a Chinese Class

VOCABULARY

1.	平常	píngcháng	adv	usually
2.	早	zǎo	adj	early
3.	怎么	zěnme	qpr	how come (used to inquire about the cause of something, implying a degree of surprise or disapproval)
4.	这么	zhème	pr	so; such
5.	半夜	bànyè	t	midnight
	夜	yè	n	night
6.	功课	gōngkè	n	schoolwork; homework

7.	朋友	péngyou	n	friend
8.	真	zhēn	adv	really
9.	大家	dàjiā	pr	everybody
10.	早	zǎo		Good morning!
11.	开始	kāishǐ	v	to start
12.	上课	shàng kè	vo	to go to class; to start a class
13.	念	niàn	v	to read aloud
14.	课文	kèwén	n	text of a lesson
15.	#录音	lùyīn/lù yīn	n/vo	sound recording; to record
16.	男的	nán de		male
17.	#帅	shuài	adj	handsome

DIALOGUE II

(Lǐ Yǒu gēn Xiǎo Bái shuō huà.)

Lǐ Yǒu: Xiǎo Bái, nǐ píngcháng lái de hěn zǎo, jīntiān zěnme(G6) lái de zhème wǎn?

Xiǎo Bái: Wǒ zuótiān yùxí Zhōngwén, bànyè yì diǎn cái(G3) shuì jiào, nǐ yě shuì de hěn wǎn ma?

Lǐ Yǒu: Wǒ zuótiān shí diǎn jiù(G3) shuì le. Yīnwèi Wáng Péng bāng wǒ liànxí Zhōngwén, suǒyǐ wǒ gōngkè zuò de hěn kuài.

Xiǎo Bái: Yǒu ge Zhōngguó péngyou zhēn(G2) hǎo.

(Shàng Zhōngwén kè.)

Lǎoshī: Dàjiā zǎo(1), xiànzài wǒmen kāishǐ shàng kè. Dì qī kè nǐmen dōu yùxí le ma?

Xuésheng: Yùxí le.

Lǎoshī: Lǐ Yǒu, qǐng nǐ niàn kèwén.... Nǐ niàn de hěn hǎo. Nǐ zuótiān wǎnshang tīng lùyīn le ba?

Lǐ Yǒu: Wǒ méi tīng.
Xiǎo Bái: Dànshì tā de péngyou chángcháng bāngzhù tā.
Lǎoshī: Nǐ de péngyou shì Zhōngguórén ma?
Lǐ Yǒu: Shì de.
Xiǎo Bái: Tā shì yí ge nán de(2), hěn shuài(3), jiào Wáng Péng(G7).

DIALOGUE II

(李友跟小白说话。)

李友：小白，你平常来得很早，今天怎么(G6)来得这么晚？

小白：我昨天预习中文，半夜一点才(G3)睡觉，你也睡得很晚吗？

李友：我昨天十点就(G3)睡了。因为王朋帮我练习中文，所以我功课做得很快。

小白：有个中国朋友真(G2)好。

(上中文课。)

老师：大家早(1)，现在我们开始上课。第七(G4)课你们都预习了吗？

学生：预习了。

老师：李友，请你念课文。...你念得很好。你昨天晚上听录音了吧？

李友：我没听。

小白：但是她的朋友常常帮助她。

老师：你的朋友是中国人吗？

李友：是的。

小白：他是一个男的(2)，很帅(3)，叫王朋(G7)。

Notes

▲1▲ 早 (Zǎo! Good morning!), and the more formal 早安 (Zǎo ān! Good morning!) may strike some people in mainland China as rather Western, but these greetings are gradually gaining acceptance among young and educated people.

▲2▲ If the referent is obvious from the context, the noun following the particle 的 (de) can often be omitted, as in the sentence: 他是一个男的 (Tā shì yí ge nán de). It is understood from the context that 男的 (nán de, male) refers to 朋友 (péngyou, friend). The word 朋友 is left out. Another example: 我写了十个字，五个难的，五个容易的。 (Wǒ xiěle shí ge zì, wǔ ge nán de, wǔ ge róngyì de; I wrote ten characters, five difficult ones and five easy ones). See Lesson 9, Grammar Note 3.

▲3▲ 帅 (shuài) is used to describe a handsome—usually young—man. To describe an attractive girl one uses the word 漂亮 (piàoliang, pretty). The term 好看 (hǎokàn, good looking), is gender neutral, and can be used for either sex.

What is Little Bai telling Li You?

What is Li You telling Little Bai?

What is Li You doing?

What is Little Bai trying to tell the teacher?

SUPPLEMENTARY VOCABULARY

1. 铅笔	qiānbǐ	n	pencil
2. 钢笔	gāngbǐ	n	fountain pen
3. 毛笔	máobǐ	n	writing brush
4. 纸	zhǐ	n	paper
5. 本子	běnzi	n	notebook
6. 午觉	wǔjiào	n	nap

Grammar

1. Descriptive Complements (I)

The particle 得 (de) can be used after a verb or an adjective. This lesson mainly deals with 得 (de) as it appears after a verb. What follows 得 (de) in the construction introduced in this lesson is called a descriptive complement, which can be an adjective, an adverb, or a verb phrase. In this lesson, the words that function as descriptive complements are all adjectives. These complements serve as comments on the actions expressed by the verbs that precede 得 (de).

(1) 他写字写得很好。

Tā xiě zì xiě de hěn hǎo.

(He writes characters well.)

[很好 (hěn hǎo, very well) is a comment on the action 写 (xiě, to write).]

(2) 他昨天睡觉睡得很晚。

Tā zuótiān shuì jiào shuì de hěn wǎn.

(He went to bed late last night.)

[很晚 (hěn wǎn, very late) is a comment on the action 睡觉 (shuì jiào, to sleep).]

(3) 妹妹歌唱得很好。

Mèimei gē chàng de hěn hǎo.

(My younger sister sings beautifully.)

[很好 (hěn hǎo, very well) is a comment on the action 唱 (chàng, to sing).]

If the complement is an adjective, it is usually preceded by 很 (hěn, very), as is the case when an adjective is used as a predicate. If the verb is followed by an object, the verb has to be repeated before it can be followed by the "得 (de) + Complement" structure, e.g., 写字写得 (xiě zì xiě de) in (1). By repeating the verb, the "verb + object" combination preceding it becomes a "topic" and the complement that follows serves as a comment on it. The first verb can be omitted if the meaning is clear from the context. See (3).

2. 太 (tài, too) and 真 (zhēn, really)

When the adverbs 太 (tài, too) and (zhēn, really) are used in exclamatory sentences, they convey in most cases not new factual information but the speaker's approval, disapproval, or other emotional reaction. If the speaker wants to make a more "objective" statement or description, other intensifiers such as 很 (hěn, very), or 特别 (tèbié, especially) are often used in place of 太 (tài, too) or (zhēn, really).

(1) A: 他写字写得怎么样?

Tā xiě zì xiě de zěnmeyàng?

(How well does he write characters?)

One would normally answer:

B: 他写字写得很好。

Tā xiě zì xiě de hěn hǎo.

(He writes characters very well.)

Compare "B" with "C" below:

C: 小张：小李，你写字写得真好！你可以帮助我吗?

Xiǎo Zhāng: Xiǎo Lǐ, nǐ xiě zì xiě de zhēn hǎo! Nǐ kěyǐ bāngzhù wǒ ma?

(Xiao Zhang: Xiao Li, you write characters really well! Could you help me?)

When 太 (tài, too) is used in an exclamatory sentence, 了 (le) usually appears at the end of the sentence:

(2) 这本书太有意思了！

Zhè běn shū tài yǒu yìsi le!

(This book is really interesting!)

(3) 我的语法太不好了！我得多练习。

Wǒ de yǔfǎ tài bù hǎo le! Wǒ děi duō liànxí.

(My grammar is indeed awful! I have to practice more.)

Can you describe this photo in Chinese?

(4) 你跳舞跳得太好了。

Nǐ tiào wǔ tiào de tài hǎo le!

(You really dance beautifully!)

3. The Adverb 就 (jiù) (I)

The adverb 就 (jiù) is used before a verb to suggest the earliness, briefness, or quickness of the action.

(1) 他明天早上八点就得上课。

Tā míngtiān zǎoshang bā diǎn jiù děi shàng kè.

(He has to go to class [as early as] at 8 o'clock tomorrow morning.)

(2) 他昨天就来了。

Tā zuótiān jiù lái le.

(He came [as early as] yesterday.)

就 (jiù) and 才 (cái) Compared [See also L.5 G6]

The adverb 就 (jiù) suggests the earliness or promptness of an action in the speaker's judgment. The adverb 才 (cái) is the opposite. It suggests the tardiness or lateness of an action as perceived by the speaker.

(1) A: 八点上课，他七点就来了。

Bā diǎn shàng kè, tā qī diǎn jiù lái le.

(Class starts at eight, but he came [as early as] seven.)

B: 八点上课，他八点半才来。

Bā diǎn shàng kè, tā bā diǎn bàn cái lái.

(Class started at eight, but he didn't come until eight thirty.)

(2) A: 我昨天五点钟就回家了。

Wǒ zuótiān wǔ diǎnzhōng jiù huí jiā le.

(Yesterday I went home when it was only five o'clock.)

B: 我昨天五点才回家。

Wǒ zuótiān wǔ diǎn cái huí jiā.

(Yesterday I didn't go home until five o'clock.)

Note: When commenting on a past action, 就 (jiù) is always used with 了 (le) to indicate promptness, but not 才 (cái).

4. Ordinal Numbers

Ordinal numbers in Chinese are formed by placing 第 (dì) before the cardinal numbers, e.g., 第一 (dì yī; the first) 、第二杯茶 (dì èr bēi chá; the second cup of tea)、第三个月 (dì sān ge yuè; the third month)....However, 第 (dì) is not used in names of months: 一月、二月、三月 (yīyuè, èryuè, sānyuè; January, February, March)....Neither is it used to indicate the birth order of siblings: 大哥、二哥、三哥 (dàgē, èrgē, sāngē; oldest brother, second oldest brother, third oldest brother)...;大姐、二姐、三姐 (dàjiě, èrjiě, sānjiě; oldest sister, second oldest sister, third oldest sister)....

5. 有(一)点儿 (yǒu {yì}diǎnr, somewhat, rather; a little bit)

The phrase 有一点儿 (yǒu yìdiǎnr) precedes adjectives or verbs, indicating a slight degree. It often carries a negative tone. The 一 in the phrase is optional.

(1) 我觉得中文有(一)点儿难。

Wǒ juéde Zhōngwén yǒu (yì)diǎnr nán.

(I think Chinese is a little bit difficult.)

*我觉得中文有(一)点儿容易。

*Wǒ juéde Zhōngwén yǒu (yì)diǎnr róngyì.

*(I think Chinese is a little bit easy.)

(2) 我觉得这一课生词有点儿多。

Wǒ juéde zhè yí kè shēngcí yǒu diǎnr duō.

(I think there are a few too many new words in this lesson.)

[The speaker complains about it.]

(3) 我有(一)点儿不喜欢他。

Wǒ yǒu (yī)diǎnr bǔ xǐhuan tā.

(I somewhat dislike him.)

*我有(一)点儿喜欢他。

*Wǒ yǒu (yī)diǎnr xǐhuan tā.

*(I somewhat like him.)

However, when the sentence suggests a change of the situation, the phrase 有一点儿 (yǒu yìdiǎnr) can carry a positive tone, e.g.:

(4) 我以前不喜欢他，现在有(一)点儿喜欢他了。

Wǒ yǐqián bù xǐhuan tā, xiānzāi yǒu (yī)diǎnr xǐhuan tā le.

(I used to dislike him, but now I somewhat like him.)

Note: 以前 yǐqián = previously or before. See "An Entry from Li You's Diary" in L.8.

Take care not to confuse 有一点儿 (yǒu yìdiǎnr, a little), which is an adverbial used to modify adjectives, with 一点儿 (yìdiǎnr, a little), which usually modifies nouns. In the above sentences, 有一点儿 (yǒu yìdiǎnr) cannot be replaced by 一点儿 (yìdiǎnr). Compare:

Learning to read Chinese characters.

(5) 给我一点儿咖啡。

Gěi wǒ yìdiǎnr kāfēi.

(Give me a little coffee.)

(6) 给我一点儿时间。

Gěi wǒ yìdiǎnr shíjiān.

(Give me a little time.)

(7) 我有一点儿忙。

Wǒ yǒu yìdiǎnr máng.

(I am kind of busy.)

*我一点儿忙。

*Wǒ yìdiǎnr máng.

(8) 她有一点儿不高兴。

Tā yǒu yìdiǎnr bù gāoxìng.

(She is a little bit unhappy.)

*她一点儿不高兴。

*Tā yìdiǎnr bù gāoxìng.

6. 怎么 (zěnme, how come) in Questions

怎么 (zěnme, how come) is an interrogative adverb. It is often used to ask about the manner—and sometimes the reason or the cause—of an action.

(1) 你怎么才来?

Nǐ zěnme cái lái?

(How come you've just arrived?)

(2) 你怎么没去看电影?

Nǐ zěnme méi qù kàn diànyǐng?

(Why didn't you go to the movie?)

(3) 怎么，你不认识他? 他不是你的老师吗?

Zěnme, nǐ bú rènshi tā? Tā bú shì nǐ de lǎoshī ma?

(What? You don't know him? Isn't he your teacher?)

Both 怎么 (zěnme, how come) and 为什么 (wèishénme, why) are used to ask about the cause of or reason for something. However, 怎么 (zěnme, how come) conveys the speaker's bewilderment or surprise whereas 为什么 (wèishénme, why) does not.

怎么 (zěnme, how come) can stand alone as a clause, as in (3).

7. The Use of Nouns and Pronouns in Continuous Discourse

If the subject remains the same in a continuous discourse, it is to be substituted with an appropriate pronoun in the second clause or sentence. In the third clause or sentence, even the pronoun can sometimes be omitted.

小白很喜欢学中文。她晚上预习课文，常常半夜一点才睡觉。

Xiǎo Bái hěn xǐhuan xué Zhōngwén. Tā wǎnshang yùxí kèwén, chángcháng bànyè yì diǎn cái shuì jiào.

(Little Bai likes to study Chinese very much. She previews the text at night, and often doesn't sleep until 1:00 a.m.)

If we keep repeating the subject, the sentence will become choppy and read like a bunch of unrelated sentences.

小白很喜欢学中文。小白晚上预习课文。小白常常半夜一点才睡觉。

Xiǎo Bái hěn xǐhuan xué Zhōngwén. Xiǎo Bái wǎnshang yùxí kèwén. Xiǎo Bái chángcháng bànyè yì diǎn cái shuì jiào.

(Little Bai likes to study Chinese very much. Little Bai previews the text at night. Little Bai often doesn't sleep until 1:00 a.m.)

PATTERN DRILLS

A. Verb + 得 (de) + Complement

1.	Tā kǎo	de	hěn hǎo.
2.	Xiǎo Gāo zuótiān shuì		hěn wǎn.
3.	Nàge xuésheng yùxí		búcuò.
4.	Wǒ dìdi chī		hěn duō.
5.	Lǎoshī lái		hěn zǎo.

1.	她考	得	很好。
2.	小高昨天睡		很晚。
3.	那个学生预习		不错。
4.	我弟弟吃		很多。
5.	老师来		很早。

B. Verb + Object + Verb + 得 (de) + Complement

1.	Wáng Péng shuō huà	shuō	de	hěn kuài.
2.	Xiǎo Bái hē píjiǔ	hē		hěn duō.
3.	Tā niàn kèwén	niàn		búcuò.
4.	Wǒ xiě Zhōngguó zì	xiě		bú tài hǎo.
5.	Nǐ mèimei chàng gē	chàng		hěn hǎo.

1. 王朋说话	说	<u>得</u>	很快。
2. 小白喝啤酒	喝		很多。
3. 他念课文	念		不错。
4. 我写中国字	写		不太好。
5. 你妹妹唱歌	唱		很好。

C. 太 (tài, too)

1. Zhège zì	<u>tài</u>	nán	<u>le</u>.
2. Wáng Lǎoshī		máng	
3. Zhè yí kè de shēngcí		duō	
4. Wǒ de jiā		xiǎo	
5. Nǐ		kèqi	
6. Zhège diànyǐng		yǒuyìsi	
7. Xiǎo Gāo de jiā		piàoliang	
8. Jīntiān de Zhōngwén kè		róngyì	

1. 这个字	<u>太</u>	难	<u>了</u>。
2. 王老师		忙	
3. 这一课的生词		多	
4. 我的家		小	
5. 你		客气	
6. 这个电影		有意思	
7. 小高的家		漂亮	
8. 今天的中文课		容易	

D. 有一点儿 (yǒu yì diǎnr, a little bit) + Adjective

1.	Jīntiān de yǔfǎ	yǒu yì diǎnr	nán.
2.	Dì wǔ kè de shēngcí		duō.
3.	Wáng Lǎoshī míngtiān		máng.
4.	Wǔ diǎnzhōng chī wǎnfàn		zǎo.
5.	Bànyè yì diǎn cái shuì jiào		wǎn.
6.	Lǐ Xiǎojie shuō huà		kuài.

1.	今天的语法	有一点儿	难。
2.	第五课的生词		多。
3.	王老师明天		忙。
4.	五点钟吃晚饭		早。
5.	半夜一点才睡觉		晚。
6.	李小姐说话		快。

E. 怎么 (zěnme, how come)

1.	Zuótiān de diànyǐng hěn hǎo,	nǐ zěnme	méi qù kàn?
2.	Shí diǎn shàngkè,		shí diǎn bàn cái lái?
3.	Zuótiān shì Xiǎo Gāo de shēngrì		méiyǒu lái?
4.	Jīntiān de kǎoshì hěn róngyì		kǎo de zhème bù hǎo?
5.	Míngtiān yǒu kǎoshì		bú fùxí?
6.	Gāo Xiǎoyīn zài túshūguǎn gōngzuò		bú rènshi tā?
7.	Bā diǎn bàn cái kāi huì		qī diǎn jiù lái le?
8.	Jīntiān shì xīngqīyī		méi qù shàng kè?

1.	昨天的电影很好，	你怎么	没去看？
2.	十点上课，		十点半才来？

3.	昨天是小高的生日	没有来?
4.	今天的考试很容易	考得这么不好?
5.	明天有考试	不复习?
6.	高小音在图书馆工作	不认识她?
7.	八点半才开会	七点就来了?
8.	今天是星期一	没去上课?

F. 才 (cái; indicating that something takes place later than expected)

1.	Māma hěn wǎn	cái	huílai.
2.	Xiǎo Gāo shí diǎn		chī zǎofàn.
3.	Wǒ gēge zuótiān wǎnshang bā diǎn		chī wǎnfàn.
4.	Tā de tóngxué zuótiān bànyè		shuì jiào.
5.	Bā diǎn bàn kǎoshì, tā jiǔ diǎn		lái.
6.	Bàba jīntiān hěn máng, zhōumò		yǒu kòngr.
7.	Wǒ yào zài xuéxiào tīng lùyīn, wǔ diǎnzhōng		huí jiā.

1.	妈妈很晚	才	回来。
2.	小高十点		吃早饭。
3.	我哥哥昨天晚上八点		吃晚饭。
4.	他的同学昨天半夜		睡觉。
5.	八点半考试，他九点		来。
6.	爸爸今天很忙，周末		有空儿。
7.	我要在学校听录音，五点钟		回家。

G. 就 (jiù; indicating that something takes place sooner than expected)

1.	Wǒ zuótiān wǎnshang shí diǎn	jiù	shuì le.
2.	Tā zǎoshang qī diǎn bàn		kāishǐ fùxí kèwén le.
3.	Xiǎo Wáng zǎoshang wǔ diǎn		qù xuéxiào le.
4.	Tā chī fàn yǐhòu		qù túshūguǎn kàn shū le.
5.	Jiǔ diǎn kǎoshì, Xiǎo Bái bā diǎn		lái le.
6.	Tā píngcháng liù diǎn chī wǎnfàn, jīntiān wǔ diǎn		chī le.

1.	我昨天晚上十点	就	睡了。
2.	他早上七点半		开始复习课文了。
3.	小王早上五点		去学校了。
4.	她吃饭以后		去图书馆看书了。
5.	九点考试，小白八点		来了。
6.	他平常六点吃晚饭，今天五点		吃了。

H. 真 (zhēn, really)

1.	Zhège xuéxiào	zhēn	hǎo.
2.	Jīntiān de fàn		bù hǎo chī.
3.	Wáng Lǎoshī		máng.
4.	Zhège zì		nán.
5.	Nǐ de Zhōngwén		búcuò.
6.	Zhè yí kè de yǔfǎ		róngyì.
7.	Zhège diànyǐng		yǒu yìsi.
8.	Zuótiān de gōngkè		duō.

1.	这个学校	真	好。
2.	今天的饭		不好吃。

3. 王老师 忙。
4. 这个字 难。
5. 你的中文 不错。
6. 这一课的语法 容易。
7. 这个电影 有意思。
8. 昨天的功课 多。

English Texts

DIALOGUE I

(Wang Peng is talking with Li You.)

Wang Peng: How did you do on last week's exam?

Li You: Pretty well. Because you helped me review, I did pretty well, but the teacher said I was too slow at writing the Chinese characters.

Wang Peng: Really? I'll practice writing characters with you from now on. I'll teach you how to write Chinese characters. How's that sound?

Li You: That would be great! Let's do it right now. Here's a pen.

Wang Peng: O.K., I'll teach you how to write the character "nán" (difficult).

Li You: You write characters really well, and fast, too.

Wang Peng: You flatter me. Do you have Chinese tomorrow?

Li You: Yes. Tomorrow we'll study Lesson Seven.

Wang Peng: Have you prepared it?

Li You: Yes, I have. The grammar in Lesson Seven is very easy. I can understand all of it, but there are too many new words, and the Chinese characters are rather difficult, too.

Wang Peng: Let me practice with you tonight.

Li You: Great. Thank you.

Wang Peng: Don't mention it. See you tonight.

Tell a story based on this picture.

DIALOGUE II

(Li You is talking with Xiao Bai.)

Li You: Xiao Bai, you usually come very early. How come you got here so late today?

Xiao Bai: Yesterday I was preparing Chinese. I didn't go to bed till one o'clock. Did you go to bed very late, too?

Li You: No, yesterday I went to bed at ten. Because Wang Peng helped me practice Chinese, I finished my homework very quickly.

Xiao Bai: It's great to have a Chinese friend.

(In the Chinese class.)

Teacher: Good morning, everyone. Let's begin. Have you all prepared Lesson Seven?

Students: Yes, we have.

Teacher: Li You, would you please read the text aloud?...You read very well. Did you listen to the tape recording last night?

Li You: No, I didn't.

Xiao Bai: But her friend often helps her.

Teacher: Is your friend Chinese?

Li You: Yes.

Xiao Bai: It's a he. He's really handsome. His name is Wang Peng.

LESSON 8 ▲ School Life

第八课 ▲ 学校生活

Dì bā kè ▲ *Xuéxiào shēnghuó*

下课以后，你想去打球吗？

Xià kè yǐhòu, nǐ xiǎng qù dǎ qiú ma?

A Diary: A Typical School Day

VOCABULARY

1.	#篇	piān	m	(a measure for essays, articles, etc.)
2.	日记	rìjì	n	diary
3.	早上	zǎoshang	t	morning
4.	起床	qǐ chuáng	vo	to get up
	床	chuáng	n	bed
5.	洗#澡	xǐ zǎo	vo	to take a bath/shower

6.	早饭	zǎofàn	n	breakfast
7.	一边...一边	yìbiān...yìbiān		(a parallel construction indicating two simultaneous actions)
8.	教室	jiàoshì	n	classroom
9.	发音	fāyīn	n	pronunciation
10.	新	xīn	adj	new
11.	电#脑	diànnǎo	n	computer
	脑	nǎo	n	brain
12.	中午	zhōngwǔ	n	noon
13.	#餐#厅	cāntīng	n	dining room; cafeteria
14.	午饭	wǔfàn	n	lunch; midday meal
15.	报	bào	n	newspaper
16.	#宿#舍	sùshè	n	dormitory
17.	到	dào	v	to arrive
18.	那儿	nàr	pr	there
19.	...的时候	...de shíhou		when...; at the time of...
20.	正在	zhèngzài	adv	in the middle of (doing something)
21.	以前	yǐqián	t	before; ago; previously
22.	告诉	gàosu	v	to tell
23.	已经	yǐjīng	adv	already

李友的一天

Lǐ Yǒu de yì tiān

AN ENTRY FROM LI YOU'S DIARY

Lǐ Yǒu de yì piān rìjì

Bāyuè jiǔrì, xīngqīyī

Wǒ jīntiān zǎoshang(1) qī diǎn bàn qǐ chuáng(G1), xǐle zǎo yǐhòu jiù(G2) chī zǎofàn. Wǒ yìbiān chī fàn, yìbiān(G3) tīng lùyīn. Jiǔ diǎnzhōng dào jiàoshì qù shàng kè(G4).

Dì yī jié kè shì Zhōngwén, lǎoshī jiāo wǒmen fāyīn(G5), shēngcí hé yǔfǎ, yě jiāo wǒmen xiě zì, hái gěile(G6) wǒmen yì piān xīn kèwén(2), zhè piān kèwén hěn yǒu yìsi. Dì èr jié kè shì diànnǎo(3) kè, hěn nán. Zhōngwǔ wǒ hé tóngxuémen yìqǐ dào cāntīng qù chī wǔfàn. Wǒmen yìbiān chī, yìbiān liànxí shuō Zhōngwén. Xiàwǔ wǒ dào túshūguǎn qù kàn bào. Sì diǎnzhōng Wáng Péng lái zhǎo wǒ qù dǎ qiú. Wǔ diǎn sān kè chī wǎnfàn. Qī diǎn bàn wǒ qù Xiǎo Bái de sùshè gēn tā liáo tiān(r). Dào nàr de shíhou, tā zhèngzài(G7) zuò gōngkè. Wǒ bā diǎn bàn huí jiā. Shuì jiào yǐqián, gěi Wáng Péng dǎle yí ge diànhuà, gàosu tā míngtiān yào kǎoshì. Tā shuō tā yǐjīng zhīdao le.

AN ENTRY FROM LI YOU'S DIARY

李友的一篇日记

八月九日　星期一

我今天早上(1)七点半起床(G1)，洗了澡以后就(G2)吃早饭。我一边吃饭，一边(G3)听录音。九点钟到教室去上课(G4)。

第一节课是中文，老师教我们发音(G5)、生词和语法，也教我们写字，还给了(G6)我们一篇新课文(2)，这篇课文很有意思。第二节课是电脑(3)课，很难。中午我和同学们一起到餐厅去吃午饭。我们一边吃，一边练习说中文。下午我到图书馆去看报。四点钟王朋来找我去打球。五点三刻吃晚饭。七点半我去小白的宿舍跟他聊天(儿)。到那儿的时候，他正在(G7)做功课。我八点半回家。睡觉以前，给王朋打了一个电话，告诉他明天要考试。他说他已经知道了。

Notes

1 Both 早上 (zǎoshang) and 上午 (shàngwǔ) are usually translated as "morning," but the two Chinese words are not interchangeable. 早上 (zǎoshang) refers to the early morning; and 上午 (shàngwǔ) to the latter part of the morning or to the first half of the day (until noon).

2 When a disyllabic adjective modifies a noun, the particle 的 (de) is usually inserted between the adjective and the noun, e.g. 漂亮的学校 (piàoliang

Describe what Li You did yesterday. Don't forget to mention the time!

de xuéxiào, beautiful school), 容易的汉字 (róngyì de Hànzì, easy characters). However, with monosyllabic adjectives, 的 (de) is often omitted, e.g., 新课文 (xīn kèwén, new lesson text), 新电脑 (xīn diànnǎo, new computer), 大教室 (dà jiàoshì, big classroom), and 好老师 (hǎo lǎoshī, good teacher). If the adjective is preceded by 很 (hěn), however, 的 (de) cannot be dropped, e.g., 很新的电脑 (hěn xīn de diànnǎo, very new computer); 很大的教室 (hěn dà de jiàoshì, very big classroom); 很好的老师 (hěn hǎo de lǎoshī, very good teacher).

▲**3**▲ The usual colloquial term for computer is 电脑 (diànnǎo), literally "electric brain." A more formal term, especially in mainland China, is 电子计算机 (diànzǐ jìsuànjī) or "electronic computing machine" or simply 计算机 (jìsuànjī).

A Letter: Talking about Studying Chinese

VOCABULARY

1.	封	fēng	m	(a measure word for letters)
2.	信	xìn	n	letter (mail)
3.	最近	zuìjìn	tw	recently
	最	zuì	adv	(an adverb of superlative degree; most, -est)
	近	jìn	adj	near
4.	学期	xuéqī	n	school term; semester/quarter
5.	除了…以外	chúle...yǐwài	conj	in addition to; besides [see G8]
6.	专#业	zhuānyè	n	major (in college); specialty
7.	会	huì	av	can; to know how to [see G9]
8.	开始	kāishǐ	n/v	in the beginning; to begin; to start
9.	习#惯	xíguàn	v/adj/n	to be accustomed to; habit
10.	后来	hòulái	t	later
11.	清#楚	qīngchu	adj	clear
12.	进步	jìnbù	v/n	to make progress; progress
13.	音乐会	yīnyuèhuì	n	concert
14.	希望	xīwàng	v/n	to hope; hope
15.	能	néng	av	can; be able to
16.	用	yòng	v/n	to use; use
17.	笑	xiào	v	to laugh; to laugh at
18.	#祝	zhù	v	to express good wishes

Proper Noun

19. 意文 Yìwén n (a given name)

A Letter

YÌ FĒNG XÌN

Zhāng Xiǎojie:

Nǐ hǎo! Hǎo jiǔ bú jiàn, zuìjìn zěnmeyàng?

Zhège xuéqī wǒ hěn máng, chúle zhuānyè kè yǐwài, hái(G8) děi xué Zhōngwén. Wǒmen de Zhōngwén kè hěn yǒu yìsi. Yīnwei wǒmen de Zhōngwén lǎoshī zhǐ huì(G9) shuō Zhōngwén, bú huì shuō Yīngwén, suǒyǐ shàngkè de shíhou wǒmen zhǐ shuō Zhōngwén, bù shuō Yīngwén. Kāishǐ wǒ bù xíguàn, hòulái, wǒ yǒule yí ge Zhōngguó péngyou, tā shuō huà shuō de hěn qīngchu, chángcháng gēn wǒ yìqǐ liànxí shuō Zhōngwén, suǒyǐ wǒ de Zhōngwén jìnbù de hěn kuài.

Nǐ xǐhuan tīng yīnyuè ma? Xià xīngqīliù, wǒmen xuéxiào yǒu yí ge yīnyuèhuì, xīwàng nǐ néng(G9) lái. Wǒ yòng Zhōngwén xiě xìn xiě de hěn bù hǎo, qǐng bié xiào wǒ. Zhù

Hǎo

Nǐ de péngyou

Yìwén

Bāyuè shírì

Culture Notes

Colleges and universities in China and Taiwan are on the semester system. Typically, the fall semester starts in late August or early September, and ends in mid January. The winter break lasts about a month. Since the Chinese New Year usually falls in late January or early February, college students can take advantage of the break to go home and celebrate the most important holiday of the year with their families. The spring semester starts around mid February and lasts till early July. A semester at a Chinese college is about three weeks longer than that at an American college.

一封信

张小姐：

你好！好久不见，最近怎么样？

这个学期我很忙，除了专业课以外，还(G8)得学中文。我们的中文课很有意思。因为我们的中文老师只会(G9)说中文，不会说英文，所以上课的时候我们只说中文，不说英文。开始我不习惯，后来，我有了一个中国朋友，他说话说得很清楚，常常跟我一起练习说中文，所以我的中文进步得很快。

你喜欢听音乐吗？下星期六，我们学校有一个音乐会，希望你能(G9)来。我用中文写信写得很不好，请别笑我。祝

好

你的朋友

意文

八月十日

音乐会

Yīnyuèhuì

Grammar

1. The Position of Time-When Expressions

Time-when expressions come before the verb.

(1) 我们十点上课。

Wǒmen shí diǎn shàng kè.

(Our class starts at ten.)

(2) 我们几点钟去？

Wǒmen jǐ diǎnzhōng qù?

(What time are we going?)

(3) 你什么时候睡觉？

Nǐ shénme shíhou shuì jiào?

(What time do you go to bed?)

(4) 他明天上午八点来。

Tā míngtiān shàngwǔ bā diǎn lái.

(He will come at eight tomorrow morning.)

2. 就 (jiù) (II) [See also L.7 G3]

The adverb 就 (jiù) connecting two verb phrases indicates that the second action happens as soon as the first one is completed.

(1) 他今天早上起床以后就听中文录音。

Tā jīntiān zǎoshang qǐchuáng yǐhòu jiù tīng Zhōngwén lùyīn.

(He listened to the Chinese recordings right after he got up this morning.)

(2) 写了信以后就去睡觉。

Xiěle xìn yǐhòu jiù qù shuì jiào.

(Go to bed right after you finish writing the letter.)

(3) 我做了功课以后就去朋友家玩。

Wǒ zuòle gōngkè yǐhòu jiù qù péngyou jiā wán.

(I will go to my friend's for a visit right after I have done my homework.)

3. 一边...一边... (yìbiān...yìbiān...)

This structure denotes the simultaneity of two ongoing actions. Usually, the word or phrase for the action that started earlier follows the first 一边 (yìbiān), while that for the action that started later follows the second 一边 (yìbiān).

(1) 我们一边吃饭，一边练习说中文。

Wǒmen yìbiān chī fàn, yìbiān liànxí shuō Zhōngwén.

(We practiced speaking Chinese while having dinner.)

(2) 他常常一边吃饭一边看电视。

Tā chángcháng yìbiān chī fàn yìbiān kàn diànshì.

(He often watches TV while eating.)

Sometimes, the action that follows the second 一边 (yìbiān) is slightly more important, while the first 一边 (yìbiān) conveys the background action.

(3) 我一边唱歌一边写字。

Wǒ yìbiān chàng gē, yìbiān xiě zì.

(I write characters while singing.)

(4) 我妹妹喜欢一边听音乐一边看书。

Wǒ mèimei xǐhuan yìbiān tīng yīnyuè, yìbiān kàn shū.

(My younger sister loves reading while listening to music.)

4. Serial Verbs/Verb Phrases

A number of verbs or verb phrases can be used in succession to represent a series of actions. The sequential order of these verbs or verb phrases usually coincides with the temporal order of the actions.

(1) 他常常去餐厅吃饭。

Tā chángcháng qù cāntīng chī fàn.

(He often goes to the cafeteria to eat.)

(2) 下午我要到图书馆去看书。

Xiàwǔ wǒ yào dào túshūguǎn qù kàn shū.

(This afternoon I want to go to the library to read.)

(3) 我想找同学去打球。

Wǒ xiǎng zhǎo tóngxué qù dǎ qiú.

(I'd like to find some classmates to play ball with me.)

(4) 你明天来我家吃晚饭吧。

Nǐ míngtiān lái wǒ jiā chī wǎnfàn ba.

(Come and have dinner at my home tomorrow.)

Sometimes the first verb indicates the means or manner of the action.

(5) 他常常用中文写信。

Tā chángcháng yòng Zhōngwén xiě xìn.

(He often writes letters in Chinese.)

A student dorm at a Chinese university.

5. Double Objects

Some verbs can take two objects. The object representing a person or persons precedes the one representing an inanimate thing.

(1) 老师教我们发音、生词和语法。

Lǎoshī jiāo wǒmen fāyīn, shēngcí hé yǔfǎ.

(The teacher teaches us pronunciation, vocabulary, and grammar.)

(2) 哥哥给了我一张照片。

Gēge gěile wǒ yì zhāng zhàopiàn.

(My brother gave me a photo.)

(3) 你教我电脑，可以吗？

Nǐ jiāo wǒ diànnǎo, kěyǐ ma?

(Teach me how to use a computer, O.K.?)

(4) 我想问你一个问题。

Wǒ xiǎng wèn nǐ yí ge wèntí.

(I'd like to ask you a question.)

学生餐厅

Xuésheng cāntīng

6. More on the Particle 了 (le) (II) [See also L.5 G5 and L.10 G2]

If a statement enumerates a series of realized actions or events, 了 (le) usually appears at the end of the series, rather than after each of the verbs.

昨天第一节课是中文。老师教我们发音、生词和语法，也教我们写字，还给了我们一篇新课文。那篇课文很有意思。

Zuótiān dì yī jié kè shì Zhōngwén. Lǎoshī jiāo wǒmen fāyīn, shēngcí hé yǔfǎ, yě jiāo wǒmen xiězì, hái gěile wǒmen yì piān xīn kèwén. Nà piān kèwén hěn yǒu yìsi.

(Yesterday the first class was Chinese. Our teacher taught us pronunciation, vocabulary, and grammar. She taught us how to write the characters, and gave us a new text. That text was very interesting.)

上中文课

Shàng Zhōngwén kè

7. ...的时候， 正在... (...de shíhou, zhèngzài...; when...be doing...)

This structure expresses an ongoing or progressive action at a certain point in time.

(1) 我到他宿舍的时候，他正在做功课。

Wǒ dào tā sùshè de shíhou, tā zhèngzài zuò gōngkè.

(When I got to his dorm, he was doing his homework.)

(2) 老师到教室的时候，我们正在看书。

Lǎoshī dào jiàoshì de shíhou, wǒmen zhèngzài kàn shū.

(When the teacher came into the classroom, we were reading.)

(3) 我进他的宿舍的时候，他正在听音乐。

Wǒ jìn tā de sùshè de shíhou, tā zhèngzài tīng yīnyuè.

(When I entered his dorm, he was listening to music.)

(4) 我给他打电话的时候，他正在练习发音。

Wǒ gěi tā dǎ diànhuà de shíhou, tā zhèngzài liànxí fāyīn.

(When I called him, he was practicing pronunciation.)

8. 除了...以外,还(chúle...yǐwài, hái, in addition to..., also...)

(1) 我除了学中文以外，还学日文。

Wǒ chúle xué Zhōngwén yǐwài, hái xué Rìwén.

(Besides Chinese, I also study Japanese.)

(2) 上个周末我们除了看电影以外，还听了音乐。

Shàngge zhōumò wǒmen chúle kàn diànyǐng yǐwài, hái tīngle yīnyuè.

(Last weekend, besides seeing a movie we also listened to some music.)

(3) 他除了喜欢听音乐以外，还喜欢打球。

Tā chúle xǐhuan tīng yīnyuè yǐwài, hái xǐhuan dǎ qiú.

(In addition to listening to music, he also likes to play ball.)

9. 能 (néng) and 会 (huì) (I) Compared

Both 能 (néng) and 会 (huì) have several meanings. The basic meaning of 能 (néng) is "to be capable of (the action named by the following verb)." It can also be an indication of whether circumstances allow the execution of an action. Additional meanings will be introduced in subsequent lessons.

(1) 我能喝十杯咖啡。

Wǒ néng hē shí bēi kāfēi.

(I can drink ten cups of coffee.)

What is the student in the middle doing?

(2) 今天下午我要开会，不能去听音乐。

Jīntiān xiàwǔ wǒ yào kāi huì, bù néng qù tīng yīnyuè.

(I have a meeting this afternoon. I cannot go to listen to music.)

(3) 我的宿舍没有电话，所以不能打电话。

Wǒ de sùshè méiyǒu diànhuà, suǒyǐ bù néng dǎ diànhuà.

(There's no phone in my dorm, so I cannot make any phone calls.)

会 (huì), as used in this lesson, means having the skill to do something through learning or instruction. However, when referring to particular language skills, we can also use 能 (néng): 我能用中文写信 (Wǒ néng yòng Zhōngwén xiě xìn; I can write letters in Chinese).

(4) 小张会说英文。

Xiǎo Zhāng huì shuō Yīngwén.

(Little Zhang can speak English.)

(5) 李友会唱很多美国歌。

Lǐ Yǒu huì chàng hěn duō Měiguó gē.

(Li You can sing many American songs.)

(6) 谁会打球?

Shéi huì dǎ qiú?

(Who can play ball?)

PATTERN DRILLS

A. Time Expression + Verb

Rephrase the sentences below using the words in parentheses.

Example: Wǒmen shàngwǔ jiǔ diǎn shàngkè. (qī diǎn bàn qǐchuáng)

→ Wǒmen qī diǎn bàn qǐchuáng.

我们上午九点上课。(七点半, 起床)

→我们七点半起床。

1.	Wáng Péng wǎnshang shí diǎn shuì jiào.	(shàngwǔ bā diǎn, shàng kè)
2.	Wǒmen shàng kè yǐqián yùxí kèwén.	(huí jiā yǐqián, tīng lùyīn)
3.	Wǒde péngyou míngtiān xiàwǔ lái.	(míngtiān shàngwǔ, lái)
4.	Xià kè yǐhòu, wǒ xiǎng qù dǎ qiú.	(wǎnfàn yǐhòu, kàn diànyǐng)
5.	Wǒ huí jiā yǐqián gēn péngyou liáo tiān.	(shàng kè yǐqián, liànxí Zhōngwén)
6.	Nǐ shénme shíhou kàn diànyǐng?	(jǐ diǎnzhōng, kǎoshì)
7.	Wǒ shí'èr diǎn bàn dào cāntīng chī fàn.	(liǎngdiǎn, dào túshūguǎn kàn shū)

1.	王朋晚上十点睡觉。	(上午八点, 上课)
2.	我们上课以前预习课文。	(回家以前, 听录音)
3.	我的朋友明天下午来。	(明天上午, 来)
4.	下课以后, 我想去打球。	(晚饭以后, 看电影)
5.	我回家以前跟朋友聊天。	(上课以前, 练习中文)
6.	你什么时候看电影?	(几点钟, 考试)
7.	我十二点半到餐厅吃饭。	(两点, 到图书馆看书)

看中文报

Kàn Zhōngwén bào

B. 一边...一边... (yìbiān…yìbiān…)

Use the groups of words below to create sentences with 一边...一边....

Example: Wǒ dìdi zuò gōngkè kàn diànshì

→ Wǒ dìdi yìbiān zuò gōngkè yìbiān kàn diànshì.

我弟弟 做功课 看电视

→我弟弟一边做功课一边看电视。

1.	Wǒ mèimei chángcháng	chī fàn	shuō huà
2.	Wáng Xiānsheng chángcháng	xǐ zǎo	chàng gē
3.	Wǒ dìdi xǐhuan	xiě Hànzì	tīng lùyīn
4.	Xiǎo Gāo yǒu shíhou	kàn bào	hē kāfēi
5.	Wǒ hé Lǎo Lǐ	liáo tiānr	hē kělè
6.	Tāmen	chī wǔfàn	liànxí shuō Zhōngwén
7.	Wǒ gēn wǒde tóngxué	dǎ qiú	liáo tiānr
8.	Wáng Péng hé Lǐ Yǒu	hē chá	tīng yīnyuè

在图书馆
Zài túshūguǎn

1.	我妹妹常常	吃饭	说话
2.	王先生常常	洗澡	唱歌
3.	我弟弟喜欢	写汉字	听录音
4.	小高有时候	看报	喝咖啡
5.	我和老李	聊天儿	喝可乐
6.	他们	吃午饭	练习说中文
7.	我跟我的同学	打球	聊天儿
8.	王朋和李友	喝茶	听音乐

C. Subject + Verb 1 + Verb 2

Rephrase the sentences below using the words in parentheses.

Example: Wáng Péng qù xuéxiào shàng kè. (dào Xiǎo Gāo jiā, chī fàn)

→ Wáng Péng dào Xiǎo Gāo jiā chī fàn.

王朋去学校上课。(到小高家，吃饭)

→王朋到小高家吃饭。

1. Wǒ dìdi chángcháng dào péngyou jiā kàn diànshì. (qù túshūguǎn, kàn shū)
2. Tā xǐhuan qù túshūguǎn kàn bào. (qù jiàoshì, liànxí fāyīn)
3. Xià kè yǐhòu tā qù zhǎo Wáng Péng dǎ qiú. (qù zhǎo péngyou, liáo tiānr)
4. Tā gēn péngyou qù xuéxiào tīng lùyīn. (qù lǎoshī jiā, wèn wèntí)
5. Wǒ de tóngxué yào lái wǒ jiā wánr. (lái wǒmen xuéxiào, kàn diànyǐng)

1. 我弟弟常常到朋友家看电视。 (去图书馆，看书)
2. 他喜欢去图书馆看报。 (去教室，练习发音)
3. 下课以后他去找王朋打球。 (去找朋友，聊天儿)
4. 她跟朋友去学校听录音。 (去老师家，问问题)
5. 我的同学要来我家玩儿。 (来我们学校，看电影)

D. Verb + Object 1 + Object 2

D1:

1.	<u>Lǎoshī</u>	<u>jiāo</u>	xuésheng	shēngcí.
2.			xuésheng	hànzì.
3.			Lǐyǒu	Zhōngwén.
4.			Xiǎo Bái	fāyīn.

D1:

1.	<u>老师</u>	<u>教</u>	学生	生词
2.			学生	汉字
3.			李友	中文
4.			小白	发音

D2:

1.	<u>Wǒ de péngyou</u>	<u>gěi</u>	lǎoshī	yì piān rìjì.
2.			tā dìdi	yí ge diànnǎo.
3.			lǎoshī	yì fēng xìn.
4.			tā bàba	yì zhāng zhàopiàn.
5.			wǒ	yì běn shū.
6.			Xiǎo Gāo	yì bēi kělè.

D2:

1.	<u>我的朋友</u>	<u>给</u>	老师	一篇日记。
2.			他弟弟	一个电脑。
3.			老师	一封信。
4.			他爸爸	一张照片。
5.			我	一本书。
6.			小高	一杯可乐。

E. ...的时候，正在... (...de shíhou, zhèngzài...)

1.	Wǒ huí jiā	<u>de shíhou,</u>	dìdi	<u>zhèngzài</u>	kàn diànshì.
2.	Wǒmen qù zhǎo Lǐ Yǒu		tā		shuì jiào.
3.	Wǒ qù tā sùshè		tā		kàn diànshì.

4.	Wáng Péng gěi dìdi dǎ diànhuà	tā dìdi	xiě xìn.
5.	Lǎoshī jìn jiàoshì	wǒmen	niàn kèwén.
6.	Wǒ huí sùshè	Xiǎo Bái	gēn péngyou liáo tiānr.
7.	Wǒ dào túshūguǎn	Lǐ Yǒu	kàn shū.
8.	Lǐ Yǒu qù zhǎo Wáng Péng	Wáng Péng	yùxí gōngkè.

1.	我回家	<u>的时候</u>,	弟弟	<u>正在</u>	看电视。
2.	我们去找李友		她		睡觉。
3.	我去他宿舍		他		看电视。
4.	王朋给弟弟打电话		他弟弟		写信。
5.	老师进教室		我们		念课文。
6.	我回宿舍		小白		跟朋友聊天儿。
7.	我到图书馆		李友		看书。
8.	李友去找王朋		王朋		预习功课。

F. 除了…以外，还…(chúle … yǐwài, hái…)

1.	<u>Tā</u>	<u>chúle</u>	tīng lùyīn	<u>yǐwài, hái</u>	niàn kèwén.
2			xué Yīngwén		xué Zhōngwén.
3.			huì shuō Zhōngwén		huì yòng Zhōngwén xiě xìn.
4.			shì wǒ de lǎoshī		shì wǒ de péngyou.
5.			hē kělè		hē chá.
6.			xǐhuan tīng yīnyuè		xǐhuan tiào wǔ.

1.	<u>他</u>	<u>除了</u>	听录音	<u>以外，还</u>	念课文。
2.			学英文		学中文。
3.			会说中文		会用中文写信。

4.	是我的老师	是我的朋友。
5.	喝可乐	喝茶。
6.	喜欢听音乐	喜欢跳舞。

G. 用 (yòng) + Object + Verb + Object

1.	Wǒmen	yòng	Zhōngwén	xiě rìjì.
2.	Xiǎo Gāo		Yīngwén	gěi tā gēge xiě xìn.
3.	Wǒ de tóngxué		diànnǎo	liànxí fāyīn.
4.	Wǒ bàba		píjiǔbēi	hē chá.

1.	我们	用	中文	写日记。
2.	小高		英文	给他哥哥写信。
3.	我的同学		电脑	练习发音。
4.	我爸爸		啤酒杯	喝茶。

English Texts

AN ENTRY FROM LI YOU'S DIARY

August 9, Monday

I got up at seven thirty this morning. After a shower I had breakfast. While I was eating, I listened to the tape recording. I went to the classroom at nine o'clock.

The first period was Chinese. The teacher taught us pronunciation, new vocabulary, and grammar. (He/she) also taught us how to write Chinese characters, and gave us a new text. The text was very interesting. The second period was Computer Science. It was very difficult. At noon I went to the cafeteria with my classmates for lunch. While we were eating, we practiced speaking Chinese. In the afternoon I went to the library to read newspapers.

At four o'clock Wang Peng came looking for me to play ball. I had dinner at a quarter to six. At seven thirty I went to Little Bai's dorm for a chat. When I got there, he was doing his homework. I got home at eight thirty. Before I went to bed, I gave Wang Peng a call. I told him there'd be an exam tomorrow. He said he already knew that.

A LETTER: TALKING ABOUT STUDYING CHINESE

August 10

Dear Miss Zhang,

How are you? Long time no see. How are things recently?

This semester I'm very busy. Besides the classes required for my major, I also need to study Chinese. Our Chinese class is really interesting. Because our Chinese teacher can only speak Chinese and does not know how to speak English, in the class we speak only Chinese, and no English. At the beginning I wasn't used to that. Then I made a Chinese friend. He speaks very clearly, and often speaks Chinese with me. As a result, I have made a lot of progress with my Chinese.

Do you like to listen to music? Next Saturday there will be a concert at our school. I hope you can come. I do not write well in Chinese. Please don't make fun of me.

Best wishes,

Your friend,

Yiwen

LESSON 9 ▲ Shopping

第九课 ▲ 买东西

Dì jiǔ kè ▲ *Mǎi dōngxi*

这件衬衫怎么样?

Zhè jiàn chènshān zěnmeyàng?

Dialogue I: Buying Clothes

VOCABULARY

1.	买	mǎi	v	to buy
2.	东西	dōngxi	n	things; objects
3.	#售#货员	shòuhuòyuán	n	shop assistant; salesclerk
4.	要	yào	av	to want to; to have a desire for [see G1]
5.	衣服	yīfu	n	clothes
6.	件	jiàn	m	(a measure word for shirts, dresses, jackets, coats, etc.)

7.	#衬#衫	chènshān	n	shirt
8.	#颜色	yánsè	n	color
9.	黄	huáng	adj	yellow
10.	红	hóng	adj	red
11.	穿	chuān	v	to wear; to put on
12.	条	tiáo	m	(a measure word for long, thin objects)
13.	#裤子	kùzi	n	pants
14.	号	hào	m	number; size
15.	中	zhōng	adj	medium
16.	贵	guì	adj	expensive
17.	便#宜	piányi	adj	cheap; inexpensive
18.	#付钱	fù qián	vo	to pay money
	钱	qián	n	money
19.	这儿	zhèr	pr	here
20.	一共	yígòng	adv	altogether
21.	多少	duōshao	qw	how much; how many
22.	块	kuài	m	colloquial term for the basic Chinese monetary unit
23.	毛	máo	m	$\frac{1}{10}$ of a kuai (similar to the U.S. dime)
24.	分	fēn	m	$\frac{1}{100}$ of a kuai, cent
25.	百	bǎi	nu	hundred
26.	找(钱)	zhǎo(qián)	v	to give change [see also L.4 Dialogue II]

DIALOGUE I

(Mǎi dōngxi)

Shòuhuòyuán: Xiǎojie(1), nín yào(G1) mǎi shénme yīfu?

Lǐ Xiǎojie: Wǒ xiǎng mǎi yí jiàn(G2) chènshān.

Shòuhuòyuán: Nín xǐhuan shénme yánsè de(G3), huáng de háishi hóng de?

Lǐ Xiǎojie: Wǒ xǐhuan chuān(2) hóng de. Wǒ hái xiǎng mǎi yì tiáo(3) (G2) kùzi.

Shòuhuòyuán: Duō(G4) dà de? Dà hào, zhōng hào háishi xiǎo hào de?

Lǐ Xiǎojie: Zhōng hào de. Bú yào tài guì de, yě bú yào tài piányi(4) de.

Shòuhuòyuán: Zhè tiáo kùzi hé zhè jiàn chènshān zěnmeyàng?

Lǐ Xiǎojie: Hěn hǎo, zài nǎr fù qián?

Shòuhuòyuán: Zài zhèr.

Lǐ Xiǎojie: Yígòng duōshao qián?

Shòuhuòyuán: Chènshān èrshí kuài wǔ, kùzi sānshí'èr kuài jiǔ máo jiǔ, yígòng shì wǔshísān kuài sì máo jiǔ fēn(G5).

Lǐ Xiǎojie: Hǎo, zhè shì yìbǎi kuài qián.

Shòuhuòyuán: Zhǎo nín sìshíliù kuài wǔ máo yī. Xièxie.

No Taxes and No Tipping in China

There is no sales tax in mainland China. It is also not customary to tip in a restaurant, although fancier restaurants often charge a service fee.

DIALOGUE I

(买东西)

售货员： 小姐(1)，您要(G1)买什么衣服？

李小姐： 我想买一件(G2)衬衫。

售货员： 您喜欢什么颜色的(G3)，黄的还是红的？

李小姐： 我喜欢穿(2)红的。我还想买一条(3) (G2)裤子。

售货员： 多(G4)大的？大号、中号还是小号的？

李小姐：　中号的。不要太贵的，也不要太便宜(4)的。

售货员：　这条裤子和这件衬衫怎么样？

李小姐：　很好，在哪儿付钱？

售货员：　在这儿。

李小姐：　一共多少钱？

售货员：　衬衫二十块五，裤子三十二块九毛九，一共是五十三块四毛九分(G5)。

李小姐：　好，这是一百块钱。

售货员：　找您四十六块五毛一。谢谢。

Notes

▲**1**▲ In mainland China a salesperson in a department store or a server in a restaurant is usually addressed as 服务员 (fúwùyuán, "Service Person") or, for speakers who like to be more "modern," 小姐 (xiǎojie, Miss) or 先生 (xiānsheng, Mr.). In speaking to bus drivers and ticket sellers, as well as taxi drivers, the most common form of address (for women as well as men) is 师傅 (shīfu, an old term of respect for a master craftsman or skilled worker). However, these terms vary according to age and preference of the speaker as well as the status or function of the person spoken to, and usage is very much in flux now at the beginning of the twenty-first century. As in so many matters of language usage, students should carefully observe actual usage and follow suit. In Taiwan the terms 小姐 (xiǎojie, Miss) and 先生 (xiānsheng, Mr.) have very broad usage, including the contexts mentioned above.

▲**2**▲ Note that the verb 穿 (chuān) can mean both "to wear" and "to put on." However, for most accessories, especially those for the upper part of the body, 戴 (dài) is used instead of 穿 (chuān). Compare: 穿衣服 (chuān yīfu, to wear clothes); 穿裤子 (chuān kùzi, to wear pants); 穿裙子 (chuān qúnzi, to wear a skirt); 穿西装 (chuān xīzhuāng, to wear a suit); 穿鞋 (chuān xié, to wear shoes); 穿袜子 (chuān wàzi, to wear socks); but 戴帽子 (dài màozi, to wear a hat); 戴眼镜 (dài yǎnjìng, to wear eyeglasses); 戴手套 (dài shǒutào, to wear gloves); and 戴手表 (dài shǒubiǎo, to wear a wristwatch).

▲3▲ In Chinese, a pair of pants is just one single piece of clothing. Hence 一条裤子 (yì tiáo kùzi, lit. a trouser) instead of *一双裤子 (*yì shuāng kùzi, lit. a pair of trousers).

▲4▲ The character 便 in 便宜 (piányi) is pronounced "pián." However, in 方便 (fāngbiàn) the same character is pronounced "biàn." It is not uncommon in Chinese for the same character to be pronounced differently and carry different meanings. Other examples include 乐 (yuè/lè) in 音乐 (yīnyuè, music) and 可乐 (kělè, cola); and 觉 (jué/jiào) in 觉得 (juéde, to feel) and 睡觉 (shuì jiào, to sleep).

Using this picture as a guide, talk about Miss Li's shopping experience.

Dialogue II: Exchanging Shoes

VOCABULARY

1.	双	shuāng	m	a pair of
2.	#鞋	xié	n	shoes
3.	#换	huàn	v	to change; to exchange
4.	一样	yíyàng	adj	same; alike
5.	虽然	suīrán	conj	although
6.	大小	dàxiǎo	n	size
7.	合#适	héshì	adj	suitable
8.	咖啡色	kāfēisè	n	coffee color; brown
9.	黑	hēi	adj	black
10.	不用	bú yòng	ce	need not

DIALOGUE II

Lǐ Xiǎojie: Duìbuqǐ, zhè shuāng xié tài xiǎo le. Néng bu néng huàn yì shuāng?

Shòuhuòyuán: Méi wèntí. Nín kàn, zhè shuāng zěnmeyàng?

Lǐ Xiǎojie: Yě bù xíng, zhè shuāng gēn nà shuāng yíyàng(G6) dà.

Shòuhuòyuán: Nà zhè shuāng hēi de ne?

Lǐ Xiǎojie: Zhè shuāng xié suīrán dàxiǎo héshì, kěshì(G7) yánsè bù hǎo. Yǒu méiyǒu kāfēisè de?

Shòuhuòyuán: Duìbuqǐ, zhǐ yǒu hēi de.

Lǐ Xiǎojie: Nà hǎo ba. Wǒ hái yào fù qián ma?

Shòuhuòyuán: Bú yòng, zhè shūang de qián gēn nà shuāng yíyàng.

DIALOGUE II

李小姐：对不起，这双鞋太小了。能不能换一双？

售货员：没问题。您看，这双怎么样？

李小姐：也不行，这双<u>跟</u>那双<u>一样</u>(G6)大。

售货员：那这双黑的呢？

李小姐：这双鞋<u>虽然</u>大小合适，<u>可是</u>(G7)颜色不好。有没有咖啡色的？

售货员：对不起，只有黑的。

李小姐：那好吧。我还要付钱吗？

售货员：不用，这双的钱跟那双一样。

Culture Notes

The traditional dress-up attire for Chinese men was a long robe called 长袍 (chángpáo, long gown) and a short jacket called 马褂 (mǎguà, Mandarin jacket), while women (in the cities) wore a modified Manchu-style dress called 旗袍 (qípáo, close-fitting woman's dress with a high neck and a slit skirt) until 1949 in China and into the 1960s and 70s in Taiwan. Through the early decades of the People's Republic men wore the 中山装 (Zhōngshānzhuāng, "Sun Yatsen suit") the top part of which came to be called in the West a "Mao jacket." Nowadays Chinese men and women dress in about the same way as Westerners, wearing suits and ties, or dresses on formal occasions and jeans and shirts, or T-shirts, for more casual purposes.

What is Miss Li trying to tell the salesclerk?

What does Miss Li say about the shoes the salesclerk recommends?

What does the salesclerk tell Miss Li about the cost of the shoes?

SUPPLEMENTARY VOCABULARY

1.	卖	mài	v	to sell
2.	裙子	qúnzi	n	skirt
3.	大衣	dàyī	n	overcoat
4.	夹克	jiákè	n	jacket
5.	外套	wàitào	n	coat; jacket
6.	西装	xīzhuāng	n	suit
7.	毛衣	máoyī	n	sweater

8.	T-恤衫	T-xùshān	n	T-shirt
9.	戴	dài	v	to wear (hat, eyeglasses, etc.)
10.	帽子	màozi	n	hat
11.	顶	dǐng	m	(a measure word for hat)
12.	袜子	wàzi	n	socks
13.	长	cháng	adj	long
14.	短	duǎn	adj	short
15.	蓝	lán	adj	blue
16.	绿	lǜ	adj	green
17.	紫	zǐ	adj	purple
18.	粉红色	fěnhóngsè	n	pink
19.	橘红色	júhóngsè	n	orange
20.	灰	huī	adj	grey

Name the clothing items in the picture.
Don't forget to use the appropriate measure words.

Yangshuo, Guangxi, China.

Grammar

1. The Auxiliary Verb 要 (yào) (II) [See also L.6 G2]

One of the meanings of 要 (yào) is "to desire to do something."

(1) 明天是周末，你要做什么？

Míngtiān shì zhōumò, nǐ yào zuò shénme?

(Tomorrow is the weekend. What do you want to do?)

(2) 我要去图书馆看书，你去不去？

Wǒ yào qù túshūguǎn kàn shū, nǐ qù bu qù?

(I want to go to the library to read. Are you going?)

(3) 我要喝可乐，他要喝水。

Wǒ yào hē kělè, tā yào hē shuǐ.

(I want to have a cola. He wants water.)

To negate it, use 不想 (bù xiǎng).

(4) 我不想去图书馆。

Wǒ bù xiǎng qù túshūguǎn.

(I don't feel like going to the library.)

(5) 今天我不想做功课。

Jīntiān wǒ bù xiǎng zuò gōngkè.

(I don't feel like doing my homework today.)

For (4), however, some Chinese, particularly in the South, would say: "我不要去图书馆" (Wǒ bú yào qù túshūguǎn).

Note: Both modal verbs 想 (xiǎng) and 要 (yào) can express a desire or an intention, but 要 (yào) carries a stronger tone.

2. Measure Words (II) [See also L.2 G1]

The following are the "measure word + noun" combinations that we have covered so far.

一杯茶	yì bēi chá	a cup of tea
一封信	yì fēng xìn	a letter
一个人	yí ge rén	a person
一节课	yì jié kè	a class period
一件衬衫	yí jiàn chènshān	a shirt
一篇日记	yì piān rìjì	a diary entry
一瓶啤酒	yì píng píjiǔ	a bottle of beer
一双鞋	yì shuāng xié	a pair of shoes
一条裤子	yì tiáo kùzi	a pair of pants
一位先生	yí wèi xiānsheng	a gentleman
一张照片	yì zhāng zhàopiàn	a picture

SUPPLEMENTARY EXPRESSIONS

一本书	yì běn shū	a book
一张纸	yì zhāng zhǐ	a piece of paper
一枝笔	yì zhī bǐ	a pen
一只鞋	yì zhī xié	a shoe (one of a pair) [see also "a pair of shoes" above]

3. 的 (de) Structure

We have a 的 (de) structure when a noun, a pronoun, or an adjective is followed by the structural particle 的 (de). Grammatically, a 的 (de) structure is equivalent to a noun, e.g., 老师的 (lǎoshī de, the teacher's), 我的 (wǒ de, mine), 大的 (dà de, the big one), etc. Also see G3 in Lesson 3.

4. 多 (duō) Used Interrogatively

(1) 你今年多大? [see L.3, Dialogue I, Note 2]

Nǐ jīnnián duō dà?

(How old are you this year?)

(2) 你穿多大的衣服?

Nǐ chuān duō dà de yīfu?

(What size clothes do you wear?)

(3) 你弟弟多高?

Nǐ dìdi duō gāo?

(How tall is your younger brother?)

5. Amounts of Money

Chinese monetary units are 元 (yuán, the Chinese dollar), 角 (jiǎo, ⅒ of a *yuan*), and 分 (fēn, one cent or ¹⁄₁₀₀ of a *yuan*). In colloquial speech, alternative terms 块 (kuài) and 毛 (máo) are usually used instead of 元 (yuán) and 角 (jiǎo), but price markings in stores are likely to be in 元 (yuán) and 角 (jiǎo), and many store clerks also use 元 (yuán) in their speech. Using the colloquial terms, ¥5.99 is 五块九毛九分钱 (wǔ kuài jiǔ máo jiǔ fēn qián). However, in casual conversation abbreviated forms are often used.

Renminbi: from top to bottom

五元，二角，一元 *(wǔ yuán, èr jiǎo, yī yuán)*.

The rules for abbreviation of monetary terms are as follows: begin by omitting the last element 钱 (qián) in the expression and then the second to the last element: 五块九毛九分 (wǔ kuài jiǔ máo jiǔ fēn) omitting 钱 (qián), or 五块九毛九 (wǔ kuài jiǔ máo jiǔ) omitting both 钱 (qián) and 分 (fēn). Note that if 钱 is included the preceding measure (e.g., 分) must also be included; one doesn't say *五块九毛九钱 (*wǔ kuài jiǔ máo jiǔ qián). One or more zeros occurring internally in a complex number are read as 零 (líng, zero).

(1) $8.55 八块五毛五(分)(钱)
bā kuài wǔ máo wǔ (fēn) (qián)

(2) $15.30 十五块三(毛)(钱)
shíwǔ kuài sān (máo) (qián)

(3) $103 一百零三块(钱)
yì bǎi líng sān kuài (qián)

(4) $100.30 一百块零三毛(钱)
yì bǎi kuài líng sān máo (qián)

(5) $100.03 一百块零三分(钱)
yìbǎi kuài líng sān fēn (qián)

Note: To avoid ambiguity, 毛 (máo) and 分 (fēn) cannot be omitted in (4) or (5) above.

6. 跟/和...(不) 一样 (gēn/hé...{bù} yíyàng, {not the} same as...)

To express similarity or dissimilarity between two objects or people, we use the structure 跟/和...(不) 一样 (gēn/hé...{bù} yíyàng).

(1) 你的衬衫跟我的一样。

Nǐ de chènshān gēn wǒ de yíyàng.

(Your shirt is the same as mine.)

(2) 贵的衣服和便宜的衣服不一样。

Guì de yīfu hé piányi de yīfu bù yíyàng.

(Expensive clothes are different from cheap ones.)

Following 一样 (yíyàng), an adjective can be used:

(3) 弟弟跟哥哥一样高。

Dìdi gēn gēge yíyàng gāo.

(The younger brother is as tall as the older one.)

7. 虽然..., 可是/但是... (suīrán..., kěshì/dànshì..., although...yet...)

This pair of conjunctions links the two clauses of a complex sentence. Note, however, that 虽然 (suīrán) is often optional.

(1) 虽然这双鞋很便宜，可是大小不合适。

Suīrán zhè shuāng xié hěn piányi, kěshì dàxiǎo bù héshì.

(Although this pair of shoes is inexpensive, it's not the right size.)

(2) 这本书很有意思，可是太贵了。

Zhè běn shū hěn yǒu yìsi, kěshì tài guì le.

(This book is very interesting, but it's too expensive.)

(3) 中文不容易，但是很有意思。

Zhōngwén bù róngyì, dànshì hěn yǒu yìsi.

(Chinese is not easy, but it's very interesting.)

Whether or not 虽然 (suīrán) is used in the first clause, 可是 (kěshì) cannot be omitted in the second. The following sentence is, therefore, **incorrect**:

(2a) *虽然这本书很有意思，太贵了。

*Suīrán zhè běn shū hěn yǒu yìsi, tài guì le.

PATTERN DRILLS

A. 要 (yào, to want to; to desire to do {something})

1.	Tā de péngyou	yào	mǎi yì tiáo hóng qúnzi.
2.	Lǐ Yǒu		chuān kāfēisè de yīfu qù tiào wǔ.
3.	Dìdi zhège zhōumò		kàn wàiguó diànyǐng.
4.	Jiějie xǐle zǎo yǐhòu		qù túshūguǎn kàn shū.
5.	Wǒ xué Zhōngwén de shíhou		yòng diànnǎo liànxí fāyīn.
6.	Wǒ mèimei xīngqītiān		qù tóngxué jiā wánr.
7.	Nǐ gēge		mǎi shénme yīfu?

1.	她的朋友	要	买一条红裙子。
2.	李友		穿咖啡色的衣服去跳舞。
3.	弟弟这个周末		看外国电影。
4.	姐姐洗了澡以后		去图书馆看书。
5.	我学中文的时候		用电脑练习发音。
6.	我妹妹星期天		去同学家玩儿。
7.	你哥哥		买什么衣服？

A shopping district in Shanghai.

B. 想 (xiǎng, to want to; to feel like; would like to)

1.	Tā	xiǎng	xué Zhōngwén.
2.	Wǒ		kàn Zhōngguó diànyǐng.
3.	Wǒ wǎnshang		yùxí shēngcí.
4.	Xiǎo Gāo		qǐng péngyou chī fàn.
5.	Lǐ Yǒu wǎnfàn yǐhòu		qù Xiǎo Gāo jiā kàn diànshì.
6.	Wáng Péng jīntiān bù		qù kàn diànyǐng.
7.	Zhè jiàn yīfu wǒ bù		mǎi.
8.	Míngtiān yǒu kǎoshì, Xiǎo Bái		gēn péngyou fùxí yǔfǎ.

1.	他	想	学中文。
2.	我		看中国电影。
3.	我晚上		预习生词。
4.	小高		请朋友吃饭。
5.	李友晚饭以后		去小高家看电视。
6.	王朋今天不		去看电影。
7.	这件衣服我不		买。
8.	明天有考试，小白		跟朋友复习语法。

A fruit shop in Taipei.

C. 的 (de) Structure

Complete the sentences with 的.

Example: Zhè jiàn yīfu / wǒ

→ Zhè jiàn yīfu shì wǒ de.

这件衣服 / 我

→ 这件衣服是我的。

1. Nà běn shū / lǎoshī
2. Zhè tiáo qúnzi hé zhè jiàn yīfu / mèimei
3. Tā yào mǎi / qī hào
4. Tā xǐhuan chuān / kāfēisè

1. 那本书 / 老师
2. 这条裙子和这件衣服 / 妹妹
3. 她要买 / 七号
4. 他喜欢穿 / 咖啡色

A traditional market in Taipei.

D. 多 (duō)

1. Nǐ de dìdi jīnnián duō dà?
2. Tā de kùzi ____ guì?
3. Tā chuān de yīfu ____ dà?
4. Nǐ de péngyou ____ gāo?
5. Nà jiàn chènshān ____ guì?

1. 你的弟弟今年 多 大?
2. 他的裤子 ____ 贵?
3. 她穿的衣服 ____ 大?
4. 你的朋友 ____ 高?
5. 那件衬衫 ____ 贵?

E. 跟...一样 (gēn…yíyàng; the same as...)

1.	Zhè jiàn yīfu	gēn	nà jiàn	yíyàng	piàoliang.
2.	Tā		wǒ gēge		gāo.
3.	Měiguó fàn		Zhōngguó fàn		hǎochī.
4.	Tā de chènshān		wǒ de		guì.
5.	Zhōngwén		Rìwén		nán.
6.	Zhè shuāng xié		nà shuāng		héshì.
7.	Jīntiān de shēngcí		zuótiān de		duō.
8.	Zhège xuéxiào		nàge		hǎo.

1.	这件衣服	跟	那件	一样	漂亮。
2.	他		我哥哥		高。
3.	美国饭		中国饭		好吃。
4.	他的衬衫		我的		贵。
5.	中文		日文		难。
6.	这双鞋		那双		合适。
7.	今天的生词		昨天的		多。
8.	这个学校		那个		好。

F. 虽然...可是/但是 (suīrán...kěshì/dànshì; although...yet)

1.	Suīrán	Zhōngwén hěn nán,	kěshì	wǒ juéde hěn yǒu yìsi.
2.		tā de yīfu hěn duō,		méiyǒu héshì de.
3.		dì bā kè de yǔfǎ hěn nán,		wǒ dōu dǒng le.
4.		jīntiān de gōngkè hěn duō,		tā dōu zuò le.
5.		zhè jiàn yīfu de yánsè hěn hǎokàn,		tài xiǎo le.
6.		wǎnshang de diànshì hěn búcuò,		wǒ méiyǒu shíjiān kàn.
7.		Lǐ Yǒu hěn xǐhuan tiào wǔ,		tā jīntiān méiyǒu kòngr.

1.	虽然	中文很难，	可是	我觉得很有意思。
2.		她的衣服很多，		没有合适的。
3.		第八课的语法很难，		我都懂了。
4.		今天的功课很多，		他都做了。
5.		这件衣服的颜色很好看，		太小了。
6.		晚上的电视很不错，		我没有时间看。
7.		李友很喜欢跳舞，		她今天没有空儿。

English Texts

DIALOGUE I

(Shopping for clothes.)

Salesperson: Miss, what are you looking for?

Miss Li: I'd like to buy a shirt.

Salesperson: What color do you like, yellow or red?

Miss Li: I like red. I'd also like to get a pair of pants.

Salesperon: What size, large, medium or small?

Miss Li: Medium. Something not too expensive, but not too cheap, either.

Salesperson: How about these pants and this shirt?

Miss Li: Great. Where do I pay?

Salesperson: Here.

Miss Li: How much altogether?

Salesperson: Twenty dollars and fifty cents for the shirt, and thirty-two ninety-nine for the pants. Fifty-three dollars and forty-nine cents altogether.

Miss Li: O.K. Here's one hundred.

Salesperson: Forty-six fifty-one is your change. Thank you.

DIALOGUE II

Miss Li: Excuse me, this pair of shoes is too small. Can I exchange them for another pair?

Salesperson: No problem. How about this pair?

Miss Li: No, that won't do. This pair is the same size as the other pair.

Salesperson: What about this pair in black?

Miss Li: Although this pair is the right size, it's not a good color. Do you have any in brown?

Salesperson: I'm sorry. We have only black ones.

Miss Li: All right then. Do I have to pay any more money?

Salesperson: No, that won't be necessary. This pair is the same price as the other one.

LESSON 10 ▲ Talking about the Weather

第十课 ▲ 谈天气

Dì shí kè ▲ *Tán tiānqì*

今天天气怎么样？

Jīntiān tiānqì zěnmeyàng?

Dialogue I: The Weather Is Getting Better

VOCABULARY

1.	天气	tiānqì	n	weather
2.	比	bǐ	prep	comparison marker [see G1]
3.	下雨	xià yǔ	vo	to rain
4.	报上	bàoshang		in the newspaper
5.	预报	yùbào	n	forecast
6.	更	gèng	adv	even more

7.	不但…而且	búdàn..., érqiě	conj	not only..., but also
8.	会	huì	av	will [see G3]
9.	#暖和	nuǎnhuo	adj	warm
10.	一点儿	yìdiǎnr		a bit
11.	约	yuē	v	to make an appointment
12.	公#园	gōngyuán	n	park
13.	红#叶	hóngyè	n	red autumn leaves
14.	怎么办	zěnme bàn	qw	what to do
15.	录#像	lùxiàng	n	video recording

Proper Nouns

16.	谢	xiè	n/v	(a surname); thanks
17.	上海	Shànghǎi	pn	Shanghai
	海	hǎi	n	sea; ocean

DIALOGUE I

Xiè Xiǎojie: Jīntiān tiānqì bǐ(G1) zuótiān hǎo, bú xià yǔ le(G2).

Gāo Xiānsheng: Míngtiān tiānqì zěnmeyàng? Xīwàng míngtiān yě bú xià yǔ.

Xiè Xiǎojie: Wǒ kànle bàoshang de tiānqì yùbào, míngtiān tiānqì bǐ jīntiān gèng hǎo. Búdàn bú huì(G3) xià yǔ, érqiě huì nuǎnhuo yìdiǎnr.

Gāo Xiānsheng: Tài hǎo le! Wǒ yuēle Lǐ Xiǎojie míngtiān qù gōngyuán kàn hóngyè.

Xiè Xiǎojie: Shì ma? Kěshì Lǐ Xiǎojie jīntiān zǎoshang gēn Wáng Xiānsheng qù Shànghǎi le.

Gāo Xiānsheng: Zhēn de a? Nà wǒ míngtiān zěnme bàn?

Xiè Xiǎojie: Nǐ zài jiā kàn lùxiàng ba!

今日大陸天氣

城市	廣州	福州	昆明	重慶	漢口	杭州	上海	南京	青島	北京	開封	西安	瀋陽	蘭州	海口
天氣	雨天	雨天	多雲	多雲	多雲	雨或雪	陰天	陰天	晴天	晴天	晴天	晴天	晴天	晴天	雨天
高温	16	15	9	8	4	5	3	3	2	2	4	0	-3	-8	22
低温	11	6	-2	2	-2	-1	0	-2	-3	-7	-5	-10	-14	-15	17

What is the weather like in Shanghai today?

DIALOGUE I

谢小姐：今天天气比(G1)昨天好，不下雨了(G2)。

高先生：明天天气怎么样？希望明天也不下雨。

谢小姐：我看了报上的天气预报，明天天气比今天更好。不但不会(G3)下雨，而且会暖和一点儿。

高先生：太好了！我约了李小姐明天去公园看红叶。

谢小姐：是吗？可是李小姐今天早上跟王先生去上海了。

高先生：真的啊？那我明天怎么办？

谢小姐：你在家看录像吧！

What is Miss Xie telling Mr. Gao?

What is Mr. Gao telling Miss Xie?

Tell what is happening in this picture.

What is Miss Xie suggesting to Mr. Gao, and why?

Culture Notes

In China the climatic conditions differ drastically from one part of the country to another. Generally speaking, just as in America, the north is cold and snowy in winter; the south, hot and wet in summer. Three cities, 重庆 (Chóngqìng), 武汉 (Wǔhàn), and 南京 (Nánjīng), are nicknamed "furnaces" for their notoriously hot temperatures in summer. Other cities, such as 昆明 (Kūnmíng), are known for their year-round balmy weather. In the lower 长江 (Chángjiāng, the longest river in China, also known as the Yangtze) valley, there is a 黄梅 (huángméi, lit. yellow plum) season in May and June characterized by copious rain and high humidity. But the major rainy season for most of southern China is in July and August, when almost all the rivers swell to flood level. In winter, the island of 海南 (Hǎinán) provides warmth and appealing resorts for tourists from the north, while many southerners brave the cold and pour into the northern city of 哈尔滨 (Hā'ěrbīn) for its annual exhibition of ice sculptures.

Dialogue II: Complaining about the Weather

VOCABULARY

1.	糟糕	zāogāo	adj	in a terrible mess; too bad
2.	又	yòu	adv	again
3.	刚才	gāngcái	t	just now; a short moment ago
4.	出去	chūqu	vc	to go out
5.	热	rè	adj	hot
6.	舒服	shūfu	adj	comfortable
7.	夏天	xiàtiān	n	summer
8.	这样	zhèyàng	pr	so; like this
9.	凉快	liángkuai	adj	pleasantly cool (weather)
10.	春天	chūntiān	n	spring
11.	冬天	dōngtiān	n	winter
12.	又…又…	yòu...yòu		both...and...
13.	冷	lěng	adj	cold
14.	闷	mēn	adj	stuffy
15.	下次	xià cì		next time
	次	cì	m	time; (a measure word for occurrence)
16.	最好	zuìhǎo	adv	had better
17.	秋天	qiūtiān	n	autumn; fall

Proper Nouns

18.	台北	Táiběi	n	Taipei
19.	台湾	Táiwān	n	Taiwan

DIALOGUE II

Xiǎo Yè: Zhēn zāogāo, yòu(G4) xià dà yǔ le.

Xiǎo Xià: Gāngcái wǒ kàn bào le, bàoshang shuō, zhège xīngqī tiānqì dōu bù hǎo, xiàge xīngqī tiānqì cái huì(G3) hǎo.

Xiǎo Yè: Zhēn de a? Nà zhège zhōumò bù néng chūqu wán le. Zuìjìn tiānqì tài rè, zhēn bù shūfu.

Xiǎo Xià: Táiběi xiàtiān de tiānqì jiù shi zhèyàng. Liǎng ge yuè yǐhòu, tiānqì jiù huì bǐ xiànzài liángkuai yìdiǎnr le.

Xiǎo Yè: Liǎng ge yuè yǐhòu? Xiàge yuè, wǒ jiù huí Měiguó qu le.

Xiǎo Xià: Táiwān chūntiān chángcháng xià yǔ, dōngtiān hěn lěng, xiàtiān yòu mēn yòu rè(G5). Nǐ xià cì zuìhǎo qiūtiān lái.

DIALOGUE II

小叶：真糟糕，又(G4)下大雨了。

小夏：刚才我看报了，报上说，这个星期天气都不好，下个星期天气才会(G3)好。

小叶：真的啊？那这个周末不能出去玩了。最近天气太热，真不舒服。

小夏：台北夏天的天气就是这样。两个月以后，天气就会比现在凉快一点儿了。

小叶：两个月以后？下个月我就回美国去了。

小夏：台湾春天常常下雨，冬天很冷，夏天又闷又热(G5)。你下次最好秋天来。

Using the information in Dialogue I, tell a story about the pictures above.

Do the pictures above accurately depict Dialogue II? Explain each picture separately.

Describe what the weather is like in each of the four seasons.

SUPPLEMENTARY VOCABULARY

1.	潮湿	cháoshī	adj	wet; humid
2.	云	yún	n	cloud
3.	雪	xuě	n	snow
4.	晴	qíng	adj	sunny; clear
5.	阴	yīn	adj	overcast
6.	台中	Táizhōng	n	Taichung (name of a city in Taiwan)
7.	加拿大	Jiānádà	n	Canada
8.	温哥华	Wēngēhuá	n	Vancouver
9.	香港	Xiānggǎng	n	Hong Kong
10.	北京	Běijīng	n	Beijing

Grammar

1. Comparative Sentences with 比 (bǐ)

Specific comparison of two entities is usually expressed with the basic pattern A 比 (bǐ) B + Adj.

(1) 李友比她姐姐高。

Lǐ Yǒu bǐ tā jiějie gāo.

(Li You is taller than her older sister.)

(2) 今天比昨天冷。

Jīntiān bǐ zuótiān lěng.

(It's colder today than yesterday.)

(3) 这本书比那本书有意思。

Zhè běn shū bǐ nà běn shū yǒu yìsi.

(This book is more interesting than that one.)

There are two ways in which the basic comparative construction may be further modified: (a) by adding a modifying term or construction after the adjective (see 4 and 5 below); and (b) by inserting the adverbs 更 (gèng) or 还 (hái) in front of the adjective (see 6 below).

(4) 今天比昨天冷<u>一点儿</u>。

Jīntiān bǐ zuótiān lěng <u>yìdiǎnr</u>.

(It's <u>a bit</u> colder today than yesterday.)

Note that the modifying term must be placed after the adjective (see 4 above), not before it (see 4a below).

(4a) *今天比昨天<u>一点儿</u>冷。

*Jīntiān bǐ zuótiān <u>yìdiǎnr</u> lěng.

(5) 明天会比今天冷<u>得多</u>。

Míngtiān huì bǐ jīntiān lěng <u>de duō</u>.

(It will be <u>much</u> colder tomorrow than today.)

(6) 昨天冷，今天比昨天<u>更</u>冷。

Zuótiān lěng, jīntiān bǐ zuótiān <u>gèng</u> lěng.

(It was cold yesterday. Today is <u>even</u> colder than yesterday.)

To express "much colder" in a comparative construction, 冷多了 (lěng duō le) or 冷得多 (lěng de duō) is used (see 7 below), not 很冷 (hěn lěng, very cold) (see 7a).

(7) 今天比昨天<u>冷多了</u>(or <u>冷得多</u>)。

Jīntiān bǐ zuótiān lěng <u>duō le</u> (*or* lěng <u>de duō</u>).

(Today is much colder than yesterday.)

The following sentences are **incorrect**:

(7a) *今天比昨天很冷。

*Jīntiān bǐ zuótiān hěn lěng.

(*Today is very cold than yesterday.)

Note: While 跟 (gēn) and 和 (hé) are also used in sentences of comparison, they only denote that two things are the same or different without indicating the specific disparity as does 比 (bǐ). Compare the following two sentences:

(8a) 这个教室和那个教室一样大。

Zhège jiàoshì hé nàge jiàoshì yíyàng dà.

(This classroom and that one are the same size.)

The Bund in Shanghai.

(8b) 这个教室跟那个教室不一样大。

Zhège jiàoshì gēn nàge jiàoshì bù yíyàng dà.

(This classroom and that one are not the same size.)

(8c) 这个教室比那个教室大。

Zhège jiàoshì bǐ nàge jiàoshì dà.

(This classroom is larger than that one.)

(8d) 这个教室比那个教室大得多。

Zhège jiàoshì bǐ nàge jiàoshì dà de duō.

(This classroom is much larger than that one.)

2. The Particle 了 (le) (III): 了 (le) as a Sentence-Final Particle [See also L.5 G5 and L.8 G6]

When 了 (le) occurs at the end of a sentence, it usually indicates a change of status or the realization of a new situation.

(1) 下雨了。

Xià yǔ le.

(It's raining now.)

At 1,667 feet, Taipei 101 towers above the city.

(2) 妹妹的衣服小了。

Mèimei de yīfu xiǎo le.

(My sister's clothes have become small [i.e., too small for her].)

(3) 我昨天没有空儿，今天有空儿了。

Wǒ zuótiān méiyǒu kòngr, jīntiān yǒu kòngr le.

(I didn't have time yesterday, but I do today.)

(4) 你看，老师来了。

Nǐ kàn, lǎoshī lái le.

(Look, the teacher has come.)

When used in this sense, 了 (le) can still be used at the end of a sentence even if the sentence is in the negative.

(5) 我没有钱了，不买了。

Wǒ méiyǒu qián le, bù mǎi le.

(I don't have any money [left]. I won't buy it anymore.)
[Indicating that I intended to buy it originally, but I changed my mind.]

Note: Remember that to negate 有 (yǒu, to have), one uses 没 (méi), not 不 (bù).

A Shanghai street scene.

3. The Auxiliary Verb 会 (huì, will) (II) [See also L.8 G9]

会 (huì) indicates an anticipated event or action in the future.

(1) 白老师现在不在办公室，可是他明天会在。

Bái Lǎoshī xiànzài bú zài bàngōngshì, kěshì tā míngtiān huì zài.

(Teacher Bai is not in the office now, but he will be tomorrow.)

(2) A: 你明年做什么？

Nǐ míngnián zuò shénme?

(What will you do next year?)

B: 我明年会去中国学中文。

Wǒ míngnián huì qù Zhōngguó xué Zhōngwén.

(I'll go to China to learn Chinese next year.)

(3) 他说他晚上会给你打电话。

Tā shuō tā wǎnshang huì gěi nǐ dǎ diànhuà.

(He said he will call you this evening.)

The negative form of 会 (huì) is 不会 (bú huì):

(4) 小王觉得不舒服，今天不会来上课。

Xiǎo Wáng juéde bù shūfu, jīntiān bú huì lái shàngkè.

(Xiao Wang is not feeling well. She won't come to class today.)

(5) 她很忙，晚上不会去看电影。

Tā hěn máng, wǎnshang bú huì qù kàn diànyǐng.

(She is very busy. She won't be going to see the movie tonight.)

4. The Adverb 又 (yòu, again)

又 (yòu, again) indicates repetition of an action.

(1) 他昨天看电影了，今天又看电影了。

Tā zuótiān kàn diànyǐng le, jīntiān yòu kàn diànyǐng le.

(He saw a movie yesterday, and saw another one today.)

(2) 前天下雨，昨天又下雨了。

Qiántiān xià yǔ, zuótiān yòu xià yǔ le.

(It rained the day before yesterday. Yesterday it rained again.)

(3) 妈妈昨天又给我打电话了。

Māma zuótiān yòu gěi wǒ dǎ diànhuà le.

(My mom called me again yesterday.)

Note: Both 又 (yòu, again) and 再 (zài, again) indicate repetition of an action, but in a sentence with 又 (yòu, again), both the original action and the repetition usually have occurred in the past, whereas 再 (zài, again) indicates an anticipated repetition of an action.

Compare:

(4) 我上个周末跳舞了，昨天我又去跳舞了。

Wǒ shàngge zhōumò tiào wǔ le, zuótiān wǒ yòu qù tiào wǔ le.

(I danced last weekend. Yesterday I went dancing again.)

(5) 我昨天跳舞了，我想明天晚上再去跳舞。

Wǒ zuótiān tiào wǔ le, wǒ xiǎng míngtiān wǎnshang zài qù tiào wǔ.

(I danced yesterday. I'm thinking of going dancing again tomorrow night.)

5. 又...又... (yòu...yòu..., both...and...)

The two adjectives used in this structure are either both commendatory or both derogatory, e.g., 又闷又热 (yòu mēn yòu rè, both stuffy and humid) [both adjectives are perceived to be derogatory], 又便宜又好 (yòu piányi yòu hǎo, both inexpensive and good) [both adjectives are commendatory].

PATTERN DRILLS

A. Comparative Sentences with 比 (bǐ)

1.	Yīngwén	<u>bǐ</u>	Zhōngwén	róngyì.
2.	Dì liù kè		dì wǔ kè	nán.
3.	Tiào wǔ		tīng yīnyuè	yǒu yìsi.
4.	Lǐ Xiǎojie		Wáng Xiānsheng	máng.
5.	Tā gēge		tā dìdi	gāo.
6.	Tā dìdi		tā gēge	shuài.
7.	Zhè jiàn yīfu		nà jiàn yīfu	piányi.
8.	Nà běn shū		zhè běn shū	guì.
9.	Tā de qián		wǒ de qián	duō.
10.	Jīntiān de tiānqì		zuótiān de tiānqì	nuǎnhuo.
11.	Shànghǎi		Táiběi	lěng.

1.	英文	<u>比</u>	中文	容易。
2.	第六课		第五课	难。
3.	跳舞		听音乐	有意思。
4.	李小姐		王先生	忙。
5.	她哥哥		她弟弟	高。

6. 他弟弟 他哥哥 帅。
7. 这件衣服 那件衣服 便宜。
8. 那本书 这本书 贵。
9. 她的钱 我的钱 多。
10. 今天的天气 昨天的天气 暖和。
11. 上海 台北 冷。

B. 了 (le) as Sentence-final Particle

Example: Zuótiān xià yǔ. (jīntiān, bú xià yǔ)

→ Jīntiān bú xià yǔ le.

昨天下雨。(今天， 不下雨)

→今天不下雨了。

1.	Wǒ qùnián xué Yīngwén.	(jīnnián	xué Zhōngwén)
2.	Tā zǎoshang xǐ zǎo le.	(wǎnshang	bù xǐ zǎo)
3.	Wǒ zuótiān chī Zhōngguó fàn le.	(jīntiān	bù chī Zhōngguó fàn)
4.	Lǐ Yǒu yǐqián xǐhuan chàng gē.	(xiànzài	xǐhuan tiào wǔ)
5.	Tā yǐqián xǐhuan Zhōngguó yīnyuè.	(xiànzài	xǐhuān Měiguó yīnyuè)
6.	Wǒ yǐqián bú huì yòng Zhōngwén xiě xìn.	(xiànzài	huì yòng Zhōngwén xiě xìn)
7.	Wǒ mèimei yǐqián chuān báisè de xié.	(xiànzài	chuān hēisè de xié)
8.	Shàngge xīngqī zhèr hěn rè.	(xiànzài	liángkuai)

1. 我去年学英文。 (今年 学中文)
2. 他早上洗澡了。 (晚上 不洗澡)
3. 我昨天吃中国饭了。 (今天 不吃中国饭)
4. 李友以前喜欢唱歌。 (现在 喜欢跳舞)

A Taipei street scene.

5. 他以前喜欢中国音乐。　(现在　喜欢美国音乐)
6. 我以前不会用中文写信。　(现在　会用中文写信)
7. 我妹妹以前穿白色的鞋。　(现在　穿黑色的鞋)
8. 上个星期这儿很热。　(现在　凉快)

C. 不但...而且 (búdàn…érqiě)

C1:

1.	Tā búdàn	huì shuō Zhōngwén,	érqiě	huì shuō Yīngwén.
2.		xǐhuan chàng gē,		xǐhuan tiào wǔ.
3.		huì zuò Měiguó fàn,		huì zuò Zhōngguó fàn.
4.		xiǎng kàn diànyǐng,		xiǎng kàn diànshì.
5.		xǐhuan bái yánsè,		xǐhuan hóng yánsè.
6.		liànxí le fāyīn,		tīng le kèwén lùyīn.
7.		fùxí le dì qī kè,		yùxí le dì bā kè.

C1:

1.	他不但	会说中文，	而且	会说英文。
2.		喜欢唱歌，		喜欢跳舞。

3.	会做美国饭，	会做中国饭。
4.	想看电影，	想看电视。
5.	喜欢白颜色，	喜欢红颜色。
6.	练习了发音，	听了课文录音。
7.	复习了第七课，	预习了第八课。

C2:

1.	Tāde dìdi	<u>búdàn</u>	hěn gāo,	<u>érqiě</u>	hěn shuài.
2.	Zhè jiàn yīfu		tài dà,		yánsè yě bù hǎo.
3.	Jīntiān de tiānqì		hěn mēn,		hěn rè.
4.	Táiwān de dōngtiān		hěn lěng,		hěn cháoshī.
5.	Dì shí kè de shēngcí		hěn duō,		hěn nán.
6.	Zhè shuāng xié		hěn guì,		hěn bù shūfu.
7.	Tā xiě zì		hěn hǎo,		hěn kuài.
8.	Xiǎo Gāo de jiā		hěn dà,		hěn piàoliang.

C2:

1.	他的弟弟	<u>不但</u>	很高，	<u>而且</u>	很帅。
2.	这件衣服		太大，		颜色也不好。
3.	今天的天气		很闷，		很热。
4.	台湾的冬天		很冷，		很潮湿。
5.	第十课的生词		很多，		很难。
6.	这双鞋		很贵，		很不舒服。
7.	他写字		很好，		很快。
8.	小高的家		很大，		很漂亮。

D. 会 (huì)

For each group of words below, write both a positive and a negative sentence using 会.

Example: Tiānqì yùbào shūo míngtiān xià yǔ

→Tiānqì yùbào shūo míngtiān huì xià yǔ.

→Tiānqì yùbào shūo míngtiān bú huì xià yǔ.

天气预报说 明天 下雨

→天气预报说明天会下雨。

→天气预报说明天不会下雨。

1.	Xiǎo Wáng	míngnián	qù Táiwān.
2.	Wáng Péng	jīntiān wǎnshang	jiāo Lǐ Yǒu xiě zì.
3.	Wǒmen	zhōumò	liànxí Zhōngwén.
4.	Lǐ Lǎoshī	xiàwǔ	qù kāi huì.
5.	Wáng Lǎoshī	míngtiān	qù kàn hóngyè.
6.	Xiǎo Gāo	xīngqīliù	qù tiào wǔ.
7.	Xiǎo Bái	xīngqītiān	qǐng wǒmen chī fàn.
8.	Lǐ Xiǎojie	míngtiān xiàwǔ	qù mǎi yīfu.

1.	小王	明年	去台湾。
2.	王朋	今天晚上	教李友写字。
3.	我们	周末	练习中文。
4.	李老师	下午	去开会。
5.	王老师	明天	去看红叶。
6.	小高	星期六	去跳舞。
7.	小白	星期天	请我们吃饭。
8.	李小姐	明天下午	去买衣服。

E. 又 (yòu)

For each group of words below, write a sentence using the 又 structure.

Example: xīngqīyī/xīngqī'èr yǒu Zhōngwénkè

→ Wǒ xīngqīyī yǒu Zhōngwénkè, xīngqī'èr yòu yǒu Zhōngwénkè.

星期一/星期二 有中文课

→我星期一有中文课，星期二又有中文课。

1. zuótiān shàngwǔ/jīntiān xiàwǔ dǎle yí ge diànhuà
2. zuótiān/jīntiān mǎile yí jiàn yīfu
3. shàng kè yǐqián/xià kè yǐhòu tīngle yí cì lùyīn
4. qùnián/jīnnián chūntiān qùle yí cì Táiwān
5. zuótiān/jīntiān qù kàn hóngyè le
6. zuótiān wǎnshang/jīntiān wǎnshang tiào wǔ le
7. shàngge xīngqī/zhège xīngqī kàn le yí ge Rìběn diànyǐng

1. 昨天上午/今天下午 打了一个电话
2. 昨天/今天 买了一件衣服
3. 上课以前/下课以后 听了一次录音
4. 去年/今年春天 去了一次台湾
5. 昨天/今天 去看红叶了

6. 昨天晚上/今天晚上　　跳舞了

7. 上个星期/这个星期　　看了一个日本电影

F. 又…又… (yòu…yòu…)

1.	Zhè shuāng xié	yòu	piányi	yòu	hǎokàn.
2.	Zhè jiàn yīfu		guì		nánkàn.
3.	Zhège diànnǎo		hǎo		piányi.
4.	Shànghǎi de xiàtiān		rè		mēn.
5.	Táiwān de dōngtiān		lěng		cháoshī.
6.	Tā de dìdi		gāo		shuài.
7.	Zhè běn shū		guì		méi yìsi.
8.	Dì bā kè		róngyì		yǒu yìsi.
9.	Xiǎo Gāo de jiā		shūfu		piàoliang.

1.	这双鞋	又	便宜	又	好看。
2.	这件衣服		贵		难看。
3.	这个电脑		好		便宜。
4.	上海的夏天		热		闷。
5.	台湾的冬天		冷		潮湿。
6.	他的弟弟		高		帅。

7.	这本书	贵	没意思。
8.	第八课	容易	有意思。
9.	小高的家	舒服	漂亮。

English Texts

DIALOGUE I

Miss Xie: The weather is better today than yesterday. It's no longer raining.

Mr. Lan: What's the weather going to be like tomorrow? I hope it won't rain tomorrow, either.

Miss Xie: I read the weather forecast in today's paper. The weather will be even better tomorrow than today. Not only will it not rain, but it will also be a bit warmer.

Mr. Lan: That's great. I asked Miss Li to go to the park with me to see the red autumn leaves tomorrow.

Miss Xie: Really? But Miss Li went to Shanghai this morning with Mr. Wang.

Mr. Lan: You don't say! What shall I do tomorrow?

Miss Xie: You can watch a video at home!

DIALOGUE II

Xiao Ye: Too bad. It's pouring again.

Xiao Xia: I just read the newspaper. The paper says the weather is going to be bad all week. It won't get better until next week.

Xiao Ye: Really? Then we can't go out this weekend. It's been too hot lately. It's really uncomfortable.

Xiao Xia: The weather is like this in the summer in Taipei. In two months the weather will be a bit cooler than it is now.

Xiao Ye: In two months? I'm going back to the United States next month.

Xiao Xia: In Taiwan it rains often in spring, and it's cold in winter. In summer it's hot and muggy. Next time you'd better come in the fall.

LESSON 11 ▲ Transportation
第十一课 ▲ 交通
Dì shíyī kè ▲ *Jiāotōng*

坐公共汽车

Zuò gōnggòng qìchē

Dialogue: Going Home for the Winter Vacation

VOCABULARY

1.	#寒假	hánjià	n	winter vacation
2.	飞机	fēijī	n	airplane
	飞	fēi	v	to fly
	机	jī	n	machine
3.	票	piào	n	ticket
4.	(飞)机场	(fēi)jīchǎng	n	airport

5.	坐	zuò	v	to travel by [see also L.5]
6.	公共汽车	gōnggòng qìchē	n	bus
	公共	gōnggòng	adj	public
	汽车	qìchē	n	automobile
	车	chē	n	vehicle; car
7.	或者	huòzhě	conj	or [see G2]
8.	地#铁	dìtiě	n	subway
9.	走	zǒu	v	to walk; to go by way of
10.	先	xiān	adv	first; before
11.	(车)站	(chē)zhàn	n	(bus, train, etc.) stop; station
12.	下车	xià chē	vo	to get off (a bus, train, etc.)
13.	然后	ránhòu	adv	then
14.	#绿	lǜ	adj	green
15.	#线	xiàn	n	line
16.	最后	zuìhòu	adv	finally
17.	#蓝	lán	adj	blue
18.	#麻#烦	máfan	adj	troublesome
19.	还是	háishi	conj	had better [see G4]
20.	出#租汽车	chūzū qìchē	n	taxi
	出租	chūzū	v	to rent out; to let
	租	zū	v	to rent
21.	开车	kāi chē	vo	to drive a car
	开	kāi	v	to drive; to operate
22.	送	sòng	v	to see off or out; to take someone (somewhere)

DIALOGUE

Wáng Péng:	Hánjià nǐ huí jiā ma?
Lǐ Yǒu:	Wǒ yào huí jiā.
Wáng Péng:	Fēijī piào nǐ mǎi le ma (G1)?
Lǐ Yǒu:	Yǐjīng mǎi le. Shì èrshíyī hào de.
Wáng Péng:	Fēijī shì jǐ diǎn de?
Lǐ Yǒu:	Wǎnshang bā diǎn de.
Wáng Péng:	Nǐ zěnme qù jīchǎng?
Lǐ Yǒu:	Wǒ xiǎng zuò gōnggòng qìchē huòzhě(G2) zuò dìtiě. Nǐ zhīdao zěnme zǒu ma?
Wáng Péng:	Nǐ xiān zuò yí hào(1) qìchē, zuò sān zhàn xià chē, ránhòu huàn dìtiě. Xiān zuò hóngxiàn, zài(G3) huàn lǜ xiàn, zuìhòu huàn lán xiàn.
Lǐ Yǒu:	Bù xíng, bù xíng, tài máfan le. Wǒ háishi(G4) zuò chūzū qìchē(2) ba.
Wáng Péng:	Zuò chūzū qìchē tài guì, wǒ kěyǐ kāi chē sòng nǐ qù.
Lǐ Yǒu:	Xièxie nǐ.
Wáng Péng:	Bú yòng kèqi.

DIALOGUE

王朋：	寒假你回家吗？
李友：	我要回家。
王朋：	飞机票你买了吗(G1)？
李友：	已经买了。是二十一号的。
王朋：	飞机是几点的？
李友：	晚上八点的。
王朋：	你怎么去机场？
李友：	我想坐公共汽车或者(G2)坐地铁。你知道怎么走吗？

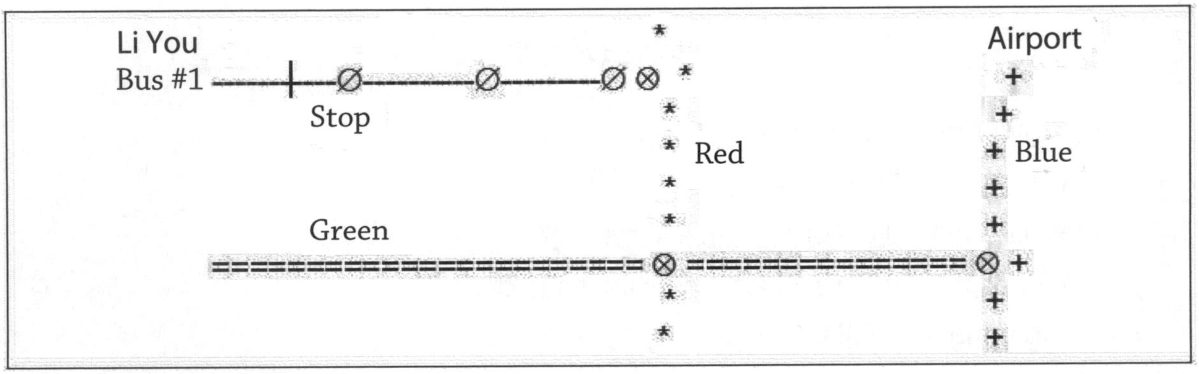

The route from Li You's home to the airport.

王朋：你先坐一号(1)汽车，坐三站下车，然后换地铁。先坐红线，再(G3)换绿线，最后换蓝线。

李友：不行，不行，太麻烦了。我还是(G4)坐出租汽车(2)吧。

王朋：坐出租汽车太贵，我可以开车送你去。

李友：谢谢你。

王朋：不用客气。

Notes

▲1▲ Both 号 (hào) and 路 (lù) are used to refer to bus routes. Therefore, 一路车 (yí lù chē) also refers to bus route #1.

▲2▲ In Taiwan taxis are called 计程车 (jìchéngchē) or 出租车 (chūzūchē).

▲3▲ In addition to 公共汽车 (gōnggòng qìchē): 公轿车 (gōngjiāochē) and 公车 (gōngchē) are also used for buses.

A Letter: Thanking Someone for a Ride

VOCABULARY

1.	不过	búguò	conj	however; but
2.	让	ràng	v	to allow or cause (somebody to do something)
3.	花	huā	v	to spend
4.	不好意思	bù hǎoyìsi	ce	to feel embarrassed
5.	这几天	zhè jǐ tiān	np	the past few days
6.	每天	měitiān		every day
	每	měi	prep	every; each (usually followed by a measure word)
7.	高速公路	gāosù gōnglù		super highway; highway
	高速	gāosù	adj	high speed
	公路	gōnglù	n	highway; road
	路	lù	n	road; path
8.	紧张	jǐnzhāng	adj	nervous, anxious
9.	自己	zìjǐ	pr	oneself
10.	新年	xīnnián	n	new year
11.	快	kuài	adv	soon; be about to; before long (usually takes 了 {le} at the end of the sentence)
12.	快乐	kuàilè	adj	happy

A LETTER

Wáng Péng:

Xièxie nǐ nà tiān kāi chē sòng wǒ dào jīchǎng. Búguò, ràng nǐ huā nàme duō shíjiān, zhēn bù hǎoyìsi. Wǒ zhè jǐ tiān <u>měi</u> tiān <u>dōu</u>(G5) kāi chē chūqu kàn lǎo péngyou. Zhèr de rén kāi chē kāi de hěn kuài. Wǒ zài gāosù gōnglù shang kāi chē, zhēn yǒu diǎnr jǐnzhāng. Kěshì zhèr méiyǒu gōnggòng qìchē, yě méiyǒu dìtiě, hěn bù fāngbiàn, zhǐ néng zìjǐ kāi chē.

Xīnnián kuài dào le, zhù(F) nǐ xīnnián kuàilè!

Lǐ Yǒu

Shí'èryuè èrshíliù rì

A LETTER

王朋：

谢谢你那天开车送我到机场。不过，让你花那么多时间，真不好意思。我这几天<u>每</u>天<u>都</u>(G5)开车出去看老朋友。这儿的人开车开得很快。我在高速公路上开车，真有点儿紧张。可是这儿没有公共汽车，也没有地铁，很不方便，只能自己开车。

新年快到了，祝(F)你新年快乐！

李友

十二月二十六日

FUNCTIONAL EXPRESSIONS

祝 **(zhù, to offer good wishes)**

祝你新年快乐！ (I wish you a happy New Year!)

Zhù nǐ xīnnián kuàilè!

祝你生日快乐！ (Happy Birthday to you!)

Zhù nǐ shēngrì kuàilè!

祝你考试考得好！ (I wish you success with the exam!)

Zhù nǐ kǎoshì kǎo de hǎo!

祝寒假快乐！ (Have a happy winter break!)

Zhù hánjià kuàilè!

祝圣诞快乐！ (Merry Christmas!)

Zhù Shèngdàn kuàilè!

祝春节快乐！ (Happy Chinese New Year!)

Zhù Chūnjié kuàilè!

Culture Notes

▲1▲ In China the railroad system has long constituted the principal means of travel as well as transport in general. However, in recent years both the highway system and airline travel have expanded very rapidly. China now ranks second only to the United States in total roadway miles covered by the highway system.

▲2▲ Chinese New Year, which is determined by the lunar calendar and usually falls in late January or early February, is the most important annual holiday in China and Taiwan. However, nowadays the January 1 international New Year is also recognized. The most common New Year greetings are "新年好" (xīnnián hǎo) and "新年快乐" (xīnnián kuàilè), which can be used for both New Years, but for the Chinese New Year many people prefer the traditional greeting: 恭喜发财 (gōngxǐ fācái). The phrase, which literally means "Congratulations and may you make a fortune," can be translated as "May you be happy and prosperous!"

SUPPLEMENTARY VOCABULARY

1.	走路	zǒu lù	vo	to walk
2	火车	huǒchē	n	train
3.	计程车	jìchéngchē	n	taxi (in Taiwan)
4.	电车	diànchē	n	cable car; trolley bus; tram
5.	船	chuán	n	boat; ship

6.	辆	liàng	m	(a measure for vehicles)
7.	暑假	shǔjià	n	summer vacation

A( )

B( )

C( )

D( )

Review Dialogue I and put the above pictures in the correct sequence by using the numbers 1–4.

Grammar

1. Topic-Comment Sentences

When a noun or noun phrase has become established as a known element in a conversation, it can occur at the beginning of the sentence, serving as the "topic," with the rest of the sentence functioning as a "comment" on it. This forms what is known as a "topic-comment sentence." In such a sentence the object of the verb can be brought forward to serve as the topic of the sentence.

(1) A: 我昨天买了一本书。

Wǒ zuótiān mǎile yì běn shū.

(I bought a book yesterday.)

B: 那本书你看了吗?

Nà běn shū nǐ kànle ma?

(Have you read that book?)

(2) A: 你知道我的衬衫在哪儿吗?

Nǐ zhīdao wǒ de chènshān zài nǎr ma?

(Do you know where my shirt is?)

B: 你的衬衫我给你妈妈了。

Nǐ de chènshān wǒ gěi nǐ māma le.

(I have given your shirt to your mother.)

(3) A: 你有朋友吗?

Nǐ yǒu péngyou ma?

(Do you have friends?)

B: 朋友我有很多,可是都不在这儿。

Péngyou wǒ yǒu hěn duō, kěshì dōu bú zài zhèr.

(I have many friends, but none of them are here.)

(4) 她不想去日本,可是飞机票她妈妈已经买好了。

Tā bù xiǎng qù Rìběn, kěshì fēijīpiào tā māma yǐjīng mǎi hǎo le.

(She does not want to go to Japan, but her mother has already booked the airplane ticket.)

2. 或者 (huòzhě, or) and 还是 (háishi, or)

While both 或者 (huòzhě, or) and 还是 (háishi, or) link up two words or phrases that indicate different alternatives, the former usually appears in statements and the latter in questions.

A subway entrance in Beijing.

(1) A: 你今天晚上做什么？

Nǐ jīntiān wǎnshang zuò shénme?

(What are you going to do tonight?)

B: 听音乐或者看录像。

Tīng yīnyuè huòzhě kàn lùxiàng.

(Listen to music or watch a video tape.)

(2) A: 你喜欢学中文还是喜欢学日文？

Nǐ xǐhuan xué Zhōngwén háishi xǐhuan xué Rìwén?

(Do you like studying Chinese or Japanese?)

B: 中文或者日文我都喜欢学。

Zhōngwén huòzhě Rìwén wǒ dōu xǐhuan xué.

(Whether it's Chinese or Japanese, I like studying both [equally].)

(3) A: 你喜欢什么颜色的鞋？ 黑的还是咖啡色的？

Nǐ xǐhuan shénme yánsè de xié? Hēi de háishi kāfēisè de?

(What color shoes do you like, black or brown?)

Taking a taxi.

B: 黑的或者咖啡色的我都不喜欢，我喜欢白的。

Hēi de huòzhě kāfēisè de wǒ dōu bù xǐhuan, wǒ xǐhuan bái de.

(I don't like either black or brown; I like white ones.)

(4) A: 你晚上看电影还是看电视？

Nǐ wǎnshang kàn diànyǐng háishi kàn diànshì?

(Are you going to see a movie or watch TV this evening?)

B: 看电影或者看电视都可以。

Kàn diànyǐng huòzhě kàn diànshì dōu kěyǐ.

(Either going to a movie or watching TV would be fine with me.)

(5) 明天你去开会或者他去开会都可以。

Míngtiān nǐ qù kāi huì huòzhě tā qù kāi huì dōu kěyǐ.

(Either you or he may attend tomorrow's meeting.)

3. 先. . . 再. . . (xiān...zài..., first..., then...)

Sometimes 再 (zài) indicates a sequence of actions rather than a repetition. "先看电影再吃饭" (Xiān kàn diànyǐng zài chī fàn; First go to the movie, then eat) means "看电影以后吃饭" (Kàn diànyǐng yǐhòu chī fàn; Eat after seeing the movie). More examples:

China-based Air China.

(1) A: 你什么时候给妈妈打电话?

Nǐ shénme shíhou gěi māma dǎ diànhuà?

(When are you going to call Mom?)

B: 下课以后再打。

Xiàkè yǐhòu zài dǎ.

(I'll call after class.)

(2) 我想先打球再去图书馆。

Wǒ xiǎng xiān dǎ qiú zài qù túshūguǎn.

(I'm thinking of going to the library after playing ball.)

(3) 你先做功课再看电视。

Nǐ xiān zuò gōngkè zài kàn diànshì.

(You'd better finish doing the homework before you watch TV.)

Note: As adverbs, 先 (xiān) and 再 (zài) must come immediately before a verb. They cannot be placed in front of the subject.

(3a) *先你做功课再你看电视。

*Xiān nǐ zuò gōngkè zài nǐ kàn diànshì.

Name the three forms of transportation above.

4. 还是 (háishi, had better)

还是 (háishi, had better) can be used to signify making a selection after considering two or more options. Sometimes in making such a decision one is forced to give up one's preference.

(1) A: 高先生：下雨了。怎么办？

Gāo Xiānsheng: Xià yǔ le. Zěnme bàn?

(Mr. Gao: It's raining. What shall we do?)

B: 白小姐：我们还是在家看录像吧。

Bái Xiǎojie: Wǒmen háishi zài jiā kàn lùxiàng ba.

(Miss Bai: We had better stay home and watch a video.)

(2) A: 你说，明天看电影还是看打球？

Nǐ shuō, míngtiān kàn diànyǐng háishi kàn dǎ qiú?

(What do you think we should watch tomorrow, a movie or a ball game?)

B: 还是看电影吧。

Háishi kàn diànyǐng ba.

(Let's go see a movie.)

5. 每...都...(měi...dōu..., every...)

In a sentence that contains the term 每 (měi, every), usually 都 (dōu, all) has to be inserted further along in the sentence, immediately in front of the verb.

(1) 他每天晚上都看电视。

Tā měi tiān wǎnshang dōu kàn diànshì.

(He watches TV every evening.)

Taiwan-based China Airlines.

(2) 我每节课都来。

Wǒ měi jié kè dōu lái.

(I come to every class.)

(3) 这儿每个人我都认识。

Zhèr měi gè rén wǒ dōu rènshi.

(I know everyone here.)

(4) 王老师写的字每个都好看。

Wáng Lǎoshī xiě de zì měi gè dōu hǎokàn.

(Every character written by Teacher Wang looks nice.)

PATTERN DRILLS

A. Topic-comment Sentences

Write a topic-comment sentence based on each sentence given below.

Example: Nǐ yǒu hěn duō péngyou ma?

→ Péngyou wǒ yǒu hěn duō.

你有很多朋友吗?

→朋友我有很多。

1. Nǐ chángcháng qù Xiǎo Bái jiā ma?
2. Tā dìdi huì bu huì xiě Zhōngwén xìn?

3. Nǐ yǐjīng mǎile diànnǎo ma?
4. Nǐ xiǎng kàn nàge diànyǐng ma?
5. Tā chángcháng hē píjiǔ ma?
6. Nǐ mǎi méi mǎi fēijīpiào?
7. Nǐ dìdi xǐhuan bù xǐhuan kàn Zhōngwén shū?
8. Tā chángcháng tīng Méiguó yīnyuè ma?

1. 你常常去小白家吗?
2. 她弟弟会不会写中文信?
3. 你已经买了电脑吗?
4. 你想看那个电影吗?
5. 他常常喝啤酒吗?
6. 你买没买飞机票?
7. 你弟弟喜欢不喜欢看中文书?
8. 她常常听美国音乐吗?

B. 或者 (huòzhě)

For each group of words below, write a sentence containing 或者.

Example: (jīntiān wǎnshang, kàn diànshì/kàn diànyǐng)

→ Jīntiān wǎnshang wǒ xiǎng kàn diànshì huòzhě kàn diànyǐng.

(今天晚上, 看电视/看电影)

→今天晚上我想看电视或者看电影。

1. míngtiān shàngwǔ — zhǎo Wáng Lǎoshī/zhǎo Lǐ Lǎoshī wèn wèntí
2. míngtiān xiàwǔ — qù dǎ qiú/qù tiào wǔ
3. jīntiān wǎnshang — chī Zhōngguó fàn/chī Rìběn fàn

北京的公共汽车

Běijīng de gōnggòng qìchē

4. xiàge xuéqí — xué Zhōngwén/xué Rìwén
5. xīngqīliù/xīngqītiān — kàn lùxiàng
6. zuò dìtiě/zuò gōnggòng qìchē — qù Wáng Lǎoshī jiā
7. jīnnián/míngnián — qù Táiwān
8. xiàwǔ sān diǎn/sì diǎn — qù Xiǎo Bái jiā
9. jīntiān xiàwǔ/wánshang — zuò gōngkè

1. 明天上午 — 找王老师/找李老师问问题
2. 明天下午 — 去打球/去跳舞
3. 今天晚上 — 吃中国饭/吃日本饭
4. 下个学期 — 学中文/学日文
5. 星期六/星期天 — 看录像
6. 坐地铁/坐公共汽车 — 去王老师家
7. 今年/明年 — 去台湾
8. 下午三点/四点 — 去小白家
9. 今天下午/晚上 — 做功课

Shanghai Railway Station.

C. 先 . . . 再 . . . (xiān…zài…)

For each group of words below, create a sentence containing the 先…再… pattern.

Example: (chī zǎofàn, qù túshūguǎn)

→ Wǒ xiān chī zǎofàn, zài qù túshūguǎn.

（吃早饭，去图书馆）

→我先吃早饭，再去图书馆。

1.	qù túshūguǎn	shàng Zhōngwénkè
2.	shàng Zhōngwénkè	shàng diànnǎokè
3.	chī wǎnfàn	qù kàn diànyǐng
4.	zuò gōngkè	qù dǎ qiú
5.	liànxí fāyīn	xiě Hànzì
6.	hē píjiǔ	chī fàn
7.	kàn lùxiàng	tiào wǔ
8.	tīng Měiguó yīnyuè	tīng Zhōngguó yīnyuè

1.	去图书馆	上中文课
2.	上中文课	上电脑课
3.	吃晚饭	去看电影

Entering Shanghai Railway Station.

4. 做功课　　去打球
5. 练习发音　　写汉字
6. 喝啤酒　　吃饭
7. 看录像　　跳舞
8. 听美国音乐　　听中国音乐

D. 还是 (háishi)

For each group of words below, write a question with 还是, and then answer the question using 还是. Use the underlined words in your answer.

Example: kàn hóngyè　　<u>kàn lùxiàng</u>

→ A: Wǒmen qù gōngyuán kàn hóngyè háishi zài jiā kàn lùxiàng?

→ B: Wǒmen háishi zài jiā kàn lùxiàng ba.

看红叶　　<u>看录像</u>

→A: 我们去公园看红叶还是在家看录像？

→B: 我们还是在家看录像吧。

Taipei Rapid Transit Station.

1.	kàn diànyǐng	kàn diànshì
2.	xué Zhōngwén	xué Fǎwén
3.	qù Táiběi wánr	qù Shànghǎi wánr
4.	shàng Zhōngwénkè	shàng diànnǎokè
5.	xiān dǎ qiú	xiān zuò gōngkè
6.	qù chī Zhōngguó fàn	qù chī Měiguó fàn
7.	jīnnián qù Táiwān	míngnián qù Táiwān
8.	qù túshūguǎn zuò gōngkè	zài sùshè zuò gōngkè

1.	看电影	看电视
2.	学中文	学法文
3.	去台北玩儿	去上海玩儿
4.	上中文课	上电脑课
5.	先打球	先做功课
6.	去吃中国饭	去吃美国饭
7.	今年去台湾	明年去台湾
8.	去图书馆做功课	在宿舍做功课

中国的高速公路

Zhōngguó de gāosù gōnglù

E. 每...都... (měi...dōu...)

For each group of words below, create a sentence containing the 每...都... pattern.

Example: (wǎnshang, kàn diànshì)

→ Tā měitiān wǎnshang dōu kàn diànshì.

(晚上 看电视)

→他每天晚上都看电视。

1. xiàwǔ liànxí Zhōngwén
2. zǎoshang tīng Zhōngwén lùyīn
3. zì xiě de hěn hǎo
4. yīfu shì xīn de
5. rén rènshi
6. wǎnshang shí diǎnzhōng shuì jiào
7. xīngqīliù gěi māma dǎ diànhuà
8. chènshān shì báisè de
9. shū hěn yǒuyìsi

1. 下午 练习中文
2. 早上 听中文录音

3. 字　写得很好
4. 衣服　是新的
5. 人　认识
6. 晚上　十点钟睡觉
7. 星期六　给妈妈打电话
8. 衬衫　是白色的
9. 书　很有意思

English Texts

DIALOGUE

Wang Peng:	Are you going home during the winter break?
Li You:	Yes, I am.
Wang Peng:	Have you booked a plane ticket?
Li You:	Yes. It's for the twenty-first.
Wang Peng:	When is the plane leaving?
Li You:	8 p.m.
Wang Peng:	How are you going to the airport?
Li You:	I'm thinking of taking the bus or the subway. Do you know how to get there?
Wang Peng:	You first take bus No. 1. Get off after three stops. Then take the subway. First take the red line, then change to the green line, and finally change to the blue line.
Li You:	Oh no, oh no. That's too much trouble. I'd better take a cab.
Wang Peng:	It's too expensive to take a cab. I can take you to the airport.
Li You:	Thank you very much.
Wang Peng:	Don't mention it.

A sleeper car in a Chinese train.

A LETTER

December 26

Wang Peng:

Thank you for driving me to the airport the other day. But I'm really embarrassed about having had you spend so much time. The past few days I've been going out by car to see old friends. People here drive fast. I was really nervous driving on the highway. But there are no public buses or subway. It's very inconvenient. I have to drive.

New Year is almost here. Happy New Year!

Li You

Taxi Drivers in China

Many taxi drivers in China, especially those in Beijing, are known to be very outgoing and talkative. If you go to China and your taxi driver happens to be a chatty one, it may be a good opportunity for you to learn about ordinary Chinese people's lives, and about their opinions on current affairs.

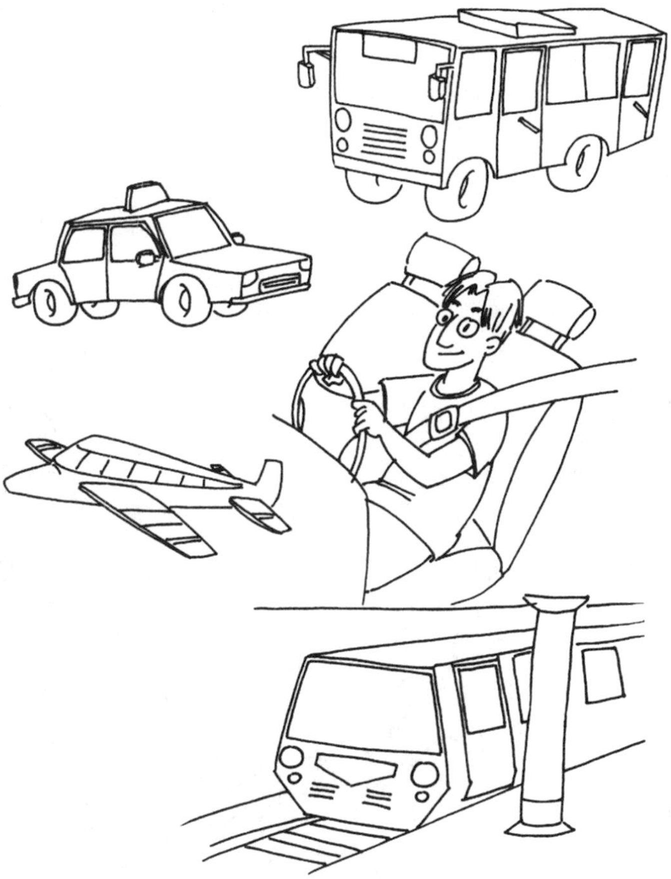

Describe the modes of transportation above.

中国地图

Map of China

APPENDIX: PLACE NAMES IN CHINA

Provinces and Their Capital Cities

Province Name		Capital City	
1. 安徽	Ānhuī	合肥	Héféi
2. 福建	Fújiàn	福州	Fúzhōu
3. 甘肃	Gānsù	兰州	Lánzhōu
4. 广东	Guǎngdōng	广州	Guǎngzhōu
5. 贵州	Guìzhōu	贵阳	Guìyáng
6. 海南	Hǎinán	海口	Hǎikǒu
7. 河北	Héběi	石家庄	Shíjiāzhuāng
8. 河南	Hénán	郑州	Zhèngzhōu
9. 黑龙江	Hēilóngjiāng	哈尔滨	Hā'ěrbīn
10. 湖北	Húběi	武汉	Wǔhàn
11. 湖南	Húnán	长沙	Chángshā
12. 吉林	Jílín	长春	Chángchūn
13. 江苏	Jiāngsū	南京	Nánjīng
14. 江西	Jiāngxī	南昌	Nánchāng
15. 辽宁	Liáoníng	沈阳	Shěnyáng
16. 青海	Qīnghǎi	西宁	Xīníng
17. 山东	Shāndōng	济南	Jǐnán
18. 山西	Shānxī	太原	Tàiyuán
19. 陕西	Shǎnxī	西安	Xī'ān
20. 四川	Sìchuān	成都	Chéngdū
21. 云南	Yúnnán	昆明	Kūnmíng
22. 浙江	Zhèjiāng	杭州	Hángzhōu
23. 台湾	Táiwān		

Municipalities Directly under the Central Government and the Provinces in Which They Are Located

Municipality		Province	
1. 北京	Běijīng	河北	Héběi
2. 上海	Shànghǎi	江苏	Jiāngsū
3. 天津	Tiānjīn	河北	Héběi
4. 重庆	Chóngqìng	四川	Sìchuān

Autonomous Regions and Their Capital Cities

Autonomous Region		Capital City	
1. 内蒙古自治区	Nèi Ménggǔ Zìzhìqū	呼和浩特	Hūhéhàotè (Huhhot)
2. 广西壮族自治区	Guǎngxī Zhuàngzú Zìzhìqū	南宁	Nánníng
3. 宁夏回族自治区	Níngxià Huízú Zìzhìqū	银川	Yínchuān
4. 新疆维吾尔自治区	Xīnjiāng Wéiwǔ'ěr (Uygur) Zìzhìqū	乌鲁木齐	Wūlǔmùqí (Urumqi)
5. 西藏自治区	Xīzàng Zìzhìqū	拉萨	Lāsà (Lhasa)

Special Administrative Regions

1. 香港特别行政区	Xiānggǎng tèbié xíngzhèng qū	Hong Kong	Xiānggǎng
2. 澳门特别行政区	Aòmén tèbié xíngzhèng qū	Macau/Macao	Aòmén

Other Major Cities in China and the Provinces in Which They Are Located

City		Province	
1. 重庆	Chóngqìng	四川	Sìchuān
2. 青岛	Qīngdǎo	山东	Shāndōng
3. 大连	Dàlián	辽宁	Liáoníng
4. 桂林	Guìlín	广西壮族自治区	Guǎngxī Zhuàngzú Zìzhìqū

Major Cities in Taiwan

1. 台北	Táiběi	Taipei
2. 高雄	Gāoxióng	Kaohsiung
3. 台中	Táizhōng	Taichung
4. 台南	Táinán	Tainan
5. 台东	Táidōng	Taitung
6. 花莲	Huālián	Hualien

Vocabulary Index (Chinese-English): Lessons 1–11

Key: c=Culture Notes; f=Functional Expressions; g=Grammar; n=Notes; s=Supplementary Vocabulary

The Chinese-English index is alphabetized by Chinese characters and their pronunciation. Words containing the same Chinese characters are first grouped together. Homonyms appear in order of their tonal pronunciation (i.e., first tones first, second tones second, third tones third, and fourth tones last).

Pinyin	Traditional Characters	Simplified Characters	Grammar	English	Lesson
A					
a	啊	啊	P	(a sentence-final particle of exclamation, interrogation, etc.)	6
B					
ba	吧	吧	P	(a "suggestion" particle; softens the tone of the sentence to which it is appended)	5
bā	八	八	Nu	eight	Intro.
bāyuè	八月	八月	N	August	3g
bàba	爸爸	爸爸	N	dad; father	2
bái	白	白	Adj	white; (a surname)	3
bǎi	百	百	Nu	hundred	9
Bǎishìkělè	百事可樂	百事可乐	N	Pepsi	5s
bàn	半	半	Nu	half; half an hour	3
bànyè	半夜	半夜	T	midnight	7
bàngōngshì	辦公室	办公室	N	office	6
bāng	幫	帮	V	to help	6
bāng máng	幫忙	帮忙	VO	to help; to do someone a favor	6
bāngzhù	幫助	帮助	V	to help	7
bàngqiú	棒球	棒球	N	baseball	4s
bào	報	报	N	newspaper	8
bàoshang	報上	报上		in the newspaper	10
bēi	杯	杯	M	cup; glass	5
Běijīng	北京	北京	PN	Beijing	10s
běnzi	本子	本子	N	notebook	7s
bǐ	筆	笔	N	pen	7
bǐ	比	比	Prep	(a comparison marker)	10

Pinyin	Traditional Characters	Simplified Characters	Grammar	English	Lesson
biǎo	錶	表	N	watch	3s
bié	別	别		don't	6
bié (de)	別(的)	别(的)	Adv	other	4
bié kèqi	別客氣	别客气	CE	Don't be so polite!	6
biérén	別人	别人	N	others; other people; another person	4
bù	不	不	Adv	not; no	1
búcuò	不錯	不错	Adj	not bad; pretty good	4
búdàn..., érqiě	不但…而且	不但…而且	Conj	not only..., but also	10
búguò	不過	不过	Conj	however; but	11
bú kèqi	不客氣	不客气	CE	You are welcome. Don't be (so) polite.	6
bú xiè	不謝	不谢	CE	Don't mention it. Not at all. You're welcome.	7
bú yòng	不用	不用	CE	need not	6g, 9
bù hǎoyìsi	不好意思	不好意思	CE	to feel embarrassed	11
bùshǒu	部首	部首	N	radical	Intro.
▴C▴					
cái	才	才	Adv	not until; only then	5
cāntīng	餐廳	餐厅	N	dining room; cafeteria	8
chá	茶	茶	N	tea	5
chà	差	差	V	to be short of; to be lacking	3s
cháng	長	长	Adj	long	9s
chángcháng	常常	常常	Adv	often	4
Chángjiāng	長江	长江	PN	Yangtze river	10c
chángpáo	長袍	长袍	N	long gown	9c
chángshòu	長壽	长寿	N	longevity	3c
chángshòu miàn	長壽麵	长寿面	N	longevity noodles	3c
chàng	唱	唱	V	to sing	4
chàng gē	唱歌	唱歌	VO	to sing (a song)	4
cháoshī	潮濕	潮湿	Adj	wet; humid	10s
chē	車	车	N	vehicle; car	11
(chē)zhàn	車站	车站	N	(bus, train, etc.) stop; station	11
chén	陳	陈	N	(a surname)	1n
chènshān	襯衫	衬衫	N	shirt	9
chī	吃	吃	V	to eat	3
chī fàn	吃飯	吃饭	VO	to eat (a meal)	3
Chóngqìng	重慶	重庆	PN	Chongqing	10c
chūqu	出去	出去	VP	to go out	10
chūzū	出租	出租	V	to rent out; to let	11
chūzū qìchē	出租汽車	出租汽车	N	taxi	11
chūzhōng	初中	初中	N	junior high (grades 7–9)	2c
chúle...yǐwài	除了…以外	除了…以外	Conj	in addition to; besides	8
chūntiān	春天	春天	N	spring	10

Pinyin	Traditional Characters	Simplified Characters	Grammar	English	Lesson
chuān	穿	穿	V	to wear; to put on	9
chuán	船	船	N	boat; ship	11s
chuáng	床	床	N	bed	2g, 8
cì	次	次	M	time; (a measure word for occurrence)	10
cuò	錯	错	Adj	wrong	4
D					
dǎ	打	打	V	to hit; to strike	4
dǎ diànhuà	打電話	打电话	VO	to make a phone call	6
dǎ gōng	打工	打工	VO	to work part-time; to do manual work	5s
dǎ qiú	打球	打球	VO	to play ball	4
dà	大	大	Adj	big; old	3
dàgē	大哥	大哥	N	oldest brother	7g
dàjiā	大家	大家	Pr	everybody	7
dàjiě	大姐	大姐	N	oldest sister	7g
dàxiǎo	大小	大小	N	size	9
dàxué	大學	大学	N	university; college	2
dàxuéshēng	大學生	大学生	N	college student	2
dàyī	大衣	大衣	N	overcoat	9s
dài	戴	戴	V	to wear (hat, glasses, etc.)	9s
dànshì	但是	但是	Conj	but	6
dào	到	到	V	to arrive	8
dào…qù	到…去	到…去		to go to (a place)	6
de	的	的	P	(a possessive, modifying, or descriptive particle)	2
de	得	得	P	(a structural particle)	7
de shíhou	的時候	的时候		when…; at the time of…	8
Déguó	德國	德国	PN	Germany	1s
Déguórén	德國人	德国人	N	German people/person	1s
Déwén	德文	德文	N	the German language	6s
děi	得	得	AV	must; to have to	6
děng	等	等	V	to wait; to wait for	6
dì	第	第	prefix	(a prefix for ordinal numbers)	7
dìdi	弟弟	弟弟	N	younger brother	2
dìtiě	地鐵	地铁	N	subway	11
diǎn	點	点	M	o'clock	3
diǎn(r)	點(兒)	点(儿)	M	a little; a bit; some	5
diǎnzhōng	點鐘	点钟	M	o'clock	3
diàn	電	电	N	electricity	4
diànchē	電車	电车	N	cable car; trolley bus; tram	11s
diànhuà	電話	电话	N	telephone	6
diànnǎo	電腦	电脑	N	computer	8
diànshì	電視	电视	N	TV	4
diànyǐng	電影	电影	N	movie	4
diànzǐ jìsuànjī	電子計算機	电子计算机	N	computer	8n

Pinyin	Traditional Characters	Simplified Characters	Grammar	English	Lesson
dǐng	頂	顶	M	(a measure word for hat)	9s
dōngtiān	冬天	冬天	N	winter	10
dōngxi	東西	东西	N	things; objects	9
dǒng	懂	懂	V	to understand	7
dōu	都	都	Adv	both; all	2
duǎn	短	短	Adj	short	9s
duì	對	对	Adj	right; correct	4
duì bu qǐ	對不起	对不起	CE	I'm sorry.	5
duì le	對了	对了	CE	That's right!	4s
duō	多	多	Adv	how many/much; to what extent	3
duō	多	多	Adj	many; much	7
duō dà	多大	多大	CE	how old	3
duōshao	多少	多少	QW	how much; how many	9
▴E▴					
Éguó	俄國	俄国	PN	Russia	6s
Éwén	俄文	俄文	N	the Russian language	6s
érzi	兒子	儿子	N	son	2
èr	二	二	Nu	two	Intro.
èrgē	二哥	二哥	N	second oldest brother	7g
èrjiě	二姐	二姐	N	second oldest sister	7g
èryuè	二月	二月	N	February	3g
▴F▴					
fācái	發財	发财	V	to make a fortune	11c
fāyīn	發音	发音	N	pronunciation	8
Fǎguó	法國	法国	PN	France	1s
Fǎguórén	法國人	法国人	N	French people/person	1s
Fǎwén	法文	法文	N	the French language	6s
fántǐzì	繁體字	繁体字	N	traditional character	7c
fàn	飯	饭	N	meal; (cooked) rice	3
fāngbiàn	方便	方便	Adj	convenient	6
fēi	飛	飞	V	to fly	11
fēijī	飛機	飞机	N	airplane	11
fēijīchǎng	飛機場	飞机场	N	airport	11
Fēilǜbīn	菲律賓	菲律宾	PN	the Philippines	6s
fēn	分	分	M	minute	3s
fēn	分	分	M	1/100 of a kuai; cent	9
fěnhóngsè	粉紅色	粉红色	N	pink	9s
fēng	封	封	M	(measure word for letters)	8
fù qián	付錢	付钱	VO	to pay money	9
fúwùyuán	服務員	服务员	N	service person; waiter; waitress	9n
fùxí	復習	复习	V	to review	7
▴G▴					
gǎnlǎn	橄欖	橄榄	N	olive	4s
gǎnlǎnqiú	橄欖球	橄榄球	N	American style football (used in Taiwan)	4s

Pinyin	Traditional Characters	Simplified Characters	Grammar	English	Lesson
gāngbǐ	鋼筆	钢笔	N	fountain pen	7s
gāngcái	刚才	刚才	T	just now; a moment ago	10
gāo	高	高		(a surname); tall	2
gāosù	高速	高速	Adj	high speed	11
gāosù gōnglù	高速公路	高速公路	N	super highway; highway	11
gāoxìng	高興	高兴	Adj	happy; pleased	5
gāozhōng	高中	高中	N	senior high (grades 10–12)	2c
gàosu	告訴	告诉	V	to tell	8
gē	歌	歌	N	song	4
gēge	哥哥	哥哥	N	older brother	2
gè	個	个	M	(a common measure word)	2
gěi	給	给	V	to give	5
gěi	給	给	Prep	to; for	6
gēn	跟	跟	Conj	and	7
gèng	更	更	Adv	even more	10
gōnggòng	公共	公共	Adj	public	11
gōngchē	公車	公车	N	bus	11
gōngjiāochē	公轎車	公轿车	N	bus	11
gōnggòng qìchē	公共汽車	公共汽车	N	bus	11
gōngkè	功課	功课	N	schoolwork; homework	7
gōnglù	公路	公路	N	highway; road	11
gōngxǐ	恭喜	恭喜	V	to congratulate	11c
gōngxǐ fācái	恭喜發財	恭喜发财	CE	Congratulations and may you make a fortune!	11n
gōngyuán	公園	公园	N	park	10
gōngzuò	工作	工作	V/N	to work; job	5
guì	貴	贵	Adj	honorable	1
guì	貴	贵	Adj	expensive	9
guì xìng	貴姓	贵姓	CE	What is your honorable surname?	1
H					
Hā'ěrbīn	哈爾濱	哈尔滨	PN	Harbin	10c
hái	還	还	Adv	also; too; as well	3
háishi	還是	还是	Conj	or	3
háishi	還是	还是	Conj	had better	11
hái yǒu	還有	还有		also there are	3
háizi	孩子	孩子	N	child	2
Hǎinán	海南	海南	PN	Hainan	10c
Hánguó	韓國	韩国	PN	Korea	6s
Hánguórén	韓國人	韩国人	N	Korean people/person	1s
Hánwén	韓文	韩文	N	the Korean language	6s
hánjià	寒假	寒假	N	winter vacation	11
Hànyǔ	漢語	汉语	N	Chinese language	6n
Hànzì	漢字	汉字	N	Chinese character	7
hǎo	好	好	Adj	fine; good; nice; O.K.	1, 3
hǎochī	好吃	好吃	Adj	good to eat; delicious	5s

Pinyin	Traditional Characters	Simplified Characters	Grammar	English	Lesson
hǎohē	好喝	好喝	Adj	good to drink; tasty	5s
hǎojiǔ	好久	好久	CE	a long time	4
hǎokàn	好看	好看	Adj	good-looking	5s, 7n
hǎowán(r)	好玩(兒)	好玩(儿)	Adj	fun	5s
hào	號	号	M	number in a series; day of the month	3
hào	號	号	N	number (bus route)	11n
hào	號	号	M	number; size	9
hē	喝	喝	V	to drink	5
hé	和	和	Conj	and	2
héshì	合適	合适	Adj	suitable	9
hēi	黑	黑	Adj	black	9
hěn	很	很	Adv	very	3
hóng	紅	红	Adj	red	9
hóngyè	紅葉	红叶	N	red autumn leaves	10
hòulái	後來	后来	T	later	8
hòunián	後年	后年	T	the year after next	3s
hòutiān	後天	后天	T	the day after tomorrow	3s
huā	花	花	V	to spend	11
huà	話	话	N	speech; talk; words	6
huàn	換	换	V	to change; to exchange	9
huáng	黃	黄	Adj	yellow	9
huángméi	黃梅	黄梅	N	raining season	10c
huī	灰	灰	Adj	gray	9s
huí	回	回	V	to return	5
huí jiā	回家	回家	VO	to go home	5
huílai	回來	回来	VC	to come back	6
huì	會	会	AV	can; to know how to	8
huì	會	会	AV	will	10
huǒchē	火車	火车	N	train	11s
huòzhě	或者	或者	Conj	or	11
▴J▴					
jī	機	机	N	machine	11
jīchǎng	機場	机场	N	airport	11
jǐ	幾	几	QW	how many	2
jǐ	幾	几	Nu	some; a few (an indefinite number, usually less than ten)	6
jìchéngchē	計程車	计程车	N	taxi (in Taiwan)	11s
jìsuànjī	計算機	计算机	N	calculator; computer	8n
jiā	家	家	N	family; home	2
Jiānádà	加拿大	加拿大	PN	Canada	10s
jiákè	夾克	夹克	N	jacket	9s
jiǎntǐzì	簡體字	简体字	N	simplified character	7c
jiàn	見	见	V	to see	3
jiàn	件	件	M	(a measure word for shirts,	9

Pinyin	Traditional Characters	Simplified Characters	Grammar	English	Lesson
				dresses, jackets, coats, etc.)	
jiāo	教	教	V	to teach	7
jiǎo	角	角	M	dime	9g
jiào	叫	叫	V	to be called; to call	1
jiàoshì	教室	教室	N	classroom	8
jié	節	节	M	(a measure word for class periods)	6
jiějie	姐姐	姐姐	N	older sister	2
jièshào	介紹	介绍	V	to introduce	5
jīnnián	今年	今年	T	this year	3
jīntiān	今天	今天	T	today	3
jǐnzhāng	緊張	紧张	Adj	nervous; anxious	11
jìn	近	近	Adj	near	8
jìn	進	进	V	to enter	5
jìnbù	進步	进步	V/N	to make progress; progress	8
jìnlai	進來	进来	VC	to come in	5
jiǔ	久	久	Adj	a long time; for a long time	4
jiǔ	酒	酒	N	wine; any alcoholic beverage	5
jiǔ	九	九	Nu	nine	Intro.
jiǔyuè	九月	九月	N	September	3
jiù	就	就	Adv	the very one (indicating verification of something mentioned before)	6
jiù	就	就	Adv	(indicates that something takes place sooner than expected)	7
júhóngsè	橘紅色	橘红色	N	orange	9s
juéde	覺得	觉得	V	to feel	4
K					
kāfēi	咖啡	咖啡	N	coffee	5
kāfēisè	咖啡色	咖啡色	N	coffee color; brown	9
kāi	開	开	V	to hold (a meeting, party, etc.)	6
kāi	開	开	V	to drive; to operate	11
kāi chē	開車	开车	VO	to drive a car	11
kāi huì	開會	开会	VO	to have a meeting	6
kāishǐ	開始	开始	N/V	in the beginning; to begin; to start	7, 8
kàn	看	看	V	to watch; to look	4
kàn shū	看書	看书	VO	to read books; to read	4
Kāngxī Zìdiǎn	康熙字典	康熙字典	N	*Kangxi Dictionary*	Intro.
kǎo	考	考	V	to give or take a test	6
kǎoshì	考試	考试	V/N	to give or take a test; test	6
Kěkǒukělè	可口可樂	可口可乐	N	Coke	5s
kělè	可樂	可乐	N	cola	5
kěshì	可是	可是	Conj	but	3
kěyǐ	可以	可以	AV	can; may	5
kè	課	课	N	class; lesson	6
kèwén	課文	课文	N	text of a lesson	7
kè	刻	刻	M	quarter (hour); 15 minutes	3

Pinyin	Traditional Characters	Simplified Characters	Grammar	English	Lesson
kèqi	客氣	客气	Adj	polite	6
kòng(r)	空(兒)	空(儿)	N	free time	6
kǒu	口	口	N/M	mouth; (measure for people)	2n
kùzi	褲子	裤子	N	pants	9
kuài	塊	块	M	colloquial term for the basic Chinese monetary unit	9
kuài	快	快	Adv	fast; quickly	5
kuài	快	快	Adj	quick; fast	7
kuài	快	快	Adv	soon; be about to; before long	11
kuàilè	快樂	快乐	Adj	happy	11
kuàngquánshuǐ	礦泉水	矿泉水	N	mineral water	5s
Kūnmíng	昆明	昆明	PN	Kunming	10c
▴L▴					
Lādīngwén	拉丁文	拉丁文	N	Latin	6s
lái	來	来	V	to come	5
lán	藍	蓝	Adj	blue	9s
lán	藍	蓝	Adj	blue	11
lánqiú	籃球	篮球	N	basketball	4s
lǎoshī	老師	老师	N	teacher	1
le	了	了	P	(a particle indicating superlative degree)	3
le (I)	了	了	P	(a dynamic particle)	5g
le (II)	了	了	P	(a dynamic particle)	8g
le (III)	了	了	P	(a sentence particle)	10g
lěng	冷	冷	Adj	cold	10
lǐ	李	李	N	(a surname); plum	1
lǐbài	禮拜	礼拜	N	week	3g
lǐbàisì	禮拜四	礼拜四	N	Thursday	3g
Lǐ Yǒu	李友	李友	PN	(a personal name)	1
liànxí	練習	练习	V	to practice	6
liángkuai	涼快	凉快	Adj	pleasantly cool (weather)	10
liǎng	兩	两	Nu	two; a couple of	2
liàng	輛	辆	M	(measure for vehicles)	11s
liáo tiān(r)	聊天(兒)	聊天(儿)	VO	to chat	5
líng	零	零	Nu	zero	3g
liú	劉	刘	N	(a surname)	1n
liù	六	六	Nu	six	Intro.
liùyuè	六月	六月	N	June	3g
lù	路	路	N	road; path	11
lù	路	路	N	number (bus route)	11n
lùxiàng	錄像	录像	N	video recording	10
lùyīn	錄音	录音	N/VO	sound recording; to record	7
lǜ	綠	绿	Adj	green	9s, 11
lǜshī	律師	律师	N	lawyer	2

▴M▴

Pinyin	Traditional Characters	Simplified Characters	Grammar	English	Lesson
ma	嗎	吗	QP	(an interrogative particle)	1
māma	媽媽	妈妈	N	mom; mother	2
máfan	麻煩	麻烦	Adj	troublesome	11
mǎguà	馬褂	马褂	N	Mandarin jacket	9c
Mǎláixīyà	馬來西亞	马来西亚	PN	Malaysia	6s
mǎi	買	买	V	to buy	9
mài	賣	卖	V	to sell	9s
màn	慢	慢	Adj	slow	7
máng	忙	忙	Adj	busy	3
máo	毛	毛	M	1/10 of a kuai (similar to the U.S. dime)	9
máobǐ	毛筆	毛笔	N	writing brush	7s
máoyī	毛衣	毛衣	N	sweater	9s
Máotái	茅台	茅台	PN	Maotai (name of a liquor)	5c
màozi	帽子	帽子	N	hat	9s
méi	沒	没	Adv	not	2
méi shìr	沒事兒	没事儿	CE	no problem; it's O.K.	8f
méi wèntí	沒問題	没问题	CE	no problem	6, 6f
měi	每	每	Prep	every; each (usually followed by a measure word)	11
měitiān	每天	每天	T	every day	11
Měiguó	美國	美国	PN	America	1
Měiguórén	美國人	美国人	N	American people/person	1
Měishì zúqiú	美式足球	美式足球	N	American style football (used in mainland China)	4s
mèimei	妹妹	妹妹	N	younger sister	2
mēn	悶	闷	Adj	stuffy	10
mén	門	门	M	(measure word for courses)	6c
miàn	麵	面	N	noodles	3c
míngnián	明年	明年	T	next year	3s
míngtiān	明天	明天	T	tomorrow	3
míngzi	名字	名字	N	name	1
N					
nǎ/něi	哪	哪	QPr	which	6
nǎli	哪裏	哪里	CE	You flatter me. Not at all. (a polite reply to a compliment)	7, 7f
nǎr	哪兒	哪儿	QPr	where	5
nà	那	那	Conj	in that case; then	4
nà/nèi	那	那	Pr	that	2
nàr	那兒	那儿	Pr	there	8
nán	男	男	N	male	2
nán de	男的	男的		male	7
nánháizi	男孩子	男孩子	N	boy	2
nán	難	难	Adj	difficult	7
Nánjīng	南京	南京	PN	Nanjing	10c

Pinyin	Traditional Characters	Simplified Characters	Grammar	English	Lesson
nǎo	腦	脑	N	brain	8
ne	呢	呢	QP	(an interrogative particle)	1
néng	能	能	AV	can; to be able to	8
nǐ	你	你	Pr	you	1
nǐ hǎo	你好	你好	CE	How do you do? Hello!	1
nián	年	年	N	year	3
niánjí	年級	年级	N	grade in school	6
niánjì	年紀	年纪	N	year (of age)	3n
niàn	念	念	V	to read aloud	7
nín	您	您	Pr	you (singular; polite)	1
nuǎnhuo	暖和	暖和	Adj	warm	10
nǚ	女	女	N	female	2
nǚ'ér	女兒	女儿	N	daughter	2
nǚháizi	女孩子	女孩子	N	girl	2
▲P▲					
páiqiú	排球	排球	N	volleyball	4s
péngyou	朋友	朋友	N	friend	1s, 7
piān	篇	篇	M	(measure for essays, articles, etc.)	8
piányi	便宜	便宜	Adj	cheap; inexpensive	9
piào	票	票	N	ticket	11
piàoliang	漂亮	漂亮	Adj	pretty	5
píjiǔ	啤酒	啤酒	N	beer	5
píng	瓶	瓶	M	bottle	5
píngcháng	平常	平常	T	usually	7
Pútáoyá	葡萄牙	葡萄牙	PN	Portugal	6s
Pútáoyáwén	葡萄牙文	葡萄牙文	N	the Portuguese language	6s
▲Q▲					
qī	七	七	Nu	seven	Intro.
qīyuè	七月	七月	N	July	3g
qípáo	旗袍	旗袍	N	(close-fitting woman's dress)	9c
qǐ chuáng	起床	起床	VO	to get up	8
qìchē	汽車	汽车	N	automobile	11
qìshuǐ(r)	汽水(兒)	汽水(儿)	N	soft drink; soda pop	5s
qiānbǐ	鉛筆	铅笔	N	pencil	7s
qián	錢	钱	N	money	9
qiánnián	前年	前年	T	the year before last	3s
qiántiān	前天	前天	T	the day before yesterday	3s
qiāo mén	敲門	敲门	VO	to knock at the door	5f
qīngchu	清楚	清楚	Adj	clear	8
qíng	晴	晴	Adj	sunny; clear	10s
qǐng	請	请	V	please (a polite form of request)	1
qǐng	請	请	V	to treat (somebody); to invite	3
qǐng kè	請客	请客	VO	to invite someone to dinner; to be the host	4
qǐng wèn	請問	请问	CE	May I ask...	1
qiūtiān	秋天	秋天	N	autumn; fall	10

Pinyin	Traditional Characters	Simplified Characters	Grammar	English	Lesson
qiú	球	球	N	ball	4
qù	去	去	V	to go	4
qùnián	去年	去年	T	last year	3s, 6n
qúnzi	裙子	裙子	N	skirt	9s
R					
ránhòu	然後	然后	Adv	then	11
ràng	讓	让	V	to allow or cause (somebody to do something)	11
rè	熱	热	Adj	hot	10
rén	人	人	N	people; person	1
rènshi	認識	认识	V	to know (someone); to recognize	3
rì	日	日	N	day; the sun	3
Rìběn	日本	日本	PN	Japan	1s
Rìběnrén	日本人	日本人	N	Japanese people/person	1s
rìjì	日記	日记	N	diary	8
Rìwén	日文	日文	N	the Japanese language	6s
róngyì	容易	容易	Adj	easy	7
S					
sān	三	三	Nu	three	Intro.
sāngē	三哥	三哥	N	third oldest brother	7g
sānjiě	三姐	三姐	N	third oldest sister	7g
sānyuè	三月	三月	N	March	3g
shàngge xīngqī	上個星期	上个星期	T	last week	6n, 7
shàngge yuè	上個月	上个月	T	last month	6n
Shànghǎi	上海	上海	PN	Shanghai	10
shàng kè	上課	上课	VO	to go to class; to start a class	7
shàngwǔ	上午	上午	T	morning	6
shéi	誰	谁	QPr	who	2
shéi ya	誰呀	谁呀	CE	Who is it?	5f
shénme	什麼	什么	QPr	what	1
shēng	生	生	V	to give birth to; to be born	3
shēngcí	生詞	生词	N	new words	7
shēngrì	生日	生日	N	birthday	3
shí	十	十	Nu	ten	Intro.
shíbā	十八	十八	Nu	eighteen	3
shí'èr	十二	十二	Nu	twelve	3
shí'èryuè	十二月	十二月	N	December	3g
shīfu	師傅	师傅	N	master craftsman; skilled worker	9n
shíyīyuè	十一月	十一月	N	November	3g
shíyuè	十月	十月	N	October	3g
shíhou	時候	时候	N	(a point in) time; moment; (a duration of) time	4
shíjiān	時間	时间	T	time	6
shì	事	事	N	matter; affair; business	3
shì	是	是	V	to be	1

Pinyin	Traditional Characters	Simplified Characters	Grammar	English	Lesson
shì	視	视	N	vision	4
shì ma	是嗎	是吗	CE	Really?	5f, 5n
shǒubiǎo	手錶	手表	N	wristwatch	9n
shǒutào	手套	手套	N	gloves	9n
shòuhuòyuán	售貨員	售货员	N	shop assistant; salesclerk	9
shū	書	书	N	book	4
shūfu	舒服	舒服	Adj	comfortable	10
shuài	帥	帅	Adj	handsome	7
shuāng	雙	双	M	a pair of	9
shuǐ	水	水	N	water	5
shuì	睡	睡	V	to sleep	4
shuì jiào	睡覺	睡觉	VO	to sleep	4
shǔjià	暑假	暑假	N	summer vacation	11s
shuō	説	说	V	to say; to speak	6
shuō huà	説話	说话	VO	to talk	7
sì	四	四	Nu	four	Intro.
sìyuè	四月	四月	N	April	3g
sòng	送	送	V	to take someone (somewhere)	11
sùshè	宿舍	宿舍	N	dormitory	8
suàn le	算了	算了	CE	Forget it. Never mind.	4
suīrán	雖然	虽然	Conj	although	9
suì	歲	岁	N	year (of age)	3
suìshù	歲數	岁数	N	year (of age)	3n
suǒyǐ	所以	所以	Conj	so	4
▲T▲					
T-xùshān	T-恤衫	T-恤衫	N	T-shirt	9s
tā	他	他	Pr	he; him	2
tā	她	她	Pr	she; her	2
Táiběi	台北	台北	PN	Taipei	10
Táiwān	台灣	台湾	PN	Taiwan	10
Táizhōng	台中	台中	PN	Taichung	10s
Tàiguó	泰國	泰国	PN	Thailand	6s
tài…(le)	太…(了)	太…(了)	Adv	too; extremely	3
tàitai	太太	太太	N	wife; Mrs.	1s
tèbié	特別	特别	Adj/Adv	special; especially	7g
tiān	天	天	N	day	3
tiānqì	天氣	天气	N	weather	10
tiáo	條	条	M	(a measure word for long, thin objects)	9
tiào	跳	跳	V	to jump	4
tiào wǔ	跳舞	跳舞	VO	to dance	4
tīng	聽	听	V	to listen	4
tóngxué	同學	同学	N	classmate	3
túshūguǎn	圖書館	图书馆	N	library	5
▲W▲					

Pinyin	Traditional Characters	Simplified Characters	Grammar	English	Lesson
wàzi	襪子	袜子	N	socks	9s
wàiguó	外國	外国	N	foreign country	4
wàitào	外套	外套	N	coat; jacket	9s
wán(r)	玩(兒)	玩(儿)	V	to have fun; to play	5
wǎn	晚	晚	N/Adj	evening; night; late	3
wǎnfàn	晚飯	晚饭	N	dinner; supper	3
wǎnshang	晚上	晚上	T	evening; night	3
wáng	王	王	N	(a surname); king	1
Wáng Péng	王朋	王朋	PN	(a personal name)	1
wǎngqiú	網球	网球	N	tennis	4s
wéi	喂	喂	Interj	Hello!; Hey!	6
wèi	喂	喂	Interj	Hello!; Hey!	6, 6f
wèi	位	位	M	(polite measure for people)	6
wèi	爲	为	Prep	for	3
wèishénme	爲什麼	为什么	QPr	why	3
Wēngēhuá	溫哥華	温哥华	PN	Vancouver	10s
wén	文	文	N	language; script; written language	6
wèn	問	问	V	to ask (a question)	1
wèntí	問題	问题	N	question; problem	6
wǒ	我	我	Pr	I; me	1
wǒmen	我們	我们	Pr	we	3
wǔ	五	五	Nu	five	Intro.
wǔ	舞	舞	N	dance	4
wǔfàn	午飯	午饭	N	lunch; midday meal	8
wǔjiào	午覺	午觉	N	nap	7s
Wǔhàn	武漢	武汉	PN	Wuhan	10c
wǔyuè	五月	五月	N	May	3g
X					
Xīlà	希臘	希腊	PN	Greece	6s
Xīlàwén	希臘文	希腊文	N	the Greek language	6s
xīwàng	希望	希望	V/N	to hope; hope	8
Xībānyá	西班牙	西班牙	PN	Spain	6s
Xībānyáwén	西班牙文	西班牙文	N	the Spanish language	6s
xīzhuāng	西裝	西装	N	suit	9s
xíguàn	習慣	习惯	V/N	to be accustomed to; habit	8
xǐhuan	喜歡	喜欢	V	to like; to prefer	3
xǐ zǎo	洗澡	洗澡	VO	to take a bath/shower	8
xià	下	下		below; next	6
xià chē	下車	下车	VO	to get off (a bus, train, etc.)	11
xià cì	下次	下次		next time	10
xiàge xīngqī	下個星期	下个星期	T	next week	6
xià(ge)yuè	下(個)月	下(个)月	T	next month	3s
xiàtiān	夏天	夏天	N	summer	10
Xiàwēiyí	夏威夷	夏威夷	PN	Hawaii	6s
xiàwǔ	下午	下午	T	afternoon	6

Pinyin	Traditional Characters	Simplified Characters	Grammar	English	Lesson
xià yǔ	下雨	下雨	VO	to rain	10
xiān	先	先	Adv	first; before	11
xiānsheng	先生	先生	N	Mr.; husband; teacher	1
xiàn	線	线	N	line	11
xiànzài	現在	现在	T	now	3
Xiānggǎng	香港	香港	PN	Hong Kong	10s
xiǎng	想	想	AV	to want to; to think	4
xiǎo	小	小	Adj	small; little	2
Xiǎo Bái	小白	小白	PN	Little Bai	3
Xiǎo Gāo	小高	小高	PN	Little Gao	2
xiǎojie	小姐	小姐	N	Miss; young lady	1
Xiǎo Lǐ	小李	小李	PN	Little Li	3
xiǎoxué	小學	小学	N	elementary school; grade school	2c
Xiǎo Zhāng	小張	小张	PN	Little Zhang	2
xiào	笑	笑	V	to laugh; to laugh at	8
xié	鞋	鞋	N	shoes	9
xiě	寫	写	V	to write	7
xiè	謝	谢	N/V	(a surname); thanks	10
xièxie	謝謝	谢谢	CE	thank you	3, 6f
xīn	新	新	Adj	new	8
xīnnián	新年	新年	N	new year	11
xìn	信	信	N	letter (mail)	8
Xīngbākè	星巴克	星巴克	PN	Starbucks	5c
xīngqī	星期	星期	N	week	3
xīngqī'èr	星期二	星期二	N	Tuesday	3g
xīngqīliù	星期六	星期六	N	Saturday	3g
xīngqīrì	星期日	星期日	N	Sunday	3g
xīngqīsān	星期三	星期三	N	Wednesday	3g
xīngqīsì	星期四	星期四	N	Thursday	3
xīngqītiān	星期天	星期天	N	Sunday	3g
xīngqīwǔ	星期五	星期五	N	Friday	3g
xīngqīyī	星期一	星期一	N	Monday	3g
xíng	行	行	Adj	all right; O.K.	6
xìng	姓	姓	V/N	(one's) surname is...; to be surnamed; surname	1
xué	學	学	V	to study	7
xuéqī	學期	学期	N	school term; semester/quarter	8
xuésheng	學生	学生	N	student	1
xuéxiào	學校	学校	N	school	5
xuéyuàn	學院	学院	N	college	2c
xuě	雪	雪	N	snow	10s
Xuěbì	雪碧	雪碧	N	Sprite	5s

▴Y▴

Pinyin	Traditional Characters	Simplified Characters	Grammar	English	Lesson
ya	呀	呀	P	(an interjectory particle used to soften a question)	5

Pinyin	Traditional Characters	Simplified Characters	Grammar	English	Lesson
yánsè	顏色	颜色	N	color	9
yǎnjìng	眼鏡	眼镜	N	eye glasses; glasses	9n
yào	要	要	V/AV	to want to; to have a desire for	5, 9
yào	要	要	AV	will; to be going to	6
yàoshi	要是	要是	Conj	if	6
yě	也	也	Adv	too; also	1
yè	夜	夜	N	night	7
yī	一	一	Nu	one	Intro.
yīyuè	一月	一月	N	January	3g
yīfu	衣服	衣服	N	clothes	9
yīshēng	醫生	医生	N	doctor; physician	2
yígòng	一共	一共	Adv	altogether	9
yí xià	一下	一下	M	(a measure word used after a verb indicating short duration)	5
yíyàng	一樣	一样	Adj	same; alike	9
yǐhòu	以後	以后	T	after	6
yǐjīng	已經	已经	Adv	already	8
yǐqián	以前	以前	T	before; ago; previously	7g, 8
yìbiān...yìbiān	一邊...一邊	一边...一边		(a parallel construction indicating two simultaneous actions)	8
yìdiǎnr	一點兒	一点儿		a bit	5g, 10
yìqǐ	一起	一起	Adv	together	5
Yìdàlì	意大利	意大利	PN	Italy	6s
Yìdàlìwén	意大利文	意大利文	N	the Italian language	6s
yìsi	意思	意思	N	meaning	4
Yìwén	意文	意文	PN	(a given name)	8
yīn	陰	阴	Adj	overcast	10s
yīnwei	因爲	因为	Conj	because	3
yīnyuè	音樂	音乐	N	music	4
yīnyuèhuì	音樂會	音乐会	N	concert	8
Yīngguó	英國	英国	PN	Britain; England	1s
Yīngguórén	英國人	英国人	N	British people/person	1s
Yīngwén	英文	英文	N	the English language	2
yǐng	影	影	N	shadow	4
yòng	用	用	V/N	to use; use	8
yǒu	有	有	V	to have; to exist	2
yǒu kòng(r)	有空(兒)	有空(儿)	VO	to have free time	6
yǒu shíhou	有時候	有时候	CE	sometimes	4
yǒu yìdiǎnr	有一點兒	有一点儿	CE	a little; somewhat	7
yǒu yìsi	有意思	有意思	CE	interesting	4
yòu	又	又	Adv	again	10
yòu...yòu	又...又...	又...又...		both...and...	10
yǔ	語	语	N	speech	6n
yǔfǎ	語法	语法	N	grammar	7
yùbào	預報	预报	N	forecast	10

Pinyin	Traditional Characters	Simplified Characters	Grammar	English	Lesson
yùxí	預習	预习	V	to preview	7
yuán	元	元	M	Chinese dollar	9g
yuánzhūbǐ	圓珠筆	圆珠笔	N	ball-point pen	7c
yuánzibǐ	原子筆	原子笔	N	ball-point pen	7c
yuē	約	约	V	to make an appointment	10
yuè	月	月	N	month	3
Yuènán	越南	越南	PN	Vietnam	6s
Yuènánrén	越南人	越南人	N	Vietnamese people/person	1s
yún	雲	云	N	cloud	10s
▴Z▴					
zài	在	在	Prep	at; in; on	5
zài	在	在	V	to be present; to be at (a place)	6
zài	再	再	Adv	again	3
zàijiàn	再見	再见	CE	goodbye; see you again	3
zāogāo	糟糕	糟糕	Adj	in a terrible mess; too bad	10
zǎo	早	早	Adj	Good morning!; early	7
zǎo ān	早安	早安	CE	Good morning!	7n
zǎofàn	早飯	早饭	N	breakfast	3s, 8
zǎoshang	早上	早上	T	morning	8
zěnme	怎麼	怎么	QPr	how; how come (used to inquire about the cause of something, implying a degree of surprise or disapproval)	7
zěnme bàn	怎麼辦	怎么办	QW	what to do	10
zěnmeyàng	怎麼樣	怎么样	QPr	Is it O.K.? What is it like? How does that sound?	3
zhàn	站	站	N	(of bus, train, etc.) stop; station	11
zhāng	張	张	PN/M	(a surname); (a measure word for flat objects)	1n, 2
zhǎo	找	找	V	to look for	4
zhǎo(qián)	找(錢)	找(钱)	V	to give change	9
zhàopiàn	照片	照片	N	picture; photo	2
zhè jǐ tiān	這幾天	这几天		the past few days	11
zhè	這	这	Pr	this	2
zhège	這個	这个	Pr	this	10
zhèi	這	这	Pr	this	2
zhème	這麼	这么	Pr	so; such	7
zhēn	眞	真	Adv	really	7
zhèngzài	正在	正在	Adv	in the middle of (doing something)	8
zhèr	這兒	这儿	Pr	here	9
zhèyàng	這樣	这样	Pr	so; like this	10
zhī	枝	枝	M	(a measure for pen and long items); twig	9g
zhī	隻	只	M	(a measure for bird, shoe, etc.)	9g
zhīdao	知道	知道	V	to know	6

Pinyin	Traditional Characters	Simplified Characters	Grammar	English	Lesson
zhǐ	只	只	Adv	only	4
zhǐ	紙	纸	N	paper	2g, 7s
zhōng	鐘	钟	N	clock	3
zhōng	中	中	Adj	medium	9
zhōngfàn	中飯	中饭	N	lunch	3s
Zhōngguó	中國	中国	PN	China	1
Zhōngguórén	中國人	中国人	N	Chinese people/person	1
Zhōngguózì	中國字	中国字	N	Chinese character	Intro.
Zhōngshānzhuāng	中山裝	中山装	N	Sun Yatsen suit	9c
Zhōngwén	中文	中文	N	the Chinese language	6
zhōngwǔ	中午	中午	T	noon	6s; 8
zhōngxué	中學	中学	N	middle school	2c
zhōu	週	周	N	week	3g
zhōu'èr	週二	周二	N	Tuesday	3g
zhōumò	週末	周末	T	weekend	4
zhōurì	週日	周日	N	Sunday	3g
zhōuyī	週一	周一	N	Monday	3g
zhù	祝	祝	V	to express good wishes	8, 11f
zhuānyè	專業	专业	N	major (in college); specialty	8
zǐ	紫	紫	Adj	purple	9s
zì	字	字	N	character	7
zìjǐ	自己	自己	Pr	oneself	11
zǒu	走	走	V	to walk; to go by way of	11
zǒu lù	走路	走路	VO	to walk	11s
zū	租	租	V	to rent	11
zúqiú	足球	足球	N	soccer	4s
zuì	最	最	Adv	(an adverb of superlative degree; most, -est)	8
zuìhǎo	最好	最好	Adv	had better	10
zuìhòu	最後	最后	Adv	finally	11
zuìjìn	最近	最近	T	recently	8
zuótiān	昨天	昨天	T	yesterday	3s, 4
zuò	做	做	V	to do	2
zuò	坐	坐	V	to sit	5
zuò	坐	坐	V	to travel by	11

Vocabulary Index (English to Chinese): Lessons 1–11

Key: c=Culture Notes; f=Functional Expressions; g=Grammar; n=Notes; s=Supplementary Vocabulary

English	Pinyin	Traditional Characters	Simplified Characters	Grammar	Lesson
A					
a bit	yìdiǎnr	一點兒	一点儿		10
a bit; a little; some	diǎn(r)	點(兒)	点(儿)	M	5
a couple of; two	liǎng	兩	两	Nu	2
a little; a bit; some	diǎn(r)	點(兒)	点(儿)	M	5
a little; somewhat	yǒu yìdiǎnr	有一點兒	有一点儿	CE	7
able to; can	néng	能	能	AV	8
affair; matter; business	shì	事	事	N	3
after	yǐhòu	以後	以后	T	6
afternoon	xiàwǔ	下午	下午	T	6
again	yòu	又	又	Adv	10
again	zài	再	再	Adv	3
age	niánjì	年紀	年纪	N	3n
ago; before; previously	yǐqián	以前	以前	T	8
airplane	fēijī	飛機	飞机	N	11
airport	fēijīchǎng	飛機場	飞机场	N	11
airport	jīchǎng	機場	机场	N	11
alike; same	yíyàng	一樣	一样	Adj	9
all; both	dōu	都	都	Adv	2
allow or cause (somebody to do something)	ràng	讓	让	V	11
already	yǐjīng	已經	已经	Adv	8
also; too	yě	也	也	Adv	1
also; too; as well	hái	還	还	Adv	3
although	suīrán	雖然	虽然	Conj	9
altogether	yígòng	一共	一共	Adv	9
America	Měiguó	美國	美国	PN	1
American people/person	Měiguórén	美國人	美国人	N	1
American style football (used in mainland China)	Měishì zúqiú	美式足球	美式足球	N	4s
American style football (used in Taiwan)	gǎnlǎnqiú	橄欖球	橄榄球	N	4s
and	gēn	跟	跟	Conj	7
and	hé	和	和	Conj	2
another person; other people; others	biérén	別人	别人	Adv	4
anxious; nervous	jǐnzhāng	緊張	紧张	Adj	11

English	Pinyin	Traditional Characters	Simplified Characters	Grammar	Lesson
arrive	dào	到	到	V	8
ask (a question)	wèn	問	问	V	1
at; in; on	zài	在	在	Prep	5
at the time of...; when...	de shíhou	的時候	的时候		8
August	bāyuè	八月	八月	N	3g
automobile	qìchē	汽車	汽车	N	11
autumn; fall	qiūtiān	秋天	秋天	N	10
B					
ball	qiú	球	球	N	4
ball-point pen	yuánzhūbǐ	圓珠筆	圆珠笔	N	7c
ball-point pen	yuánzibǐ	原子筆	原子笔	N	7c
baseball	bàngqiú	棒球	棒球	N	4s
basketball	lánqiú	籃球	篮球	N	4s
be	shì	是	是	V	1
be about to; soon; before long	kuài	快	快	Adv	11
be accustomed to	xíguàn	習慣	习惯	V	8
be all right; O.K.	xíng	行	行	Adj	6
be at; be there	zài	在	在	V	6
be born; give birth to	shēng	生	生	V	3
be called	jiào	叫	叫	V	1
be going to; will	yào	要	要	AV	6
be host; invite someone to dinner	qǐng kè	請客	请客	VO	4
be present; be at (a place)	zài	在	在	V	6
because	yīnwei	因爲	因为	Conj	3
bed	chuáng	床	床	N	2g, 8
beer	píjiǔ	啤酒	啤酒	N	5
before; ago; previously	yǐqián	以前	以前	T	8
before; first	xiān	先	先	Adv	11
begin; in the beginning; start	kāishǐ	開始	开始	N/V	8
Beijing	Běijīng	北京	北京	PN	10s
besides; in addition to	chúle...yǐwài	除了...以外	除了...以外	Conj	8
big; old	dà	大	大	Adj	3
birthday	shēngrì	生日	生日	N	3
black	hēi	黑	黑	Adj	9
blue	lán	藍	蓝	Adj	9s
blue	lán	藍	蓝	Adj	11
boat; ship	chuán	船	船	N	11s
book	shū	書	书	N	4
both...and...	yòu...yòu	又...又...	又...又...		10
both; all	dōu	都	都	Adv	2
bottle	píng	瓶	瓶	M	5
boy	nánháizi	男孩子	男孩子	N	2
brain	nǎo	腦	脑	N	8
breakfast	zǎofàn	早飯	早饭	N	3s, 8
Britain; England	Yīngguó	英國	英国	PN	1s

English	Pinyin	Traditional Characters	Simplified Characters	Grammar	Lesson
British people/person	Yīngguórén	英國人	英国人	N	1s
brown; coffee color	kāfēisè	咖啡色	咖啡色	N	9
bus	gōngchē	公車	公车	N	11
bus	gōnggòng qìchē	公共汽車	公共汽车	N	11
bus	gōngjiāochē	公轎車	公轿车	N	11
business; matter; affair	shì	事	事	N	3
busy	máng	忙	忙	Adj	3
but	dànshì	但是	但是	Conj	6
but	kěshì	可是	可是	Conj	3
but; however	búguò	不過	不过	Conj	11
buy	mǎi	買	买	V	9
▲C▲					
cable car; trolley bus; tram	diànchē	電車	电车	N	11s
cafeteria; dining room	cāntīng	餐廳	餐厅	N	8
calculator; computer	jìsuànjī	計算機	计算机	N	8n
can; able to	néng	能	能	AV	8
can; know how to	huì	會	会	AV	8
can; may	kěyǐ	可以	可以	AV	5
Canada	Jiānádà	加拿大	加拿大	PN	10s
car, vehicle	chē	車	车	N	11
cause or allow (somebody to do something)	ràng	讓	让	V	11
cent; 1/100 of a kuai	fēn	分	分	M	9
change; exchange	huàn	换	换	V	9
character; word	zì	字	字	N	7
chat	liáo tiān(r)	聊天(兒)	聊天(儿)	VO	5
cheap; inexpensive	piányi	便宜	便宜	Adj	9
child	háizi	孩子	孩子	N	2
China	Zhōngguó	中國	中国	PN	1
Chinese character	Hànzì	漢字	汉字	N	7
Chinese character	Zhōngguózì	中國字	中国字	N	Intro.
Chinese dollar	yuán	元	元	M	9g
Chinese language	Hànyǔ	漢語	汉语	N	6n
Chinese language	Zhōngwén	中文	中文	N	6
Chinese people/person	Zhōngguórén	中國人	中国人	N	1
Chongqing	Chóngqìng	重慶	重庆	PN	10c
class; lesson	kè	課	课	N	6
classmate	tóngxué	同學	同学	N	3
classroom	jiàoshì	教室	教室	N	8
clear	qīngchu	清楚	清楚	Adj	8
clear; sunny	qíng	晴	晴	Adj	10s
clock	zhōng	鐘	钟	N	3
close-fitting woman's dress	qípáo	旗袍	旗袍	N	9c
clothes	yīfu	衣服	衣服	N	9

English	Pinyin	Traditional Characters	Simplified Characters	Grammar	Lesson
cloud	yún	雲	云	N	10s
coat; jacket	wàitào	外套	外套	N	9s
coffee	kāfēi	咖啡	咖啡	N	5
coffee color; brown	kāfēisè	咖啡色	咖啡色	N	9
Coke	Kěkǒukělè	可口可樂	可口可乐	N	5s
cola	kělè	可樂	可乐	N	5
cold	lěng	冷	冷	Adj	10
college	xuéyuàn	學院	学院	N	2c
college student	dàxuéshēng	大學生	大学生	N	2
college; university	dàxué	大學	大学	N	2
color	yánsè	顏色	颜色	N	9
come	lái	來	来	V	5
come back	huílai	回來	回来	VC	6
come in	jìnlai	進來	进来	VC	5
comfortable	shūfu	舒服	舒服	Adj	10
computer	diànnǎo	電腦	电脑	N	8
computer	diànzǐ jìsuànjī	電子計算機	电子计算机	N	8n
computer; calculator	jìsuànjī	計算機	计算机	N	8n
concert	yīnyuèhuì	音樂會	音乐会	N	8
congratulate	gōngxǐ	恭喜	恭喜	V	11c
Congratulations and may you make a fortune!	gōngxǐ fācái	恭喜發財	恭喜发财	CE	11n
convenient	fāngbiàn	方便	方便	Adj	6
correct; right	duì	對	对	Adj	4
cup; glass	bēi	杯	杯	M	5
▲D▲					
dad; father	bàba	爸爸	爸爸	N	2
dance	tiào wǔ	跳舞	跳舞	VO	4
dance	wǔ	舞	舞	N	4
daughter	nǚ'ér	女兒	女儿	N	2
day	tiān	天	天	N	3
day after tomorrow	hòutiān	後天	后天	T	3s
day before yesterday	qiántiān	前天	前天	T	3s
day of the month; number in a series; size	hào	號	号	M	3, 9
day; the sun	rì	日	日	N	3
December	shí'èryuè	十二月	十二月	N	3g
delicious; good to eat	hǎochī	好吃	好吃	Adj	5s
diary	rìjì	日記	日记	N	8
difficult	nán	難	难	Adj	7
dime; 1/10 of a kuai	jiǎo	角	角	M	9g
dime; 1/10 of a kuai	máo	毛	毛	M	9
dining room; cafeteria	cāntīng	餐廳	餐厅	N	8
dinner; supper	wǎnfàn	晚飯	晚饭	N	3
do	zuò	做	做	V	2

English	Pinyin	Traditional Characters	Simplified Characters	Grammar	Lesson
do manual work; work part-time	dǎ gōng	打工	打工	VO	5s
doctor; physician	yīshēng	醫生	医生	N	2
dollar	kuài	塊	块	M	9
don't	bié	別	别		6
Don't be so polite!	bié kèqi	別客氣	别客气		6
Don't be (so) polite. You are welcome.	bú kèqi	不客氣	不客气	CE	6
Don't mention it. Not at all. You're welcome.	bú xiè	不謝	不谢	CE	7
door; (a measure word for academic courses)	mén	門	门	N	6n
dormitory	sùshè	宿舍	宿舍	N	8
drink	hē	喝	喝	V	5
drive a car	kāi chē	開車	开车	VO	11
drive; operate	kāi	開	开	V	11
▴E▴					
each; every	měi	每	每	Prep	11
early	zǎo	早	早	Adj	7
early; Good morning!	zǎo	早	早	Adj	7
easy	róngyì	容易	容易	Adj	7
eat	chī	吃	吃	V	3
eat (a meal)	chī fàn	吃飯	吃饭	VO	3
eight	bā	八	八	Nu	Intro.
eighteen	shíbā	十八	十八	Nu	3
electricity	diàn	電	电	N	4
elementary school; grade school	xiǎoxué	小學	小学	N	2c
embarrassed	bù hǎoyìsi	不好意思	不好意思	CE	11
England; Britain	Yīngguó	英國	英国	PN	1s
English language	Yīngwén	英文	英文	N	2
enter	jìn	進	进	V	5
especially; special	tèbié	特別	特别	Adv/Adj	7g
even more	gèng	更	更	Adv	10
evening; night	wǎnshang	晚上	晚上	T	3
evening; night; late	wǎn	晚	晚	N/Adj	3
every day	měitiān	每天	每天	T	11
every; each	měi	每	每	Prep	11
everybody	dàjiā	大家	大家	Pr	7
exchange; change	huàn	換	换	V	9
exist; have	yǒu	有	有	V	2
expensive	guì	貴	贵	Adj	9
extremely; too	tài	太	太	Adv	3
eye glasses; glasses	yǎnjìng	眼鏡	眼镜	N	9n
▴F▴					
fall; autumn	qiūtiān	秋天	秋天	N	10
family; home	jiā	家	家	N	2

English	Pinyin	Traditional Characters	Simplified Characters	Grammar	Lesson
fast; quick; quickly	kuài	快	快	Adj/Adv	5, 7
father; dad	bàba	爸爸	爸爸	N	2
February	Èryuè	二月	二月	N	3g
feel embarrassed	bù hǎoyìsi	不好意思	不好意思	CE	11
feel/think that	juéde	覺得	觉得	V	4
female	nǚ	女	女	N	2
fifteen minutes; quarter (hour)	kè	刻	刻	M	3
finally	zuìhòu	最後	最后	Adv	11
fine; good; nice; O.K.	hǎo	好	好	Adj	1, 3
first; before	xiān	先	先	Adv	11
five	wǔ	五	五	Nu	Intro.
fly	fēi	飛	飞	V	11
for	wèi	爲	为	Prep	3
for; to	gěi	給	给	Prep	6
forecast	yùbào	預報	预报	N	10
foreign country	wàiguó	外國	外国	N	4
Forget it. Never mind.	suàn le	算了	算了	CE	4
fountain pen	gāngbǐ	鋼筆	钢笔	N	7s
four	sì	四	四	Nu	Intro.
France	Fǎguó	法國	法国	PN	1s
free time	kòng(r)	空(兒)	空(儿)	N	6
French language	Fǎwén	法文	法文	N	6s
French people/person	Fǎguórén	法國人	法国人	N	1s
Friday	xīngqīwǔ	星期五	星期五	N	3g
friend	péngyou	朋友	朋友	N	1s, 7
fun	hǎowán(r)	好玩(兒)	好玩(儿)	Adj	5s
G					
German language	Déwén	德文	德文	N	6s
German people/person	Déguórén	德國人	德国人	N	1s
Germany	Déguó	德國	德国	PN	1s
get off (a bus, train, etc.)	xià chē	下車	下车	VO	11
get up	qǐ chuáng	起床	起床	VO	8
girl	nǚháizi	女孩子	女孩子	N	2
give	gěi	給	给	V	5
give birth to; be born	shēng	生	生	V	3
give change	zhǎo(qián)	找(錢)	找(钱)	V	9
give or take a test	kǎo	考	考	V	6
give or take a test; test	kǎoshì	考試	考试	V/N	6
give (someone a gift)	sòng	送	送	V	11
glass; cup	bēi	杯	杯	M	5
glasses; eye glasses	yǎnjìng	眼鏡	眼镜	N	9n
gloves	shǒutào	手套	手套	N	9n
go	qù	去	去	V	4
go by way of; walk	zǒu	走	走	V	11
go home	huí jiā	回家	回家	VO	5

English	Pinyin	Traditional Characters	Simplified Characters	Grammar	Lesson
go out	chūqu	出去	出去	VP	10
go to (a place)	dào…qù	到…去	到…去		6
go to class; start a class	shàng kè	上課	上课	VO	7
good; fine; nice; O.K.	hǎo	好	好	Adj	1, 3
Good morning!	zǎo ān	早安	早安	CE	7n
Good morning!; early	zǎo	早	早	Adj	7
good to drink; tasty	hǎohē	好喝	好喝	Adj	5s
good to eat; delicious	hǎochī	好吃	好吃	Adj	5s
good-looking	hǎokàn	好看	好看	Adj	5s
goodbye; see you again	zàijiàn	再見	再见	CE	3
grade in school	niánjí	年級	年级	N	6
grade school; elementary school	xiǎoxué	小學	小学	N	2c
grammar	yǔfǎ	語法	语法	N	7
gray	huī	灰	灰	Adj	9s
Greece	Xīlà	希臘	希腊	PN	6s
Greek language	Xīlàwén	希臘文	希腊文	N	6s
green	lǜ	綠	绿	Adj	9s, 11
▴**H**▴					
habit	xíguàn	習慣	习惯	N	8
had better	háishi	還是	还是	Conj	11
had better	zuìhǎo	最好	最好	Adv	10
Hainan	Hǎinán	海南	海南	PN	10c
half; half an hour	bàn	半	半	Nu	3
handsome	shuài	帥	帅	Adj	7
happy	kuàilè	快樂	快乐	Adj	11
happy; pleased	gāoxìng	高興	高兴	Adj	5
Harbin	Hā'ěrbīn	哈爾濱	哈尔滨	PN	10c
hat	màozi	帽子	帽子	N	9s
have; exist	yǒu	有	有	V	2
have a desire for; want to	yào	要	要	V/AV	5, 9
have a meeting	kāi huì	開會	开会	VO	6
have free time	yǒu kòng(r)	有空(兒)	有空(儿)	VO	6
have fun; play	wán(r)	玩(兒)	玩(儿)	V	5
have to; must	děi	得	得	AV	6
Hawaii	Xiàwēiyí	夏威夷	夏威夷	PN	6s
he	tā	他	他	Pr	2
Hello! Hey!	wèi	喂	喂	Interj	6
Hello! How do you do?	nǐ hǎo	你好	你好	CE	1
help	bāng	幫	帮	V	6
help	bāngzhù	幫助	帮助	V	7
help; to do someone a favor	bāng máng	幫忙	帮忙	VO	6
here	zhèr	這兒	这儿	Pr	9
Hey! Hello!	wèi/wéi	喂	喂	Interj	6
high speed	gāosù	高速	高速	Adj	11
highway; road	gōnglù	公路	公路	N	11

English	Pinyin	Traditional Characters	Simplified Characters	Grammar	Lesson
highway; super highway	gāosù gōnglù	高速公路	高速公路	N	11
hit; strike	dǎ	打	打	V	4
hold (a meeting, party, etc.)	kāi	開	开	V	6
home; family	jiā	家	家	N	2
homework; schoolwork	gōngkè	功課	功课	N	7
Hong Kong	Xiānggǎng	香港	香港	PN	10s
honorable	guì	貴	贵	Adj	1
hope	xīwàng	希望	希望	V	8
hot	rè	熱	热	Adj	10
how; how come	zěnme	怎麼	怎么	QPr	7
How do you do? Hello!	nǐ hǎo	你好	你好	CE	1
How does it sound?	zěnmeyàng	怎麼樣	怎么样	QPr	3
how many	jǐ	幾	几	QW	2
how many/much; to what extent	duō	多	多	Adv	3
how many; how much	duōshao	多少	多少	QW	9
how much; how many	duōshao	多少	多少	QW	9
how old	duō dà	多大	多大	CE	3
however; but	búguò	不過	不过	Conj	11
humid; wet	cháoshī	潮濕	潮湿	Adj	10s
hundred	bǎi	百	百	Nu	9
▲I▲					
I; me	wǒ	我	我	Pr	1
I'm sorry.	duì bu qǐ	對不起	对不起	CE	5
if	yàoshi	要是	要是	Conj	6
in; at; on	zài	在	在	Prep	5
in a terrible mess	zāogāo	糟糕	糟糕	Adj	10
in addition to; besides	chúle...yǐwài	除了…以外	除了…以外	Conj	8
in that case; then	nà	那	那	Conj	4
in the beginning; begin; start	kāishǐ	開始	开始	N/V	8
in the middle of (doing something)	zhèngzài	正在	正在	Adv	8
in the newspaper	bàoshang	報上	报上		10
inexpensive; cheap	piányi	便宜	便宜	Adj	9
interesting	yǒu yìsi	有意思	有意思	CE	4
introduce	jièshào	介紹	介绍	V	5
invite; treat (somebody)	qǐng	請	请	V	3
invite someone to dinner; be the host	qǐng kè	請客	请客	VO	4
Italian language	Yìdàlìwén	意大利文	意大利文	N	6s
Italy	Yìdàlì	意大利	意大利	PN	6s
▲J▲					
jacket	jiákè	夾克	夹克	N	9s
jacket; coat	wàitào	外套	外套	N	9s
January	yīyuè	一月	一月	N	3g
Japan	Rìběn	日本	日本	PN	1s

English	Pinyin	Traditional Characters	Simplified Characters	Grammar	Lesson
Japanese language	Rìwén	日文	日文	N	6s
Japanese people/person	Rìběnrén	日本人	日本人	N	1s
job; to work	gōngzuò	工作	工作	N/V	5
July	qīyuè	七月	七月	N	3g
jump	tiào	跳	跳	V	4
June	liùyuè	六月	六月	N	3g
junior high (grades 7–9)	chūzhōng	初中	初中	N	2c
just now; a short moment ago	gāngcái	剛才	刚才	T	10
▲K▲					
Kangxi Dictionary	*Kāngxī Zìdiǎn*	康熙字典	康熙字典	N	Intro.
king; a surname	wáng	王	王	N	1
knock at the door	qiāo mén	敲門	敲门	VO	5f
know	zhīdao	知道	知道	V	6
know (someone); recognize	rènshi	認識	认识	V	3
know how to; can	huì	會	会	AV	8
Korea	Hánguó	韓國	韩国	PN	6s
Korean language	Hánwén	韓文	韩文	N	6s
Korean people/person	Hánguórén	韓國人	韩国人	N	1s
Kunming	Kūnmíng	昆明	昆明	PN	10c
▲L▲					
lacking; short of	chà	差	差	V	3s
language; written language	wén	文	文	N	6
last month	shàngge yuè	上個月	上个月	T	6n
last week	shàngge xīngqī	上個星期	上个星期	T	7
last year	qùnián	去年	去年	T	3s
late; night; evening	wǎn	晚	晚	Adj/N	3
later	hòulái	後來	后来	T	8
Latin	Lādīngwén	拉丁文	拉丁文	N	6s
laugh; laugh at	xiào	笑	笑	V	8
laugh at; laugh	xiào	笑	笑	V	8
lawyer	lǜshī	律師	律师	N	2
lesson; class	kè	課	课	N	6
letter	xìn	信	信	N	8
library	túshūguǎn	圖書館	图书馆	N	5
like; prefer	xǐhuan	喜歡	喜欢	V	3
like this; so	zhèyàng	這樣	这样	Pr	10
line	xiàn	線	线	N	11
listen	tīng	聽	听	V	4
little; small	xiǎo	小	小	Adj	2
Little Bai	Xiǎo Bái	小白	小白	PN	3
Little Gao	Xiǎo Gāo	小高	小高	PN	2
Little Li	Xiǎo Lǐ	小李	小李	PN	3
Little Zhang	Xiǎo Zhāng	小張	小张	PN	2
long	cháng	長	长	Adj	9s
long gown	chángpáo	長袍	长袍	N	9c

English	Pinyin	Traditional Characters	Simplified Characters	Grammar	Lesson
long time	hǎojiǔ	好久	好久	CE	4
long time; for a long time	jiǔ	久	久	Adj	4
longevity	chángshòu	長壽	长寿	N	3c
longevity noodles	chángshòu miàn	長壽麵	长寿面	N	3c
look; watch	kàn	看	看	V	4
look for	zhǎo	找	找	V	4
lunch	wǔfàn	午飯	午饭	N	8
lunch	zhōngfàn	中飯	中饭	N	3s
M					
machine	jī	機	机	N	11
major; specialty	zhuānyè	專業	专业	N	8
make a fortune	fācái	發財	发财	V	11c
make a phone call	dǎ diànhuà	打電話	打电话	VO	6
make an appointment	yuē	約	约	V	10
make progress	jìnbù	進步	进步	V	8
Malaysia	Mǎláixīyà	馬來西亞	马来西亚	PN	6s
male	nán	男	男	N	2
male	nán de	男的	男的		7
Mandarin jacket	mǎguà	馬褂	马褂	N	9c
many; much	duō	多	多	Adj	7
Maotai (name of a liquor)	Máotái	茅台	茅台	PN	5c
March	Sānyuè	三月	三月	N	3g
master craftsman; skilled worker	shīfu	師傅	师傅	N	9n
matter; affair; business	shì	事	事	N	3
May	wǔyuè	五月	五月	N	3g
may; can	kěyǐ	可以	可以	AV	5
May I ask...	qǐng wèn	請問	请问	CE	1
me; I	wǒ	我	我	Pr	1
meal; (cooked) rice	fàn	飯	饭	N	3
meaning	yìsi	意思	意思	N	4
medium	zhōng	中	中	Adj	9
middle school	zhōngxué	中學	中学	N	2c
midnight	bànyè	半夜	半夜	T	7
mineral water	kuàngquán shuǐ	礦泉水	矿泉水	N	5s
minute	fēn	分	分	M	3s
Miss; young lady	xiǎojie	小姐	小姐	N	1
mom; mother	māma	媽媽	妈妈	N	2
moment; (a point in) time; (a duration of) time	shíhou	時候	时候	N	4
moment ago; just now	gāngcái	剛才	刚才	T	10
Monday	xīngqīyī	星期一	星期一	N	3g
Monday	zhōuyī	週一	周一	N	3g
money	qián	錢	钱	N	9
month	yuè	月	月	N	3

English	Pinyin	Traditional Characters	Simplified Characters	Grammar	Lesson
morning	shàngwǔ	上午	上午	T	6
morning	zǎoshang	早上	早上	T	8
mother; mom	māma	媽媽	妈妈	N	2
mouth; (measure word for people)	kǒu	口	口	N/M	2n
movie	diànyǐng	電影	电影	N	4
Mr.; husband; teacher	xiānsheng	先生	先生	N	1
Mrs.; wife	tàitai	太太	太太	N	1s
much; many	duō	多	多	Adj	7
music	yīnyuè	音樂	音乐	N	4
must; have to	děi	得	得	AV	6
▴**N**▴					
name	míngzi	名字	名字	N	1
Nanjing	Nánjīng	南京	南京	PN	10c
nap	wǔjiào	午覺	午觉	N	7s
near	jìn	近	近	Adj	8
need not	bú yòng	不用	不用	CE	9
nervous; anxious	jǐnzhāng	緊張	紧张	Adj	11
Never mind. Forget it.	suàn le	算了	算了	CE	4
new	xīn	新	新	Adj	8
new words	shēngcí	生詞	生词	N	7
new year	xīnnián	新年	新年	N	11
newspaper	bào	報	报	N	8
next; under	xià	下	下		6
next month	xià(ge)yuè	下(個)月	下(个)月	T	3s
next time	xià cì	下次	下次		10
next week	xiàge xīngqī	下個星期	下个星期	T	6
next year	míngnián	明年	明年	T	3s
nice; good; fine; O.K.	hǎo	好	好	Adj	1, 3
night	yè	夜	夜	N	7
night; evening	wǎnshang	晚上	晚上	T	3
night; evening; late	wǎn	晚	晚	N/Adj	3
nine	jiǔ	九	九	Nu	Intro.
no; not	bù	不	不	Adv	1
no problem	méi shìr	沒事兒	没事儿	CE	8f
no problem	méi wèntí	沒問題	没问题	CE	6
noodles	miàn	麵	面	N	3c
noon	zhōngwǔ	中午	中午	T	6s; 8
not; no	bù	不	不	Adv	1
not	méi	沒	没	Adv	2
not bad; pretty good	búcuò	不錯	不错	Adj	4
not only..., but also	búdàn..., érqiě	不但...而且	不但...而且	Conj	10
not until; only then	cái	才	才	Adv	5
notebook	běnzi	本子	本子	N	7s
November	shíyīyuè	十一月	十一月	N	3g
now	xiànzài	現在	现在	T	3

English	Pinyin	Traditional Characters	Simplified Characters	Grammar	Lesson
number (bus route)	hào	號	号	N	11n
number (bus route)	lù	路	路	N	11n
number in a series; day of the month; size	hào	號	号	M	3, 9
O					
O.K.; be all right	xíng	行	行	Adj	6
O.K.; good; fine; nice	hǎo	好	好	Adj	1, 3
object; things	dōngxi	東西	东西	N	9
o'clock	diǎn	點	点	N	3
o'clock	-diǎnzhōng	點鐘	点钟	M	3
October	shíyuè	十月	十月	N	3g
office	bàngōngshì	辦公室	办公室	N	6
often	chángcháng	常常	常常	Adv	4
old; big	dà	大	大	Adj	3
older brother	gēge	哥哥	哥哥	N	2
older sister	jiějie	姐姐	姐姐	N	2
oldest brother	dàgē	大哥	大哥	N	7g
oldest sister	dàjiě	大姐	大姐	N	7g
olive	gǎnlǎn	橄欖	橄榄	N	4s
on; at; in	zài	在	在	Prep	5
one	yī	一	一	Nu	Intro.
1/100 of a kuai; cent	fēn	分	分	M	9
1/10 of a kuai (similar to the U.S. dime)	máo	毛	毛	M	9
oneself	zìjǐ	自己	自己	Pr	11
only	zhǐ	只	只	Adv	4
only then; not until	cái	才	才	Adv	5
operate; drive	kāi	開	开	V	11
or	háishi	還是	还是	Conj	3
or	huòzhě	或者	或者	Conj	11
orange	júhóngsè	橘紅色	橘红色	N	9s
other	bié (de)	別(的)	别(的)	Adv	4
others; other people; another person	biérén	別人	别人	Adv	4
overcast	yīn	陰	阴	Adj	10s
overcoat	dàyī	大衣	大衣	N	9s
P					
pair of	shuāng	雙	双	M	9
pants	kùzi	褲子	裤子	N	9
paper	zhǐ	紙	纸	N	2g, 7s
park	gōngyuán	公園	公园	N	10
past few days	zhè jǐ tiān	這幾天	这几天		11
path; road	lù	路	路	N	11
pay money	fù qián	付錢	付钱	VO	9
pen	bǐ	筆	笔	N	7

English	Pinyin	Traditional Characters	Simplified Characters	Grammar	Lesson
pencil	qiānbǐ	鉛筆	铅笔	N	7s
people; person	rén	人	人	N	1
Pepsi	Bǎishìkělè	百事可樂	百事可乐	N	5s
person; people	rén	人	人	N	1
Philippines (the)	Fēilǜbīn	菲律賓	菲律宾	PN	6s
photo; picture	zhàopiàn	照片	照片	N	2
physician; doctor	yīshēng	醫生	医生	N	2
picture; photo	zhàopiàn	照片	照片	N	2
pink	fěnhóngsè	粉紅色	粉红色	N	9s
play; have fun	wán(r)	玩(兒)	玩(儿)	V	5
play ball	dǎ qiú	打球	打球	VO	4
pleasantly cool (weather)	liángkuai	涼快	凉快	Adj	10
please (polite form of request)	qǐng	請	请	V	1
pleased; happy	gāoxìng	高興	高兴	Adj	5
plum; a surname	lǐ	李	李	N	1
polite	kèqi	客氣	客气	Adj	6
Portugal	Pútáoyá	葡萄牙	葡萄牙	PN	6s
Portuguese language	Pútáoyáwén	葡萄牙文	葡萄牙文	N	6s
practice	liànxí	練習	练习	V	6
pretty	piàoliang	漂亮	漂亮	Adj	5
pretty good; not bad	búcuò	不錯	不错	Adj	4
preview	yùxí	預習	预习	V	7
previously; before; ago	yǐqián	以前	以前	T	8
pronunciation	fāyīn	發音	发音	N	8
public	gōnggòng	公共	公共	Adj	11
purple	zǐ	紫	紫	Adj	9s
put on; wear	chuān	穿	穿	V	9
▴**Q**▴					
quarter (hour); 15 minutes	kè	刻	刻	M	3
question; problem	wèntí	問題	问题	N	6
quickly; fast;quick	kuài	快	快	Adv/Adj	5, 7
▴**R**▴					
radical	bùshǒu	部首	部首	N	Intro.
rain	xià yǔ	下雨	下雨	VO	10
raining season	huángméi	黃梅	黄梅	N	10c
read	niàn	念	念	V	7
read; read books	kàn shū	看書	看书	VO	4
read books; read	kàn shū	看書	看书	VO	4
really	zhēn	真	真	Adv	7
Really?	shì ma	是嗎	是吗	CE	5f, 5n
recently	zuìjìn	最近	最近	T	8
recognize; know (someone)	rènshi	認識	认识	V	3
record	lùyīn	錄音	录音	N/VO	7
red	hóng	紅	红	Adj	9
red autumn leaves	hóngyè	紅葉	红叶	N	10

English	Pinyin	Traditional Characters	Simplified Characters	Grammar	Lesson
rent	zū	租	租	V	11
rent out; to let	chūzū	出租	出租	V	11
return	huí	回	回	V	5
review	fùxí	復習	复习	V	7
rice (cooked); meal	fàn	飯	饭	N	3
right; correct	duì	對	对	Adj	4
road; highway	gōnglù	公路	公路	N	11
road; path	lù	路	路	N	11
Russia	Éguó	俄國	俄国	PN	6s
Russian language	Éwén	俄文	俄文	N	6s
S					
salesclerk; shop assistant	shòuhuòyuán	售貨員	售货员	N	9
same; alike	yíyàng	一樣	一样	Adj	9
Saturday	xīngqīliù	星期六	星期六	N	3g
say; speak	shuō	說	说	V	6
school	xuéxiào	學校	学校	N	5
school term; semester/quarter	xuéqī	學期	学期	N	8
schoolwork; homework	gōngkè	功課	功课	N	7
second oldest brother	èrgē	二哥	二哥	N	7g
second oldest sister	èrjiě	二姐	二姐	N	7g
see	jiàn	見	见	V	3
see you again; goodbye	zàijiàn	再見	再见	CE	3
sell	mài	賣	卖	V	9s
semester/quarter; school term	xuéqī	學期	学期	N	8
senior high (grades 10–12)	gāozhōng	高中	高中	N	2c
September	jiǔyuè	九月	九月	N	3
service person; waiter; waitress	fúwùyuán	服務員	服务员	N	9n
seven	qī	七	七	Nu	Intro.
shadow	yǐng	影	影	N	4
Shanghai	Shànghǎi	上海	上海	PN	10
she	tā	她	她	Pr	2
ship; boat	chuán	船	船	N	11s
shirt	chènshān	襯衫	衬衫	N	9
shoes	xié	鞋	鞋	N	9
shop assistant; salesclerk	shòuhuòyuán	售貨員	售货员	N	9
short	duǎn	短	短	Adj	9s
short of; lacking	chà	差	差	V	3s
simplified character	jiǎntǐzì	簡體字	简体字	N	7c
sing	chàng	唱	唱	V	4
sing (a song)	chàng gē	唱歌	唱歌	VO	4
sit	zuò	坐	坐	V	5
six	liù	六	六	Nu	Intro.
size	dàxiǎo	大小	大小	N	9
size; number in a series; day of the month	hào	號	号	M	3, 9

English	Pinyin	Traditional Characters	Simplified Characters	Grammar	Lesson
skirt	qúnzi	裙子	裙子	N	9s
sleep	shuì	睡	睡	V	4
sleep	shuì jiào	睡覺	睡觉	VO	4
slow	màn	慢	慢	Adj	7
small; little	xiǎo	小	小	Adj	2
snow	xuě	雪	雪	N	10s
so	suǒyǐ	所以	所以	Conj	4
so; like this	zhèyàng	這樣	这样	Pr	10
so; such	zhème	這麼	这么	Pr	7
soccer	zúqiú	足球	足球	N	4s
socks	wàzi	襪子	袜子	N	9s
soda pop; soft drink	qìshuǐ(r)	汽水(兒)	汽水(儿)	N	5s
soft drink; soda pop	qìshuǐ(r)	汽水(兒)	汽水(儿)	N	5s
some; a few (an indefinite number, usually less than ten)	jǐ	幾	几	Nu	6
sometimes	yǒu shíhou	有時候	有时候	CE	4
somewhat; a little	yǒu yìdiǎnr	有一點兒	有一点儿	CE	7
son	érzi	兒子	儿子	N	2
song	gē	歌	歌	N	4
soon; be about to; before long	kuài	快	快	Adv	11
sound recording	lùyīn	錄音	录音	N	7
Spain	Xībānyá	西班牙	西班牙	PN	6s
Spanish language	Xībānyáwén	西班牙文	西班牙文	N	6s
speak; say	shuō	說	说	V	6
special; especially	tèbié	特别	特别	Adj/Adv	7g
specialty; major	zhuānyè	專業	专业	N	8
speech; talk; words	huà	話	话	N	6
spend	huā	花	花	V	11
spring	chūntiān	春天	春天	N	10
Sprite	Xuěbì	雪碧	雪碧	N	5s
Starbucks	Xīngbākè	星巴克	星巴克	PN	5c
start	kāishǐ	開始	开始	V	7
start; begin; in the beginning	kāishǐ	開始	开始	N/V	8
start a class; go to class	shàng kè	上課	上课	VO	7
station; stop (of bus, train, etc.)	zhàn	站	站	N	11
station; stop (of bus, train, etc.)	chēzhàn	車站	车站	N	11
stop; station (of bus, train, etc.)	zhàn	站	站	N	11
stop; station (of bus, train, etc.)	chēzhàn	車站	车站	N	11
strike, hit	dǎ	打	打	V	4
student	xuésheng	學生	学生	N	1
study	xué	學	学	V	7
stuffy	mēn	悶	闷	Adj	10
subway	dìtiě	地鐵	地铁	N	11
such; so	zhème	這麼	这么	Pr	7
suit	xīzhuāng	西裝	西装	N	9s
suitable	héshì	合適	合适	Adj	9

English	Pinyin	Traditional Characters	Simplified Characters	Grammar	Lesson
summer	xiàtiān	夏天	夏天	N	10
summer vacation	shǔjià	暑假	暑假	N	11s
sun; day	rì	日	日	N	3
Sun Yatsen suit	Zhōngshān zhuāng	中山裝	中山装	N	9c
Sunday	xīngqīrì	星期日	星期日	N	3g
Sunday	xīngqītiān	星期天	星期天	N	3g
Sunday	zhōurì	週日	周日	N	3g
sunny; clear	qíng	晴	晴	Adj	10s
super highway; highway	gāosù gōnglù	高速公路	高速公路	N	11
supper; dinner	wǎnfàn	晚飯	晚饭	N	3
surname; (one's) surname is...; to be surnamed	xìng	姓	姓	N/V	1
sweater	máoyī	毛衣	毛衣	N	9s
▲T▲					
Taichung	Táizhōng	台中	台中	PN	10s
Taipei	Táiběi	台北	台北	PN	10
Taiwan	Táiwān	台灣	台湾	PN	10
take a bath/shower	xǐ zǎo	洗澡	洗澡	VO	8
take someone (somewhere)	sòng	送	送	V	11
talk	shuō huà	說話	说话	VO	7
talk; speech; words	huà	話	话	N	6
tall; (a surname)	gāo	高	高	Adj/N	2
tasty; good to drink	hǎohē	好喝	好喝	Adj	5s
taxi	chūzū qìchē	出租汽車	出租汽车	N	11
taxi (in Taiwan)	jìchéngchē	計程車	计程车	N	11s
tea	chá	茶	茶	N	5
teach	jiāo	教	教	V	7
teacher	lǎoshī	老師	老师	N	1
telephone	diànhuà	電話	电话	N	6
tell	gàosu	告訴	告诉	V	8
ten	shí	十	十	Nu	Intro.
tennis	wǎngqiú	網球	网球	N	4s
test; give or take a test	kǎoshì	考試	考试	V/N	6
text	kèwén	課文	课文	N	7
Thailand	Tàiguó	泰國	泰国	PN	6s
thank you	xièxie	謝謝	谢谢	CE	3
thanks; (a surname)	xiè	謝	谢	V/N	10
that	nà/nèi	那	那	Pr	2
That's right!	duì le	對了	对了	CE	4s
then	ránhòu	然後	然后	Adv	11
then; in that case	nà	那	那	Conj	4
there	nàr	那兒	那儿	Pr	8
things; objects	dōngxi	東西	东西	N	9
think; feel that	juéde	覺得	觉得	V	4

English	Pinyin	Traditional Characters	Simplified Characters	Grammar	Lesson
think; want to	xiǎng	想	想	AV	4
third oldest brother	sāngē	三哥	三哥	N	7g
third oldest sister	sānjiě	三姐	三姐	N	7g
this	zhè/zhèi	這	这	Pr	2
this	zhège	這個	这个	Pr	10
this year	jīnnián	今年	今年	T	3
three	sān	三	三	Nu	Intro.
Thursday	lǐbàisì	禮拜四	礼拜四	N	3g
Thursday	xīngqīsì	星期四	星期四	N	3
ticket	piào	票	票	N	11
time	shíjiān	時間	时间	T	6
time (a point in); moment; time (a duration of)	shíhou	時候	时候	N	4
to; for	gěi	給	给	Prep	6
to what extent; how many/much	duō	多	多	Adv	3
today	jīntiān	今天	今天	T	3
together	yìqǐ	一起	一起	Adv	5
tomorrow	míngtiān	明天	明天	T	3
too; also	yě	也	也	Adv	1
too; also; as well	hái	還	还	Adv	3
too; extremely	tài…(le)	太…(了)	太…(了)	Adv	3
traditional character	fántǐzì	繁體字	繁体字	N	7c
train	huǒchē	火車	火车	N	11s
travel by	zuò	坐	坐	V	11
treat (somebody); invite	qǐng	請	请	V	3
trolley bus; cable car; tram	diànchē	電車	电车	N	11s
troublesome	máfan	麻煩	麻烦	Adj	11
T-shirt	T-xùshān	T-恤衫	T-恤衫	N	9s
Tuesday	xīngqī'èr	星期二	星期二	N	3g
Tuesday	zhōu'èr	週二	周二	N	3g
TV	diànshì	電視	电视	N	4
twelve	shí'èr	十二	十二	Nu	3
two	èr	二	二	Nu	Intro.
two; a couple of	liǎng	兩	两	Nu	2
▴U▴					
under; next	xià	下	下		6
understand	dǒng	懂	懂	V	7
university; college	dàxué	大學	大学	N	2
use; to use	yòng	用	用	V/N	8
usually	píngcháng	平常	平常	T	7
▴V▴					
Vancouver	Wēngēhuá	溫哥華	温哥华	PN	10s
vehicle; car	chē	車	车	N	11
very	hěn	很	很	Adv	3
video recording	lùxiàng	錄像	录像	N	10

English	Pinyin	Traditional Characters	Simplified Characters	Grammar	Lesson
Vietnam	Yuènán	越南	越南	PN	6s
Vietnamese people/person	Yuènánrén	越南人	越南人	N	1s
vision	shì	視	视	N	4
volleyball	páiqiú	排球	排球	N	4s
W					
wait	děng	等	等	V	6
waiter; waitress; service person	fúwùyuán	服務員	服务员	N	9n
walk	zǒu lù	走路	走路	VO	11s
walk; go by way of	zǒu	走	走	V	11
want to; have a desire for	yào	要	要	V/AV	5, 9
want to; think	xiǎng	想	想	AV	4
warm (weather)	nuǎnhuo	暖和	暖和	Adj	10
watch	biǎo	錶	表	N	3s
watch; look	kàn	看	看	V	4
water	shuǐ	水	水	N	5
we	wǒmen	我們	我们	Pr	3
wear (hat, glasses, etc.)	dài	戴	戴	V	9s
wear; put on	chuān	穿	穿	V	9
weather	tiānqì	天氣	天气	N	10
week	lǐbài	禮拜	礼拜	N	3g
week	xīngqī	星期	星期	N	3
weekend	zhōumò	週末	周末	T	4
wet; humid	cháoshī	潮濕	潮湿	Adj	10s
what	shénme	什麼	什么	QPr	1
What is your honorable surname?	guì xìng	貴姓	贵姓	CE	1
what to do	zěnme bàn	怎麼辦	怎么办	QW	10
when...; at the time of...	de shíhou	的時候	的时候		8
where	nǎr	哪兒	哪儿	QPr	5
which	nǎ/něi	哪	哪	QPr	6
white; (a surname)	bái	白	白	Adj	3
who	shéi	誰	谁	QPr	2
Who is it?	shéi ya	誰呀	谁呀	CE	5f
why	wèishénme	爲什麼	为什么	QPr	3
wife; Mrs.	tàitai	太太	太太	N	1s
will	huì	會	会	AV	10
will; be going to	yào	要	要	AV	6
wine	jiǔ	酒	酒	N	5
winter	dōngtiān	冬天	冬天	N	10
winter vacation	hánjià	寒假	寒假	N	11
wish	zhù	祝	祝	V	8
word; character	zì	字	字	N	7
words; speech; talk	huà	話	话	N	6
work; job	gōngzuò	工作	工作	V/N	5
work part-time; do manual work	dǎ gōng	打工	打工	VO	5s
wristwatch	shǒubiǎo	手錶	手表	N	9n

English	Pinyin	Traditional Characters	Simplified Characters	Grammar	Lesson
write	xiě	寫	写	V	7
writing brush	máobǐ	毛筆	毛笔	N	7s
wrong	cuò	錯	错	Adj	4
Wuhan	Wǔhàn	武漢	武汉	PN	10c
▴Y▴					
Yangtze river	Chángjiāng	長江	长江	PN	10c
year	nián	年	年	N	3
year after next	hòunián	後年	后年	T	3s
year before last	qiánnián	前年	前年	T	3s
year of age	suìshù	歲數	岁数	N	3n
year (of age)	suì	歲	岁	N	3
yellow	huáng	黄	黄	Adj	9
yesterday	zuótiān	昨天	昨天	T	3s, 4
you	nǐ	你	你	Pr	1
you (singular; polite)	nín	您	您	Pr	1
You are welcome. Don't be (so) polite.	bú kèqi	不客氣	不客气	CE	6
You flatter me. Not at all.	nǎli	哪裏	哪里	CE	7
young lady; Miss	xiǎojie	小姐	小姐	N	1
younger brother	dìdi	弟弟	弟弟	N	2
younger sister	mèimei	妹妹	妹妹	N	2

Vocabulary Index (by Grammar Category): Lessons 1–11

Key: c=Culture Notes; f=Functional Expressions; g=Grammar; n=Notes; x=Supplementary Vocabulary

Grammar	Pinyin	Traditional Characters	Simplified Characters	English	Lesson
Adjectives					
Adj	bái	白	白	white; (a surname)	3
Adj	búcuò	不錯	不错	not bad; pretty good	4
Adj	cháng	長	长	long	9s
Adj	cháoshī	潮濕	潮湿	wet; humid	10s
Adj	cuò	錯	错	wrong	4
Adj	dà	大	大	big; old	3
Adj	duǎn	短	短	short	9s
Adj	duì	對	对	right; correct	4
Adj	duō	多	多	many; much	7
Adj	fāngbiàn	方便	方便	convenient	6
Adj	gāo	高	高	(a surname); tall	2
Adj	gāosù	高速	高速	high speed	11
Adj	gāoxìng	高興	高兴	happy; pleased	5
Adj	gōnggòng	公共	公共	public	11
Adj	guì	貴	贵	honorable	1
Adj	guì	貴	贵	expensive	9
Adj	hǎo	好	好	fine; good; nice; O.K.	1, 3
Adj	hǎochī	好吃	好吃	good to eat; delicious	5s
Adj	hǎohē	好喝	好喝	good to drink; tasty	5s
Adj	hǎokàn	好看	好看	good-looking	5s, 7n
Adj	hǎowán(r)	好玩(兒)	好玩(儿)	fun	5s
Adj	hēi	黑	黑	black	9
Adj	héshì	合適	合适	suitable	9
Adj	hóng	紅	红	red	9
Adj	huáng	黃	黄	yellow	9
Adj	huī	灰	灰	gray	9s
Adj	jìn	近	近	near	8
Adj	jǐnzhāng	緊張	紧张	nervous; anxious	11
Adj	jiǔ	久	久	a long time; for a long time	4
Adj	kèqi	客氣	客气	polite	6
Adj	kuài	快	快	quick; fast	7
Adj	kuàilè	快樂	快乐	happy	11
Adj	lán	藍	蓝	blue	9s, 11
Adj	lěng	冷	冷	cold	10
Adj	liángkuai	涼快	凉快	pleasantly cool (weather)	10
Adj	lǜ	綠	绿	green	9s, 11

Grammar	Pinyin	Traditional Characters	Simplified Characters	English	Lesson
Adj	máfan	麻煩	麻烦	troublesome	11
Adj	màn	慢	慢	slow	7
Adj	máng	忙	忙	busy	3
Adj	mēn	悶	闷	stuffy	10
Adj	nán	難	难	difficult	7
Adj	nuǎnhuo	暖和	暖和	warm (weather)	10
Adj	piányi	便宜	便宜	cheap; inexpensive	9
Adj	piàoliang	漂亮	漂亮	pretty	5
Adj	qíng	晴	晴	sunny; clear	10s
Adj	qīngchu	清楚	清楚	clear	8
Adj	rè	熱	热	hot	10
Adj	róngyì	容易	容易	easy	7
Adj	shuài	帥	帅	handsome	7
Adj	shūfu	舒服	舒服	comfortable	10
Adj	tèbié	特別	特别	special	7g
Adj	wǎn	晚	晚	late	3
Adj	xiǎo	小	小	small; little	2
Adj	xīn	新	新	new	8
Adj	xíng	行	行	be all right; O.K.	6
Adj	yīn	陰	阴	overcast	10s
Adj	yíyàng	一樣	一样	same; alike	9
Adj	zǎo	早	早	Good morning!; early	7
Adj	zāogāo	糟糕	糟糕	in a terrible mess; too bad	10
Adj	zhōng	中	中	medium	9
Adj	zǐ	紫	紫	purple	9s
Adverbs					
Adv	bié	別	别	don't	6
Adv	bié (de)	別(的)	别(的)	other	4
Adv	bù	不	不	not; no	1
Adv	cái	才	才	not until; only then	5
Adv	chángcháng	常常	常常	often	4
Adv	dōu	都	都	both; all	2
Adv	duō	多	多	how many/much; to what extent	3
Adv	gèng	更	更	even more	10
Adv	hái	還	还	also; too; as well	3
Adv	hěn	很	很	very	3
Adv	jiù	就	就	(indicates that something takes place sooner than expected)	7
Adv	jiù	就	就	the very one (indicating verification of something mentioned before)	6
Adv	kuài	快	快	soon; be about to; before long	11
Adv	kuài	快	快	fast; quickly	5
Adv	méi	沒	没	not	2
Adv	píngcháng	平常	平常	usually	7

Grammar	Pinyin	Traditional Characters	Simplified Characters	English	Lesson
Adv	ránhòu	然後	然后	then	11
Adv	tài...(le)	太...(了)	太...(了)	too; extremely	3
Adv	tèbié	特別	特别	especially	7g
Adv	xiān	先	先	first; before	11
Adv	yě	也	也	too; also	1
Adv	yígòng	一共	一共	altogether	9
Adv	yǐjīng	已經	已经	already	8
Adv	yìqǐ	一起	一起	together	5
Adv	yòu	又	又	again	10
Adv	zài	再	再	again	3
Adv	zhēn	眞	真	really	7
Adv	zhèngzài	正在	正在	in the middle of (doing something)	8
Adv	zhǐ	只	只	only	4
Adv	zuì	最	最	(an adverb of superlative degree; most, -est)	8
Adv	zuìhǎo	最好	最好	had better	10
Adv	zuìhòu	最後	最后	finally	11
Auxiliary Verbs					
AV	děi	得	得	must; to have to	6
AV	huì	會	会	can; to know how to	8
AV	huì	會	会	will	10
AV	kěyǐ	可以	可以	can; may	5
AV	néng	能	能	can; to be able to	8
AV	xiǎng	想	想	to want to; to think	4
AV	yào	要	要	will; to be going to	6
AV	yào	要	要	want to; to have a desire for	9
Common Expressions					
CE	bié kèqi	別客氣	别客气	Don't be so polite!	6
CE	bù hǎoyìsi	不好意思	不好意思	to feel embarrassed	11
CE	bú kèqi	不客氣	不客气	You are welcome. Don't be (so) polite.	6
CE	bú xiè	不謝	不谢	Don't mention it. Not at all. You're welcome.	7
CE	bú yòng	不用	不用	need not	6g, 9
CE	duì bu qǐ	對不起	对不起	I'm sorry.	5
CE	duì le	對了	对了	That's right!	4s
CE	duō dà	多大	多大	how old	3
CE	gōngxǐ fācái	恭喜發財	恭喜发财	Congratulations and may you make a fortune!	11n
CE	guì xìng	貴姓	贵姓	What is your honorable surname?	1
CE	hǎojiǔ	好久	好久	a long time	4
CE	méi shìr	沒事兒	没事儿	no problem; it's O.K.	8f
CE	méi wèntí	沒問題	没问题	no problem	6

Grammar	Pinyin	Traditional Characters	Simplified Characters	English	Lesson
CE	nǎli	哪裏	哪里	You flatter me. Not at all. (a polite reply to a compliment)	7
CE	nǐ hǎo	你好	你好	How do you do? Hello!	1
CE	qǐng wèn	請問	请问	May I ask...	1
CE	shéi ya	誰呀	谁呀	Who is it?	5f
CE	shì ma	是嗎	是吗	Really?	5f, 5n
CE	suàn le	算了	算了	Forget it. Never mind.	4
CE	xièxie	謝謝	谢谢	thank you	3
CE	yǒu shíhou	有時候	有时候	sometimes	4
CE	yǒu yìdiǎnr	有一點兒	有一点儿	a little; somewhat	7
CE	yǒu yìsi	有意思	有意思	interesting	4
CE	zàijiàn	再見	再见	good-bye; see you again	3
CE	zǎo ān	早安	早安	Good morning!	7n
Conjunctions					
Conj	búdàn..., érqiě	不但...而且	不但...而且	not only..., but also	10
Conj	búguò	不過	不过	however; but	11
Conj	chúle...yǐwài	除了...以外	除了...以外	in addition to; besides	8
Conj	dànshì	但是	但是	but	6
Conj	gēn	跟	跟	and	7
Conj	háishi	還是	还是	had better	11
Conj	háishi	還是	还是	or	3
Conj	hé	和	和	and	2
Conj	huòzhě	或者	或者	or	11
Conj	kěshì	可是	可是	but	3
Conj	nà	那	那	in that case; then	4
Conj	suīrán	雖然	虽然	although	9
Conj	suǒyǐ	所以	所以	so	4
Conj	yàoshi	要是	要是	if	6
Conj	yīnwei	因爲	因为	because	3
Interjections					
Interj	wèi/wéi	喂	喂	Hello!; Hey!	6
Measure Words					
M	bēi	杯	杯	cup; glass	5
M	cì	次	次	time; (a measure word for occurrence)	10
M	diǎn	點	点	o'clock	3
M	diǎn(r)	點(兒)	点(儿)	a little; a bit; some	5
M	diǎnzhōng	點鐘	点钟	o'clock	3
M	dǐng	頂	顶	(a measure word for hat)	9s
M	fēn	分	分	minute	3s
M	fēn	分	分	1/100 of a kuai; cent	9
M	fēng	封	封	(a measure word for letters)	8
M	gè	個	个	(a common measure word)	2

Grammar	Pinyin	Traditional Characters	Simplified Characters	English	Lesson
M	hào	號	号	number in a series; day of the month	3
M	hào	號	号	number; size	9
M	jiàn	件	件	(a measure word for shirts, dresses, jackets, coats, etc.)	9
M	jiǎo	角	角	dime	9g
M	jié	節	节	(a measure word for class periods)	6
M	kè	刻	刻	quarter (hour); 15 minutes	3
M	kǒu	口	口	(a measure word for people)	2n
M	kuài	塊	块	colloquial term for the basic Chinese monetary unit	9
M	liàng	輛	辆	(a measure for vehicles)	11s
M	máo	毛	毛	1/10 of a kuai (similar to the U.S. dime)	9
M	mén	門	门	(a measure word for courses)	6c
M	piān	篇	篇	(a measure word for essays, articles, etc.)	8
M	píng	瓶	瓶	bottle	5
M	shuāng	雙	双	a pair of	9
M	tiáo	條	条	(a measure word for long, thin objects)	9
M	wèi	位	位	(a polite measure word for people)	6
M	yí xià	一下	一下	(a measure word used after a verb indicating short duration)	5
M	yuán	元	元	Chinese dollar	9g
M	zhāng	張	张	(a measure word for flat objects)	2
M	zhī	枝	枝	(a measure word for pens and long items); twig	9g
M	zhī	隻	只	(a measure word for bird, shoe, etc.)	9g
Nouns					
N	bàba	爸爸	爸爸	dad; father	2
N	Bǎishìkělè	百事可樂	百事可乐	Pepsi	5s
N	bàngōngshì	辦公室	办公室	office	6
N	bàngqiú	棒球	棒球	baseball	4s
N	bào	報	报	newspaper	8
N	bāyuè	八月	八月	August	3g
N	běnzi	本子	本子	notebook	7s
N	bǐ	筆	笔	pen	7
N	biǎo	錶	表	watch	3s
N	biérén	別人	别人	others; other people; another person	4
N	bùshǒu	部首	部首	radical	Intro.

Grammar	Pinyin	Traditional Characters	Simplified Characters	English	Lesson
N	cāntīng	餐廳	餐厅	dining room; cafeteria	8
N	chá	茶	茶	tea	5
N	chángpáo	長袍	长袍	long gown	9c
N	chángshòu	長壽	长寿	longevity	3c
N	chángshòu miàn	長壽麵	长寿面	longevity noodles	3c
N	chē	車	车	vehicle; car	11
N	chén	陳	陈	(a surname)	1n
N	chènshān	襯衫	衬衫	shirt	9
N	chēzhàn	車站	车站	(bus, train, etc.) stop; station	11
N	chuán	船	船	boat; ship	11s
N	chuáng	床	床	bed	2g, 8
N	chūntiān	春天	春天	spring	10
N	chūzhōng	初中	初中	junior high (grades 7–9)	2c
N	chūzū qìchē	出租汽車	出租汽车	taxi	11
N	dàgē	大哥	大哥	oldest brother	7g
N	dàjiě	大姐	大姐	oldest sister	7g
N	dàxiǎo	大小	大小	size	9
N	dàxué	大學	大学	university; college	2
N	dàxuéshēng	大學生	大学生	college student	2
N	dàyī	大衣	大衣	overcoat	9s
N	Déguórén	德國人	德国人	German people/person	1s
N	Déwén	德文	德文	the German language	6s
N	diàn	電	电	electricity	4
N	diànchē	電車	电车	cable car; trolley bus; tram	11s
N	diànhuà	電話	电话	telephone	6
N	diànnǎo	電腦	电脑	computer	8
N	diànshì	電視	电视	TV	4
N	diànyǐng	電影	电影	movie	4
N	diànzǐ jìsuànjī	電子計算機	电子计算机	computer	8n
N	dìdi	弟弟	弟弟	younger brother	2
N	dìtiě	地鐵	地铁	subway	11
N	dōngtiān	冬天	冬天	winter	10
N	dōngxi	東西	东西	things; objects	9
N	èrgē	二哥	二哥	second oldest brother	7g
N	èrjiě	二姐	二姐	second oldest sister	7g
N	èryuè	二月	二月	February	3g
N	érzi	兒子	儿子	son	2
N	Éwén	俄文	俄文	the Russian language	6s
N	Fǎguórén	法國人	法国人	French people/person	1s
N	fàn	飯	饭	meal; (cooked) rice	3
N	fántǐzì	繁體字	繁体字	traditional character	7c
N	Fǎwén	法文	法文	the French language	6s
N	fāyīn	發音	发音	pronunciation	8
N	fēijī	飛機	飞机	airplane	11
N	fēijīchǎng	飛機場	飞机场	airport	11

Grammar	Pinyin	Traditional Characters	Simplified Characters	English	Lesson
N	fěnhóngsè	粉紅色	粉红色	pink	9s
N	fúwùyuán	服務員	服务员	service person; waiter; waitress	9n
N	gāngbǐ	鋼筆	钢笔	fountain pen	7s
N	gǎnlǎn	橄欖	橄榄	olive	4s
N	gǎnlǎnqiú	橄欖球	橄榄球	American style football (used in Taiwan)	4s
N	gāosù gōnglù	高速公路	高速公路	super highway; highway	11
N	gāozhōng	高中	高中	senior high (grades 10–12)	2c
N	gē	歌	歌	song	4
N	gēge	哥哥	哥哥	older brother	2
N	gōngchē	公車	公车	bus	11
N	gōnggòng qìchē	公共汽車	公共汽车	bus	11
N	gōngjiāochē	公轎車	公轿车	bus	11
N	gōngkè	功課	功课	schoolwork; homework	7
N	gōnglù	公路	公路	highway; road	11
N	gōngyuán	公園	公园	park	10
N	gōngzuò	工作	工作	job	5
N	háizi	孩子	孩子	child	2
N	Hánguórén	韓國人	韩国人	Korean people/person	1s
N	hánjià	寒假	寒假	winter vacation	11
N	Hánwén	韓文	韩文	the Korean language	6s
N	Hànyǔ	漢語	汉语	the Chinese language	6n
N	Hànzì	漢字	汉字	Chinese character	7
N	hào	號	号	number (bus route)	11n
N	hóngyè	紅葉	红叶	red autumn leaves	10
N	huà	話	话	speech; talk; words	6
N	huángméi	黃梅	黄梅	raining season	10c
N	huǒchē	火車	火车	train	11s
N	jī	機	机	machine	11
N	jiā	家	家	family; home	2
N	jiákè	夾克	夹克	jacket	9s
N	jiǎntǐzì	簡體字	简体字	simplified character	7c
N	jiàoshì	教室	教室	classroom	8
N	jīchǎng	機場	机场	airport	11
N	jìchéngchē	計程車	计程车	taxi (in Taiwan)	11s
N	jiějie	姐姐	姐姐	older sister	2
N	jìnbù	進步	进步	progress	8
N	jìsuànjī	計算機	计算机	calculator; computer	8n
N	jiǔ	酒	酒	wine; any alcoholic beverage	5
N	jiǔyuè	九月	九月	September	3
N	júhóngsè	橘紅色	橘红色	orange	9s
N	kāfēi	咖啡	咖啡	coffee	5
N	kāfēisè	咖啡色	咖啡色	coffee color; brown	9
N	kāishǐ	開始	开始	in the beginning	7, 8
N	*Kāngxī Zìdiǎn*	康熙字典	康熙字典	*Kangxi Dictionary*	Intro.

Grammar	Pinyin	Traditional Characters	Simplified Characters	English	Lesson
N	kǎoshì	考試	考试	test	6
N	kè	課	课	class; lesson	6
N	Kěkǒukělè	可口可樂	可口可乐	Coke	5s
N	kělè	可樂	可乐	cola	5
N	kèwén	課文	课文	text of a lesson	7
N	kòng(r)	空(兒)	空(儿)	free time	6
N	kǒu	口	口	mouth	2n
N	kǒu	口	口	mouth; (a measure word for people)	2c
N	kuàngquánshuǐ	礦泉水	矿泉水	mineral water	5s
N	kùzi	褲子	裤子	pants	9
N	Lādīngwén	拉丁文	拉丁文	Latin	6s
N	lánqiú	籃球	篮球	basketball	4s
N	lǎoshī	老師	老师	teacher	1
N	lǐ	李	李	(a surname); plum	1
N	lǐbài	禮拜	礼拜	week	3g
N	lǐbàisì	禮拜四	礼拜四	Thursday	3g
N	liùyuè	六月	六月	June	3g
N	lù	路	路	road; path	11
N	lù	路	路	number (bus route)	11n
N	lǜshī	律師	律师	lawyer	2
N	lùxiàng	錄像	录像	video recording	10
N	lùyīn	錄音	录音	sound recording	
N	mǎguà	馬褂	马褂	Mandarin jacket	9c
N	māma	媽媽	妈妈	mom; mother	2
N	máobǐ	毛筆	毛笔	writing brush	7s
N	máoyī	毛衣	毛衣	sweater	9s
N	màozi	帽子	帽子	hat	9s
N	Měiguórén	美國人	美国人	American people/person	1
N	mèimei	妹妹	妹妹	younger sister	2
N	Měishì zúqiú	美式足球	美式足球	American style football (used in mainland China)	4s
N	mén	門	门	door; (a measure word for academic courses)	6n
N	miàn	麵	面	noodles	3c
N	míngzi	名字	名字	name	1
N	nán	男	男	male	2
N	nánháizi	男孩子	男孩子	boy	2
N	nǎo	腦	脑	brain	8
N	nián	年	年	year	3
N	niánjì	年紀	年纪	age	3n
N	niánjí	年級	年级	grade in school	6
N	nǚ	女	女	female	2
N	nǚ'ér	女兒	女儿	daughter	2
N	nǚháizi	女孩子	女孩子	girl	2

Grammar	Pinyin	Traditional Characters	Simplified Characters	English	Lesson
N	páiqiú	排球	排球	volleyball	4s
N	péngyou	朋友	朋友	friend	1s, 7
N	piào	票	票	ticket	11
N	píjiǔ	啤酒	啤酒	beer	5
N	Pútáoyáwén	葡萄牙文	葡萄牙文	the Portuguese language	6s
N	qián	錢	钱	money	9
N	qiānbǐ	鉛筆	铅笔	pencil	7s
N	qìchē	汽車	汽车	automobile	11
N	qípáo	旗袍	旗袍	(a close-fitting woman's dress)	9c
N	qìshuǐ(r)	汽水(兒)	汽水(儿)	soft drink; soda pop	5s
N	qiú	球	球	ball	4
N	qiūtiān	秋天	秋天	autumn; fall	10
N	qīyuè	七月	七月	July	3g
N	qúnzi	裙子	裙子	skirt	9s
N	rén	人	人	people; person	1
N	rì	日	日	day; the sun	3
N	Rìběnrén	日本人	日本人	Japanese people/person	1s
N	rìjì	日記	日记	diary	8
N	Rìwén	日文	日文	the Japanese language	6s
N	sāngē	三哥	三哥	third oldest brother	7g
N	sānjiě	三姐	三姐	third oldest sister	7g
N	sānyuè	三月	三月	March	3g
N	shēngcí	生詞	生词	new words	7
N	shēngrì	生日	生日	birthday	3
N	shì	事	事	matter; affair; business	3
N	shì	視	视	vision	4
N	shí'èryuè	十二月	十二月	December	3g
N	shīfu	師傅	师傅	master craftsman; skilled worker	9n
N	shíhou	時候	时候	(a point in) time; moment; (a duration of) time	4
N	shíyīyuè	十一月	十一月	November	3g
N	shíyuè	十月	十月	October	3g
N	shǒubiǎo	手錶	手表	wristwatch	9n
N	shòuhuòyuán	售貨員	售货员	shop assistant; salesclerk	9
N	shǒutào	手套	手套	gloves	9n
N	shū	書	书	book	4
N	shuǐ	水	水	water	5
N	shǔjià	暑假	暑假	summer vacation	11s
N	sìyuè	四月	四月	April	3g
N	suì	歲	岁	year (of age)	3
N	suìshù	歲數	岁数	year (of age)	3n
N	sùshè	宿舍	宿舍	dormitory	8
N	tàitai	太太	太太	wife; Mrs.	1s
N	tiān	天	天	day	3
N	tiānqì	天氣	天气	weather	10

Grammar	Pinyin	Traditional Characters	Simplified Characters	English	Lesson
N	tóngxué	同學	同学	classmate	3
N	túshūguǎn	圖書館	图书馆	library	5
N	T-xùshān	T-恤衫	T-恤衫	T-shirt	9s
N	wàiguó	外國	外国	foreign country	4
N	wàitào	外套	外套	coat; jacket	9s
N	wǎn	晚	晚	evening; night	3
N	wǎnfàn	晚飯	晚饭	dinner; supper	3
N	wáng	王	王	(a surname); king	1
N	wǎngqiú	網球	网球	tennis	4s
N	wàzi	襪子	袜子	socks	9s
N	wén	文	文	language; script; written language	6
N	wèntí	問題	问题	question; problem	6
N	wǔ	舞	舞	dance	4
N	wǔfàn	午飯	午饭	lunch; midday meal	8
N	wǔjiào	午覺	午觉	nap	7s
N	wǔyuè	五月	五月	May	3g
N	xiàn	線	线	line	11
N	xiānsheng	先生	先生	Mr.; husband; teacher	1
N	xiǎojie	小姐	小姐	Miss; young lady	1
N	xiǎoxué	小學	小学	elementary school; grade school	2c
N	xiàtiān	夏天	夏天	summer	10
N	Xībānyáwén	西班牙文	西班牙文	the Spanish language	6s
N	xié	鞋	鞋	shoes	9
N	xíguàn	習慣	习惯	habit	8
N	Xīlàwén	希臘文	希腊文	the Greek language	6s
N	xìn	信	信	letter (mail)	8
N	xìng	姓	姓	surname	1
N	xīngqī	星期	星期	week	3
N	xīngqī'èr	星期二	星期二	Tuesday	3g
N	xīngqīliù	星期六	星期六	Saturday	3g
N	xīngqīrì	星期日	星期日	Sunday	3g
N	xīngqīsān	星期三	星期三	Wednesday	3g
N	xīngqīsì	星期四	星期四	Thursday	3
N	xīngqītiān	星期天	星期天	Sunday	3g
N	xīngqīwǔ	星期五	星期五	Friday	3g
N	xīngqīyī	星期一	星期一	Monday	3g
N	xīnnián	新年	新年	new year	11
N	xīwàng	希望	希望	hope	8
N	xīzhuāng	西裝	西装	suit	9s
N	xuě	雪	雪	snow	10s
N	Xuěbì	雪碧	雪碧	Sprite	5s
N	xuéqī	學期	学期	school term; semester/quarter	8
N	xuésheng	學生	学生	student	1
N	xuéxiào	學校	学校	school	5
N	xuéyuàn	學院	学院	college	2c

Grammar	Pinyin	Traditional Characters	Simplified Characters	English	Lesson
N	yǎnjìng	眼鏡	眼镜	eye glasses; glasses	9n
N	yánsè	顏色	颜色	color	9
N	yè	夜	夜	night	7
N	Yìdàlìwén	意大利文	意大利文	the Italian language	6s
N	yīfu	衣服	衣服	clothes	9
N	yǐng	影	影	shadow	4
N	Yīngguórén	英國人	英国人	British people/person	1s
N	Yīngwén	英文	英文	the English language	2
N	yīnyuè	音樂	音乐	music	4
N	yīnyuèhuì	音樂會	音乐会	concert	8
N	yīshēng	醫生	医生	doctor; physician	2
N	yìsi	意思	意思	meaning	4
N	yīyuè	一月	一月	January	3g
N	yòng	用	用	use	8
N	yǔ	語	语	speech	6n
N	yuánzhūbǐ	圓珠筆	圆珠笔	ball-point pen	7c
N	yuánzibǐ	原子筆	原子笔	ball-point pen	7c
N	yùbào	預報	预报	forecast	10
N	yuè	月	月	month	3
N	Yuènánrén	越南人	越南人	Vietnamese people/person	1s
N	yǔfǎ	語法	语法	grammar	7
N	yún	雲	云	cloud	10s
N	zǎofàn	早飯	早饭	breakfast	3s, 8
N	zhàn	站	站	(bus, train, etc.) stop; station	11
N	zhàopiàn	照片	照片	picture; photo	2
N	zhǐ	紙	纸	paper	2g, 7s
N	zhōng	鐘	钟	clock	3
N	zhōngfàn	中飯	中饭	lunch	3s
N	Zhōngguórén	中國人	中国人	Chinese people/person	1
N	Zhōngguózì	中國字	中国字	Chinese character	Intro.
N	Zhōngshānzhuāng	中山裝	中山装	Sun Yatsen suit	9c
N	Zhōngwén	中文	中文	the Chinese language	6
N	zhōngxué	中學	中学	middle school	2c
N	zhōu	週	周	week	3g
N	zhōu'èr	週二	周二	Tuesday	3g
N	zhōurì	週日	周日	Sunday	3g
N	zhōuyī	週一	周一	Monday	3g
N	zhuānyè	專業	专业	major (in college); specialty	8
N	zì	字	字	character	7
N	zúqiú	足球	足球	soccer	4s
Numerals					
Nu	bā	八	八	eight	Intro.
Nu	bǎi	百	百	hundred	9
Nu	bàn	半	半	half; half an hour	3
Nu	èr	二	二	two	Intro.

Grammar	Pinyin	Traditional Characters	Simplified Characters	English	Lesson
Nu	jǐ	幾	几	some; a few (an indefinite number, usually less than ten)	6
Nu	jiǔ	九	九	nine	Intro.
Nu	liǎng	兩	两	two; a couple of	2
Nu	líng	零	零	zero	3g
Nu	liù	六	六	six	Intro.
Nu	qī	七	七	seven	Intro.
Nu	sān	三	三	three	Intro.
Nu	shí	十	十	ten	Intro.
Nu	shí'èr	十二	十二	twelve	3
Nu	shíbā	十八	十八	eighteen	3
Nu	sì	四	四	four	Intro.
Nu	wǔ	五	五	five	Intro.
Nu	yī	一	一	one	Intro.
Particles					
P	a	啊	啊	(a sentence-final particle of exclamation, interrogation, etc.)	6
P	ba	吧	吧	(a "suggestion" particle; softens the tone of the sentence to which it is appended)	5
P	de	的	的	(a possessive, modifying, or descriptive particle)	2
P	de	得	得	(a structural particle)	7
P	le	了	了	(a particle indicating superlative degree)	3
P	le	了	了	(a dynamic particle; a sentence particle)	5g, 8g, 10g
P	ya	呀	呀	(an interjectory particle used to soften a question)	5
Proper Nouns					
PN	Běijīng	北京	北京	Beijing	10s
PN	Chángjiāng	長江	长江	Yangtze river	10c
PN	Chóngqìng	重慶	重庆	Chongqing	10c
PN	Déguó	德國	德国	Germany	1s
PN	Éguó	俄國	俄国	Russia	6s
PN	Fǎguó	法國	法国	France	1s
PN	Fēilǜbīn	菲律賓	菲律宾	the Philippines	6s
PN	Hā'ěrbīn	哈爾濱	哈尔滨	Harbin	10c
PN	Hǎinán	海南	海南	Hainan	10c
PN	Hánguó	韓國	韩国	Korea	6s
PN	Jiānádà	加拿大	加拿大	Canada	10s
PN	Kūnmíng	昆明	昆明	Kunming	10c
PN	Lǐ Yǒu	李友	李友	(a personal name)	1
PN	Mǎláixīyà	馬來西亞	马来西亚	Malaysia	6s

Grammar	Pinyin	Traditional Characters	Simplified Characters	English	Lesson
PN	Máotái	茅台	茅台	Maotai (name of a liquor)	5c
PN	Měiguó	美國	美国	America	1
PN	Nánjīng	南京	南京	Nanjing	10c
PN	Pútáoyá	葡萄牙	葡萄牙	Portugal	6s
PN	Rìběn	日本	日本	Japan	1s
PN	Shànghǎi	上海	上海	Shanghai	10
PN	Táiběi	台北	台北	Taipei	10
PN	Tàiguó	泰國	泰国	Thailand	6s
PN	Táiwān	台灣	台湾	Taiwan	10
PN	Táizhōng	台中	台中	Taichung	10s
PN	Wáng Péng	王朋	王朋	(a personal name)	1
PN	Wēngēhuá	温哥華	温哥华	Vancouver	10s
PN	Wǔhàn	武漢	武汉	Wuhan	10c
PN	Xiānggǎng	香港	香港	Hong Kong	10s
PN	Xiǎo Bái	小白	小白	Little Bai	3
PN	Xiǎo Gāo	小高	小高	Little Gao	2
PN	Xiǎo Lǐ	小李	小李	Little Li	3
PN	Xiǎo Zhāng	小張	小张	Little Zhang	2
PN	Xiàwēiyí	夏威夷	夏威夷	Hawaii	6s
PN	Xībānyá	西班牙	西班牙	Spain	6s
PN	Xiè	謝	谢	(a surname)	10
PN	Xīlà	希臘	希腊	Greece	6s
PN	Xīngbākè	星巴克	星巴克	Starbucks	5c
PN	Yìdàlì	意大利	意大利	Italy	6s
PN	Yīngguó	英國	英国	Britain; England	1s
PN	Yìwén	意文	意文	(a given name)	8
PN	Yuènán	越南	越南	Vietnam	6s
PN	Zhōngguó	中國	中国	China	1
PN	Zhāng	張	张	(a surname)	1n

Pronouns

Grammar	Pinyin	Traditional Characters	Simplified Characters	English	Lesson
Pr	dàjiā	大家	大家	everybody	7
Pr	nà/nèi	那	那	that	2
Pr	nàr	那兒	那儿	there	8
Pr	nǐ	你	你	you	1
Pr	nín	您	您	you (singular; polite)	1
Pr	tā	他	他	he; him	2
Pr	tā	她	她	she	2
Pr	wǒ	我	我	I; me	1
Pr	wǒmen	我們	我们	we	3
Pr	zhè/zhèi	這	这	this	2
Pr	zhège	這個	这个	this	10
Pr	zhème	這麼	这么	so; such	7
Pr	zhèr	這兒	这儿	here	9
Pr	zhèyàng	這樣	这样	so; like this	10
Pr	zìjǐ	自己	自己	oneself	11

Grammar	Pinyin	Traditional Characters	Simplified Characters	English	Lesson
Prefixes					
prefix	dì	第	第	(a prefix for ordinal numbers)	7
Prepositions					
Prep	bǐ	比	比	(a comparison marker)	10
Prep	gěi	給	给	to; for	6
Prep	měi	每	每	every; each (usually followed by a measure word)	11
Prep	wèi	爲	为	for	3
Prep	zài	在	在	at; in; on	5
Question Particles					
QP	ma	嗎	吗	(an interrogative particle)	1
QP	ne	呢	呢	(an interrogative particle)	1
Question Pronouns					
QPr	nǎ/něi	哪	哪	which	6
QPr	nǎr	哪兒	哪儿	where	5
QPr	shéi	誰	谁	who	2
QPr	shénme	什麼	什么	what	1
QPr	wèishénme	爲什麼	为什么	why	3
QPr	zěnme	怎麼	怎么	how; how come (used to inquire about the cause of something, implying a degree of surprise or disapproval)	7
QPr	zěnmeyàng	怎麼樣	怎么样	Is it O.K.? What is it like? How does that sound?	3
Question Words					
QW	duōshao	多少	多少	how much; how many	9
QW	jǐ	幾	几	how many	2
QW	zěnme bàn	怎麼辦	怎么办	what to do	10
Time Words					
T	bànyè	半夜	半夜	midnight	7
T	gāngcái	剛才	刚才	just now; a moment ago	10
T	hòulái	後來	后来	later	8
T	hòunián	後年	后年	the year after next	3s
T	hòutiān	後天	后天	the day after tomorrow	3s
T	jīnnián	今年	今年	this year	3
T	jīntiān	今天	今天	today	3
T	měitiān	每天	每天	every day	11
T	míngnián	明年	明年	next year	3s
T	míngtiān	明天	明天	tomorrow	3
T	qiánnián	前年	前年	the year before last	3s
T	qiántiān	前天	前天	the day before yesterday	3s
T	qùnián	去年	去年	last year	3s, 6n
T	shàngge xīngqī	上個星期	上个星期	last week	6n, 7
T	shàngge yuè	上個月	上个月	last month	6n

Grammar	Pinyin	Traditional Characters	Simplified Characters	English	Lesson
T	shàngwǔ	上午	上午	morning	6
T	shíjiān	時間	时间	time	6
T	wǎnshang	晚上	晚上	evening; night	3
T	xià(ge)yuè	下(個)月	下(个)月	next month	3s
T	xiàge xīngqī	下個星期	下个星期	next week	6
T	xiànzài	現在	现在	now	3
T	xiàwǔ	下午	下午	afternoon	6
T	yǐhòu	以後	以后	after	6
T	yǐqián	以前	以前	before; ago; previously	7g, 8
T	zǎoshang	早上	早上	morning	8
T	zhōngwǔ	中午	中午	noon	6s, 8
T	zhōumò	週末	周末	weekend	4
T	zuìjìn	最近	最近	recently	8
T	zuótiān	昨天	昨天	yesterday	3s, 4
Verbs					
V	bāng	幫	帮	to help	6
V	bāngzhù	幫助	帮助	to help	7
V	chà	差	差	to be short of; to be lacking	3s
V	chàng	唱	唱	to sing	4
V	chī	吃	吃	to eat	3
V	chuān	穿	穿	to wear; to put on	9
V	chūzū	出租	出租	to rent out; to let	11
V	dǎ	打	打	to hit; to strike	4
V	dài	戴	戴	to wear (hat, glasses, etc.)	9s
V	dào	到	到	to arrive	8
V	děng	等	等	to wait; to wait for	6
V	dǒng	懂	懂	to understand	7
V	fācái	發財	发财	to make a fortune	11c
V	fēi	飛	飞	to fly	11
V	fùxí	復習	复习	to review	7
V	gàosu	告訴	告诉	to tell	8
V	gěi	給	给	to give	5
V	gōngxǐ	恭喜	恭喜	to congratulate	11c
V	gōngzuò	工作	工作	to work	5
V	hē	喝	喝	to drink	5
V	huā	花	花	to spend	11
V	huàn	換	换	to change; to exchange	9
V	huí	回	回	to return	5
V	jiàn	見	见	to see	3
V	jiào	叫	叫	to be called; to call	1
V	jiāo	教	教	to teach	7
V	jièshào	介紹	介绍	to introduce	5
V	jìn	進	进	to enter	5
V	jìnbù	進步	进步	to make progress	8
V	juéde	覺得	觉得	to feel	4

Grammar	Pinyin	Traditional Characters	Simplified Characters	English	Lesson
V	kāi	開	开	to hold (a meeting, party, etc.)	6
V	kāi	開	开	to drive; to operate	11
V	kāishǐ	開始	开始	to begin; to start	7, 8
V	kàn	看	看	to watch; to look	4
V	kǎo	考	考	to give or take a test	6
V	kǎoshì	考試	考试	to give or take a test	6
V	lái	來	来	to come	5
V	liànxí	練習	练习	to practice	6
V	mǎi	買	买	to buy	9
V	mài	賣	卖	to sell	9s
V	niàn	念	念	to read aloud	7
V	qǐng	請	请	please (a polite form of request)	1
V	qǐng	請	请	to treat (somebody); to invite	3
V	qù	去	去	to go	4
V	ràng	讓	让	to allow or cause (somebody to do something)	11
V	rènshi	認識	认识	to know (someone); to recognize	3
V	shēng	生	生	to give birth to; to be born	3
V	shì	是	是	to be	1
V	shuì	睡	睡	to sleep	4
V	shuō	說	说	to say; to speak	6
V	sòng	送	送	to take someone (somewhere)	11
V	tiào	跳	跳	to jump	4
V	tīng	聽	听	to listen	4
V	wán(r)	玩(兒)	玩(儿)	to have fun; to play	5
V	wèn	問	问	to ask (a question)	1
V	xiào	笑	笑	to laugh; to laugh at	8
V	xiě	寫	写	to write	7
V	xiè	謝	谢	thanks	10
V	xíguàn	習慣	习惯	to be accustomed to	8
V	xǐhuan	喜歡	喜欢	to like; to prefer	3
V	xìng	姓	姓	(one's) surname is...	1
V	xīwàng	希望	希望	to hope	8
V	xué	學	学	to study	7
V	yào	要	要	to want to; to have a desire for	5
V	yòng	用	用	to use	8
V	yǒu	有	有	to have; to exist	2
V	yuē	約	约	to make an appointment	10
V	yùxí	預習	预习	to preview	7
V	zài	在	在	to be present; to be at (a place)	6
V	zhǎo	找	找	to look for	4
V	zhǎo(qián)	找(錢)	找(钱)	to give change	9
V	zhīdao	知道	知道	to know	6
V	zhù	祝	祝	to express good wishes	8
V	zǒu	走	走	to walk; to go by way of	11

Grammar	Pinyin	Traditional Characters	Simplified Characters	English	Lesson
V	zū	租	租	to rent	11
V	zuò	做	做	to do	2
V	zuò	坐	坐	to sit	5
V	zuò	坐	坐	to travel by	11
Verbs plus Complement					
VC	huílai	回來	回来	to come back	6
VC	jìnlai	進來	进来	to come in	5
Verbs plus Object					
VO	bāng máng	幫忙	帮忙	to help; to do someone a favor	6
VO	chàng gē	唱歌	唱歌	to sing (a song)	4
VO	chī fàn	吃飯	吃饭	to eat (a meal)	3
VO	dǎ diànhuà	打電話	打电话	to make a phone call	6
VO	dǎ gōng	打工	打工	to work part-time; to do manual work	5s
VO	dǎ qiú	打球	打球	to play ball	4
VO	fù qián	付錢	付钱	to pay money	9
VO	huí jiā	回家	回家	to go home	5
VO	kāi chē	開車	开车	to drive a car	11
VO	kāi huì	開會	开会	to have a meeting	6
VO	kàn shū	看書	看书	to read books; to read	4
VO	liáo tiān(r)	聊天(兒)	聊天(儿)	to chat	5
VO	lùyīn	錄音	录音	to record	7
VO	qǐ chuáng	起床	起床	to get up	8
VO	qiāo mén	敲門	敲门	to knock at the door	5f
VO	qǐng kè	請客	请客	to invite someone to dinner; to be the host	4
VO	shàng kè	上課	上课	to go to class; to start a class	7
VO	shuì jiào	睡覺	睡觉	to sleep	4
VO	shuō huà	說話	说话	to talk	7
VO	tiào wǔ	跳舞	跳舞	to dance	4
VO	xǐ zǎo	洗澡	洗澡	to take a bath/shower	8
VO	xià chē	下車	下车	to get off (a bus, train, etc.)	11
VO	xià yǔ	下雨	下雨	to rain	10
VO	yǒu kòng(r)	有空(兒)	有空(儿)	to have free time	6
VO	zǒu lù	走路	走路	to walk	11s

LESSON 1 ▲ Greetings

Dialogue I: Exchanging Greetings

DIALOGUE I

王先生[(1)]:你好[(2)]!

李小姐: 你好!

王先生: 請問,您貴姓[(3)]?

李小姐: 我姓[(G1)]李。你呢[(G2)]?

王先生: 我姓王,叫[(G3)]王朋[(4)]。你叫什麼名字[(5)]?

李小姐: 我叫李友。

Dialogue II: Asking One's Status

DIALOGUE II

李小姐: 王先生,你是[(G4)]老師嗎[(G5)]?

王先生: 不[(G6)],我不[(1)]是老師,我是學生。李小姐,你呢?

李小姐: 我也[(G7)]是學生。你是中國人嗎?

王先生: 是,我是中國人。你是美國人嗎?

李小姐: 我是美國人。

LESSON 2 ▲ Family

Dialogue I: Looking at a Family Photo

DIALOGUE I

(Wang Peng is in Little Gao's room pointing to a picture on the wall.)

王朋: 小高[1]，那張[G1]照片是你的嗎?

(They both walk toward the picture and then stand in front of it.)

小高: 是。這是我爸爸，這是我媽媽。

王朋: 這個男孩子是誰[G2]?

小高: 他是我弟弟。

王朋: 這個女孩子是你妹妹嗎?

小高: 不是，她是李先生的[2]女兒。

王朋: 李先生有[G3]兒子嗎?

小高: 他沒有兒子。

Dialogue II: Asking About Someone's Family

DIALOGUE II

李友: 小張，你家[1]有[G4]幾個[2]人?

小張: 我家有六個人。我爸爸[3]、我媽媽、一[4]個[G1]哥哥、兩[G5]個姐姐和[5]我[6]。李小姐，你家有幾個人?

李友: 我家有五個人。爸爸、媽媽、兩個妹妹和我。你爸爸媽媽是做什麼的(7)?

小張: 我媽媽是英文老師，爸爸是律師，哥哥、姐姐都(G6)是大學生。

李友: 我媽媽也是老師，我爸爸是醫生。

LESSON 3 ▲ Dates and Time

Dialogue I: Taking Someone out to Eat on His/Her Birthday

DIALOGUE I

(Little Gao is talking to Little Bai.)

小高: 小白，九月十二(1)(G1)號(G2)是星期幾(G2)?

小白: 是星期四。

小高: 那天是我的(G3)生日。

小白: 是嗎? 你今年多大(2)?

小高: 十八歲(3)。

小白: 星期四我請你吃晚飯(G4)，怎麼樣?

小高: 太好了。謝謝，謝謝(4)。

小白: 你喜歡吃中國飯還是(G5)美國飯?

小高: 我是中國人，可是我喜歡吃美國飯。

小白: 好，我們吃美國飯。

小高: 星期四幾點鐘?

小白: 七點半(G2.6)怎麼樣?

小高: 好,星期四晚上見。

小白: 再見!

Dialogue II: Inviting Someone to Dinner

DIALOGUE II

(Wang Peng and Little Bai are talking to each other.)

王朋: 小白,現在幾點鐘?

小白: 五點三刻。

王朋: 我六點一刻有事。

小白: 王朋,你明天忙不忙(G6)?

王朋: 我今天很忙(1),可是明天不忙。有事嗎?

小白: 明天我請你吃晚飯,怎麼樣?

王朋: 為什麼請我吃飯?

小白: 因為明天是小高的生日。

王朋: 是嗎? 好。還有(G7)誰?

小白: 還有我的同學小李。

王朋: 那太好了,我也認識小李。幾點鐘?

小白: 明天晚上七點半。

王朋: 好,明天七點半見。

LESSON 4 ▲ Hobbies

Dialogue I: Talking about Hobbies

DIALOGUE I

(Little Bai is talking to Little Gao.)

小白: 小高,你週末(1)喜歡做什麼(G1)?

小高: 我喜歡打球、看電視(2)。你呢?

小白: 我喜歡唱歌、跳舞,還喜歡聽音樂。

小高: 你也喜歡看書,對不對?

小白: 對,有時候也喜歡看書。

小高: 你喜歡不喜歡(G2)看電影?

小白: 喜歡。我週末常常看電影。

小高: 那(G3)我們今天晚上去看(G4)一個外國電影,怎麼樣?

小白: 好。今天我請客。

小高: 為什麼你請客?

小白: 因為昨天你請我吃飯,所以今天我請你看電影。

Dialogue II: Inviting Someone to Play Ball

DIALOGUE II

(Wang Peng is talking to Little Zhang.)

王朋: 小張，好久不見[1]，你好嗎?

小張: 我很好。你怎麼樣?

王朋: 我也不錯。這個週末你想[G5]做什麼?
想不想去打球?

小張: 打球? 我不喜歡打球。

王朋: 那我們去看電影，好嗎[G6]?

小張: 看電影? 我覺得看電影也沒有意思[2]。

王朋: 那你喜歡做什麼?

小張: 我只喜歡吃飯、睡覺。

王朋: 那算了[F]。我去找別人。

LESSON 5 ▲ Visiting Friends

Dialogue: Visiting a Friend's Home

DIALOGUE

小高: 誰呀? (F)

王朋: 是我，王朋，還有李友。

小高: 請進，請進! 李友，快進來! 來，介紹一下(G1)，這是我姐姐，高小音。

李友: 小音，你好。認識你很高興(1)。

高小音: 認識你們我也很高興。

李友: 你們家很大(G2)，也很漂亮(F)。

小高: 是嗎(2)(F)? 請坐，請坐。

王朋: 小音，你在(G3)哪兒工作?

高小音: 我在學校工作。你們想喝點兒(G1)什麼? 有茶、咖啡，還有啤酒。

王朋: 我喝啤酒吧(G4)。

李友: 我不喝酒。我要一杯可樂，可以嗎?

高小音: 對不起，我們沒有可樂。

李友: 那給我一杯水吧。

Narrative: At a Friend's House

NARRATIVE

昨天晚上，王朋和李友去小高家玩兒。在小高家，他們認識了(G5)小高的姐姐。她叫高小音，在學校的圖書館工作。小高請王朋喝(1)啤酒，王朋喝了兩瓶。李友不喝酒，只喝了一杯水。他們一起聊天兒、看電視。王朋和李友晚上十二點才(G6)回家。

LESSON 6 ▲ Making Appointments

Dialogue I: Calling One's Teacher

DIALOGUE I

(李友給(G1)老師打電話)

李友: 喂(F)，請問，王老師在嗎?

王老師: 我就是。您是哪位?

李友: 老師，您好。我是李友。

王老師: 李友，你好，有事嗎?

李友: 老師，今天下午您有時間嗎?我想問(1)您幾個問題。

王老師: 對不起，今天下午我要(G2)開會。

李友: 明天呢?

王老師: 明天上午我有兩節(2)課,下午三點鐘要給二年級考試。

李友: 您什麼時候有空?

王老師: 明天四點以後(3)才有空。

李友: 要是您方便,四點半我到您的辦公室去,行嗎?

王老師: 四點半,沒問題(F)。我在辦公室等你。

李友: 謝謝您。

王老師: 不客氣。

Dialogue II: Calling a Friend for Help

DIALOGUE II

李友: 喂,請問,王朋在嗎?

王朋: 我就是。你是李友吧(1)?有事嗎?

李友: 我想請你幫忙。

王朋: 別(G3)客氣,有什麼事?

李友: 我下個星期(2)要考中文(3),你幫我練習說中文,好嗎?

王朋: 好啊,但是你得(G4)請我喝咖啡。

李友: 喝咖啡,沒問題。今天晚上你有空兒嗎?

王朋: 今天晚上有人請我吃飯,不知道(4)什麼時候回來(G5)。我回來以後給你打電話吧。

李友: 好吧,我等你的電話。

LESSON 7 ▲ Studying Chinese

Dialogue I: Asking about an Examination

DIALOGUE I

(王朋跟李友說話)

王朋: 李友,你上個星期考試考得(G1)怎麼樣?

李友: 考得不錯,因為你幫助(1)我復習,所以考得不錯。但是老師說我中國字寫得太(G2)慢!

王朋: 是嗎? 以後我跟你一起練習寫字教你怎麼寫,好不好(2)?

李友: 那太好了!我們現在就(G3)寫。給你筆。

王朋: 好,我教你寫"難"字。

李友: 你寫字寫得很好,也很快。

王朋：哪裏，哪裏(F)。你明天有中文課嗎？

李友：有，明天我們學第七(G4)課。

王朋：你預習了嗎？

李友：預習了。第七課的語法很容易，我都懂，可是生詞太多，漢字也有一點兒(G5)難。

王朋：今天晚上我跟你一起練習吧。

李友：好，謝謝你。

王朋：不謝，晚上見。

Dialogue II: Preparing for a Chinese Class

DIALOGUE II

(李友跟小白說話)

李友：小白，你平常來得很早，今天怎麼(G6)來得這麼晚？

小白：我昨天預習中文，半夜一點才(G3)睡覺，你也睡得很晚嗎？

李友：我昨天十點就(G3)睡了。因為王朋幫我練習中文，所以我功課做得很快。

小白：有個中國朋友真(G2)好。

(上中文課)

老師: 大家早(1)，現在我們開始上課。第七(G4)課你們都預習了嗎?

學生: 預習了。

老師: 李友，請你念課文。...你念得很好。你昨天晚上聽錄音了吧?

李友: 我沒聽。

小白: 但是她的朋友常常幫助她。

老師: 你的朋友是中國人嗎?

李友: 是的。

小白: 他是一個男的(2)，很帥(3)，叫王朋(G7)。

LESSON 8 ▲ School Life

A Diary: A Typical School Day

AN ENTRY FROM LI YOU'S DIARY

李友的一篇日記

八月九日　星期一

我今天早上(1)七點半起床(G1)，洗了澡以後就(G2)吃早飯。我一邊吃飯，一邊(G3)聽錄音。九點鐘到教室去上課(G4)。

第一節課是中文，老師教我們發音(G5)、生詞和語法，也教我們寫字，還給了(G6)我們一篇新課文(2)，這篇課文很有意思。第二節課是電腦(3)課，很難。中午我和同學們一起到餐廳去吃午飯。我們一邊吃，一邊練習說中文。下午我到圖書館去看報。四點鐘王朋來找我去打球。五點三刻吃晚飯。七點半我去小白的宿舍跟他聊天(兒)。到那兒的時候，他正在(G7)做功課。我八點半回家。睡覺以前，給王朋打了一個電話，告訴他明天要考試。他說他已經知道了。

A Letter

一封信

張小姐：

你好！好久不見，最近怎麼樣？

這個學期我很忙，除了專業課以外，還(G8)得學中文。我們的中文課很有意思。因為我們的中文老師只會(G9)說中文，不會說英文，所以上課的時候我們只說中文，不說英文。開始我不習慣，後來，我有了一個中國朋友，他說話說得很清楚，常常跟我一起練習說中文，所以我的中文進步得很快。

你喜歡聽音樂嗎？下星期六，我們學校

有一個音樂會，希望你能(G9)來。我用中文寫信寫得很不好，請別笑我。祝

好

你的朋友

意文

八月十日

LESSON 9 ▲ Shopping

Dialogue I: Buying Clothes

DIALOGUE I

(買東西)

售貨員：小姐(1)，您要(G1)買什麼衣服？

李小姐：我想買一件(G2)襯衫。

售貨員：您喜歡什麼顏色的(G3)，黃的還是紅的？

李小姐：我喜歡穿(2)紅的。我還想買一條(3) (G2)褲子。

售貨員：多(G4)大的？大號、中號還是小號的？

李小姐：中號的。不要太貴的，也不要太

便宜[4]的。

售貨員: 這條褲子和這件襯衫怎麼樣?

李小姐: 很好，在哪兒付錢?

售貨員: 在這兒。

李小姐: 一共多少錢?

售貨員: 襯衫二十塊五，褲子三十二塊九毛九，一共是五十三塊四毛九分[G5]。

李小姐: 好，這是一百塊錢。

售貨員: 找您四十六塊五毛一。謝謝。

Dialogue II: Exchanging Shoes

DIALOGUE II

李小姐: 對不起，這雙鞋太小了。能不能換一雙?

售貨員: 沒問題。您看，這雙怎麼樣?

李小姐: 也不行，這雙跟那雙一樣[G6]大。

售貨員: 那這雙黑的呢?

李小姐: 這雙鞋雖然大小合適，可是[G7]顏色不好。有沒有咖啡色的?

售貨員: 對不起，只有黑的。

李小姐: 那好吧。我還要付錢嗎?

售貨員: 不用，這雙的錢跟那雙一樣。

LESSON 10 ▲ Talking about the Weather

Dialogue I: The Weather is Getting Better

DIALOGUE I

謝小姐: 今天天氣比(G1)昨天好，不下雨了(G2)。

高先生: 明天天氣怎麼樣? 希望明天也不下雨。

謝小姐: 我看了報上的天氣預報，明天天氣比今天更好。不但不會(G3)下雨，而且會暖和一點兒。

高先生: 太好了! 我約了李小姐明天去公園看紅葉。

謝小姐: 是嗎? 可是李小姐今天早上跟王先生去上海了。

高先生: 真的啊? 那我明天怎麼辦?

謝小姐: 你在家看錄像吧!

Dialogue II: Complaining about the Weather

DIALOGUE II

小葉: 真糟糕，又(G4) 下大雨了。

小夏: 剛才我看報了，報上說，這個星期天氣都不好，下個星期天氣才會(G3)好。

小葉: 真的啊? 那這個週末不能出去玩了。最近天氣太熱，真不舒服。

小夏: 台北夏天的天氣就是這樣。兩個月以後，天氣就會比現在涼快一點兒了。

小葉: 兩個月以後? 下個月我就回美國去了。

小夏: 台灣春天常常下雨，冬天很冷，夏天又悶又熱(G5) 。你下次最好秋天來。

LESSON 11 ▲ Transportation

Dialogue: Going Home for the Winter Vacation

DIALOGUE

王朋: 寒假你回家嗎?

李友: 我要回家。

王朋: 飛機票你買了嗎(G1)?

李友: 已經買了。是二十一號的。

王朋: 飛機是幾點的?

李友: 晚上八點的。

王朋: 你怎麼去機場?

李友: 我想坐公共汽車或者(G2)坐地鐵。你知道怎麼走嗎?

王朋: 你先坐一號(1)汽車，坐三站下車，然後換地鐵。先坐紅線，再(G3)換綠線，最後換藍線。

李友: 不行，不行，太麻煩了。我還是(G4)坐出租汽車(2)吧。

王朋: 坐出租汽車太貴，我可以開車送你去。

李友: 謝謝你。

王朋: 不用客氣。

A Letter: Thanking Someone for a Ride

A LETTER

王朋：

謝謝你那天開車送我到機場。不過，讓你花那麼多時間，真不好意思。我這幾天每天都(G5)開車出去看老朋友。這兒的人開車開得很快。我在高速公路上開車，真有點兒緊張。可是這兒沒有公共汽車，也沒有地鐵，很不方便，只能自己開車。

新年快到了，祝(F)你新年快樂！

李友

十二月二十六日